# South Asian Economy

***Challenges and Future Prospects***

# South Asian Economy

***Challenges and Future Prospects***

**Dr Sukanta Sarkar**

**Dr Suman Kalyan Chaudhury**

KALPAZ

First Published, 2018

*Published by*

Kalpaz Publications
C-30, Satyawati Nagar,
Delhi – 110052
E-mail: kalpaz@hotmail.com
Ph.: 9212142040

*Printed at:* G. Print Process, Delhi

**Cataloging in Publication Data—DK**
Courtesy: D.K. Agencies (P) Ltd. <docinfo@dkagencies.com>

**Sarkar, Sukanta, author.**
South Asian economy : challenges and future prospects / Dr Sukanta Sarkar, Dr Suman Kalyan Chaudhury.
pages cm
Includes bibliographical references.
ISBN 9789386397225

1. South Asia—Economic conditions. 2. South Asia—Economic policy. I. Chaudhury, Suman Kalyan, 1972- author. II. Title.

LCC HC430.6.S27 2018 | DDC 330.954 23

# Contents

# Preface

Economic development ideally refers to the sustained, concerted actions of communities and policymakers that improve the standard of living and economic health of a specific locality. It can be referred to as the quantitative and qualitative changes in an existing economy. It involves development of human capital, increasing the literacy ratio, improve important infrastructure, improvement of health and safety and others areas that aims at increasing the general welfare of the citizens. Education, entrepreneurship, physical infrastructure, and social infrastructure all play an important role in developing rural regions.

This book consists of 15 chapters. The issue covered in the book has a practical and policy significance in South Asia. However, we believe that perfection is achievable, but not an achieved one. We invite your comments and constructive suggestions, if any. Thanks are due to Dr K. B. Das, Professor P. G. Dept. of Commerce, Professor P. K. Sahoo, Vice Chancellor, Utkal University, Bhubaneswar, Dr D.P. Mishra, Professor, Dept. of MBA, F.M. University, Balasore, Dr Hitesh Shukla, Professor, Dept. of MBA, Saurashtra University, Dr R.P. Dash, Professor, Pt. Ravisankar Shukla University, Raipur, Dr P.K. Padhy, Professor, Dept. of MBA, Berhampur University, Dr P. C. Mishra, P. G. Dept. of Commerce, Berhampur University, Dr R. Prasad, Professor, Pt. Ravisankar Shukla University, Raipur, Dr N.G. Pendse, Professor, Rani Durgabati University, Jabalpur, Dr D. Pulla. Rao, Professor, Andhra University for constant encouragement, advice and help extended to us. Further, we express our heartily thankfulness to each and every person who directly/indirectly helped us in preparing this work.

Further, we express our heartily thankfulness to each and every person who directly/indirectly helped us in preparing this work. It is hoped that this book will be very useful society in general and students of developmental studies/South Asian studies in particular.

**Dr Sukanta Sarkar**

**Dr Suman Kalyan Chaudhury**

# Abbreviations

| | |
|---|---|
| ADB | : Asian Development Bank |
| AFP | : Auto Fuel Policy |
| AQM | : Air Quality Management |
| ARIA | : Agricultural Research Institute of Afghanistan |
| ATC | : Agreement on Textiles and Clothing |
| ATMs | : Automated Teller Machines |
| BIMSTEC | : Bangladesh, India, Myanmar, Singapore, and Thailand Economic Cooperation Forum |
| BLSS | : Bhutan Living Standard Survey |
| BoP | : Balance of Payments |
| BTC | : Bhutan Tourism Corporation |
| CIAL | : Cochin International Airport |
| CSF | : Coalition Support Fund |
| DAB | : Da Afghanistan Bank |
| DADF | : Department of Animal Husbandry, Dairying and Fisheries |
| DANIDA | : Danish International Development Agency |
| DGCA | : Directorate General of Civil Aviation |
| DGCI & S | : Directorate General of Commercial Intelligence and Statistics |
| DGM | : Department of Geology and Mines |
| DIPP | : Department of Industrial Policy and Promotion |
| EPC | : Environment Protection Council |
| FAO | : Food and Agriculture Organisation |
| FDI | : Foreign Direct Investment |

| | |
|---|---|
| FEMA | : Foreign Exchange Management Act |
| FICCI | : Foreign Investors' Chamber of Commerce and Industry |
| FII | : Foreign Institutional Investments |
| FIMI | : Federation of Indian Mineral Industries |
| GATT | : General Agreement on Tariffs and Trade |
| GFCF | : Gross Fixed Capital Formation |
| GSI | : Geological Survey of India |
| HACCP | : Hazard Analysis Critical Control Point |
| HDI | : Human Development Index |
| IBSL | : Institute of Bankers of Sri Lanka |
| ISE | : Improved Seed Enterprise |
| KESC | : Karachi Electric Supply Company |
| MAIL | : Ministry of Agriculture, Irrigation and Livestock |
| MCDR | : Mineral Conservation and Development Rules |
| MCR | : Mineral Concession Rules |
| MDGs | : Millennium Development Goals |
| MFA | : Multi-Fibre Arrangement |
| MFN | : Most Favoured Nation |
| MMDR | : Mines and Minerals Development and Regulation |
| MoUD | : Ministry of Urban Development |
| MPI | : Multidimensional Poverty Index |
| MSEs | : Micro and Small Enterprises |
| NCDC | : National Coal Development Corporation |
| NDC | : National Development Council |
| NEAT | : Nepal Economic Agriculture and Trade |
| NEP | : National Energy Policy |
| NEP | : National Environment Policy |
| NMFP | : National Mission on Food Processing |
| NOC | : Nepal Oil Corporation Ltd. |
| NPC | : National Planning Commission |
| NPCIL | : Nuclear Power Corporation of India Limited |

| | |
|---|---|
| NRIs | : Non-resident Indians |
| NSB | : National Statistics Bureau |
| NSIC | : National Small Industries Corporation Limited |
| NT | : Nepal Telecom |
| NUTP | : National Urban Transport Policy |
| OCHA | : Office for the Coordination of Humanitarian Affairs |
| OGDCL | : Oil and Gas Development Company Limited |
| PPP | : Public–Private Partnership |
| PR | : Pakistan Railways |
| RE | : Renewable Energy |
| RGoB | : Royal Government of Bhutan |
| RICB | : Royal Insurance Corporation of Bhutan |
| RMG | : Ready-Made Garments |
| SA | : Structural Adjustment |
| SAARC | : South Asian Association for Regional Cooperation |
| SAFTA | : South Asian Free Trade Agreement |
| SBP | : State Bank of Pakistan |
| SCO | : Shanghai Cooperation Organisation |
| SDPI | : Sustainable Development Policy Institute |
| SIDO | : Small Industries Development Organisation |
| SLBFE | : Sri Lanka Bureau of Foreign Employment |
| SLR | : Sri Lanka Railways |
| SLR | : Statutory Liquidity Ratio |
| SREP | : Sustainable Renewable Energy Project |
| SSI | : Small-Scale Industry |
| TCC | : Tashi Commercial Corp |
| TRAI | : Telecom Regulatory Authority of India |
| UCIL | : Uranium Corporation of India Limited |
| UNCTAD | : United Nations Conference on Trade and Development |
| UNDP | : United Nation Development Programme |
| UNODC | : United Nations Office on Drugs and Crime |

USAID : US Agency for International Development
USGS : United States Geological Survey
USTDA : US Trade and Development Agency
UTB : Unit Trust of Bhutan
WAPDA : Water and Power Development Authority
WB : World Bank
WTTC : World Travel and Tourism Council

# Chapter - 1

# Economic Sectors: Overview

*"Unlimited economic growth has the marvelous quality of stilling discontent while maintaining privilege, a fact that has not gone unnoticed among liberal economists."*

—***Noam Chomsky***

According to History of World (2014), the past of the world is the olden times of humanity. The Agricultural Revolution marked a change in human history, as humans began the systematic husbandry of plants and animals. Agriculture advanced, and most humans transitioned from a nomadic to a settled lifestyle as farmers in permanent settlements. As farming developed, grain agriculture became more sophisticated and prompted a division of labour to store food between growing seasons. Many cities developed on the banks of lakes and rivers; as early as 3000 BCE some of the first prominent, well-developed settlements had arisen in Mesopotamia, on the banks of Egypt's River Nile, and in the Indus River valley.[1] According to wikipedia, human evolution is a complex process. It is the evolutionary process leading up to the appearance of modern humans. The scope of economic development includes the process and policies by which a nation improves the economic, political, and social well-being of its people. Economic development originated in the post war period of reconstruction initiated by the US.

In 1949, during his inaugural speech, President Harry Truman identified the development of undeveloped areas as a priority for the west: *"More than half the people of the world are living in conditions approaching misery. Their food is inadequate, they are victims of disease. Their economic life is primitive and stagnant. Their poverty is a handicap and a threat both to them and to more prosperous areas. For the first time in history humanity possesses the knowledge and the skill to relieve the suffering of these people .... I believe that we should make available to peace-loving peoples the benefits of our store of technical knowledge in order to help them realise their aspirations for a better life.... What we envisage is a programme of development based on the concepts of democratic fair dealing.... Greater production is the key to prosperity and peace. And the key to greater production is a wider and more vigorous application of modem scientific and technical knowledge."*

## What is Economic Development?

Economic development is the sustained, concerted actions of policy-makers and communities that promote the standard of living and economic health of a specific area. It can be referred to as the quantitative and qualitative changes in the economy. It differs from economic growth. Whereas economic development is a policy intervention endeavour with aims of economic and social well-being of people, economic growth is a phenomenon of market productivity and rise in GDP. The scope of economic development includes the process and policies by which a nation improves the economic, political, and social well-being of its people.[2]

## Economic Sectors: Types

According to Managing the supply chain to meet customer needs (2012), to understand an economy better scholars like Colin Clark and Jean Fourastia have developed the three sector hypothesis, dividing the economy in to three sectors of activity, viz.

(a) The primary sector of the economy is the sector of an economy making direct use of natural resources. This includes agriculture, forestry, fishing, mining, and extraction of oil and gas. Primary industry is a larger sector in developing countries. Developed countries are allowed to maintain and develop their primary industries even further due to the excess wealth.

(b) The secondary sector of the economy or industrial sector includes those economic sectors that create a finished, tangible product: production and construction. This sector generally takes the output of the primary sector and manufactures finished goods. These products are then either exported or sold to domestic consumers and to places where they are suitable for use by other businesses. The secondary sector takes raw materials and turns them into products. In the oil and gas industry, there are two aspects to production. However, the oil and gas industry as a whole needs people with the right skills to get the products to market. These products include petrol, diesel and natural gas. Throughout the manufacturing process, sustainability and efficiency are important principles.[3]

(c) The tertiary sector of the economy is one of the three economic sectors, the others being the secondary sector and the primary sector. The service sector consists of the *"soft"* parts of the economy, i.e. activities where people offer their knowledge and time to improve productivity, performance, potential, and sustainability. The basic characteristic of this sector is the production of services instead of end products. The tertiary sector of industry involves the provision of services to other businesses as well as final consumers. Services may involve the transport, distribution and sale of goods from producer to a consumer (source: wikipedia).[4] In summary we can say that the classical breakdown of all economic sectors follows:

1. *Primary:* Involves the retrieval and production of raw materials, such as corn, coal, wood and iron.
2. *Secondary:* Involves the transformation of raw or intermediate materials into goods e.g. manufacturing steel into cars, or textiles into clothing.
3. *Tertiary:* Involves the supplying of services to consumers and businesses, such as baby-sitting, cinema and banking.

## Needs for Balancing Sectors

While a balanced growth is the desire of all economic planners, the reality is that some countries have natural advantages that make them very efficient in one of the sectors. They then go on to leverage that sector to spur growth across the economy. Canada and Australia are two good examples of developed countries that have extensive natural resources and have become strong economies by developing their primary sectors like agriculture, fishing, mining and petroleum. They became developed countries because they leveraged these strengths well and then focused on value addition through secondary and later tertiary sectors.

In contrast, there are several African countries that are rich in mineral resources (just as Canada and Australia are), but have not been able to leverage this for the benefit of their citizens, to develop vibrant secondary and tertiary sectors. Unstable political and social environments are perhaps the biggest reason why many of these countries remain under-developed.[5]

## Changing of Economic Sectors in India

According to Majumder (2012), major structural shifts in output and employment always accompany a sustained and rapid growth of per capita output of a country has been an established truism since the original studies of economic growth by Fisher, Clark and Kuznets.[6] Classical development economics emphasised the link between structural change and economic growth. Growth was seen as driven by industrialisation and by the re-allocation of labour from lower-productivity activities or sectors (e.g., traditional agriculture) to higher-productivity employment in areas such as manufacturing.[7]

According wikipedia, economic structural change refers to a long-term shift in the fundamental structure of an economy, which is often linked to growth and economic development. For example, a subsistence economy may be transformed into a manufacturing economy, or a regulated mixed economy is liberalised. The structural changes that move countries through the development process are often viewed in terms of shifts from primary, to secondary and finally, to tertiary production.[8] According Rodrik (2012), two traditions are exist side by side within growth economics. One of them has its roots in development economics and is based on the dual economy approach first formalised by Lewis (1954) and Ranis and Fei (1961). The other has its roots in macroeconomics, and derives from the neoclassical growth model of Solow (1956).[9]

According to Sectors of Indian economy (2013), during early civilisation all economic activity was in primary sector. When the food production became surplus people's need for other products increased.

This led to the development of secondary sector. The growth of secondary sector spread its influence during industrial revolution in nineteenth century. After growth of economic activity a support system was the need to facilitate the industrial activity. Certain sectors like transport and finance play an important role in supporting the industrial activity. Moreover, more shops were needed to provide goods in people's neighbourhood.

Majority of people are still employed in agricultural activities. As agriculture provides seasonal employment during cropping season so chances of hidden employment are big. Secondary and tertiary sector have failed to generate enough employment opportunities making a pressure on primary sector. Although educated and skilled workforces do get employed in secondary and tertiary sector but for unskilled and semi-skilled workers there is still shortage of employment avenues. The sector which carries out all activity through a system and follows the law of the land is called organised sector. The sectors which evade most of the laws and do not follow the system come under unorganised sector.[10]

According to Rainfed Agriculture in India (2014), agriculture plays the vital role in Indian economy. To reduce their vulnerability to rains, farmers in some areas grew crops such as jowar, bajra and pulses. These crops are low-yielding, but less affected by variations in rainfall. This saved the farmers from the risky nature of farming in rainfed and dry areas. The too much exploitation of the groundwater by tube wells led to the depletion of this finite resource. National Rainfed Area Authority was established in 2006 to give focused attention to rainfed areas of the country. This advisory body formulated some common guidelines for the Watershed Development Project and is in consultation with all the States for its implementation.[11]

According the Agricultural Biosecurity Bill 2013, the inflow of pests/diseases of plants and animals into countries through imports is considered one of the biggest threats to diversity, leading to huge economic losses. Against this backdrop, on March 11, 2013, the Agricultural Bio-security Bill, 2013 has been introduced in the Lok Sabha. The Agricultural Biosecurity Bill aims bring all aspects of plant, animal and marine protection and quarantine under a high powered statutory body Agricultural Biosecurity Authority with adequate powers.[12]

According to the National Mission on Sustainable Agriculture (2014), under the National Action Plan on Climate Change, India has launched a dedicated National Mission on Sustainable Agriculture to define its strategies for climate mitigation and adaptation within the agriculture sector.[13] According to National Mission on Food Processing (2014), the Cabinet Committee on Economic Affairs in August 2012 had approved a new Centrally Sponsored Scheme titled "National Mission on Food Processing". This scheme was announced in Union Budget 2012-13. The objective of the scheme is to have a better outreach and to provide more flexibility to suit local needs.[14]

According to Papola (2012), structural changes in an economy can be studied in respect of different outcomes like output, employment, capital investment and consumption. Economic growth in post-Independence India has certainly seen several turns and twists. Accordingly, several phases with distinctive features in terms of rates of growth and structural changes can be identified. Structural changes as reflected in the changes in the shares of agriculture, industry and services have broadly followed the same time pattern as the changes in growth rate but the contents of change have varied from period to period. No doubt, the share of agriculture has continued to consistently decline over the past six decades: from 57 per cent in 1950-51 to 40 per cent in 1980-81 to 24 per cent in 1995-96, to about 16 per cent in 2009-10.

Industry and services have both increased their share, but at different pace and in different periods. Acceleration in the growth of services was led by transport and communication and financial services since 1980: but trade, also joined the fast growing group in the later part of the period, 1995-96/2007-08. In community, social and personal services, public administration and defence saw some decline but other services a sharp acceleration in growth rate. Besides a faster structural shift from agriculture to non-agriculture and emergence of services as the dominant part of the economy, another major change that the Indian economy has seen during the past three decades, especially in the post-reform period is a sharp rise in the importance of the external sector. Exports and Imports together accounted for about 15 per cent of GDP in 1980-81. By 2009-10 the figure has gone up to 35 per cent.[15]

According to Eichengreen and Gupta (2011), among fast growing developing countries, India is distinctive for the role of the service sector. Where earlier developers grew by exporting labour-intensive manufactures, India has relied to a greater extent on services. Although there are other emerging markets where the share of services in GDP exceeds the share of manufacturing, India stands out for the dynamism of its service sector. The share of agriculture (the dashed line) has fallen from 55 per cent in 1950-51 to less than 17 per cent in 2008-09. Following an increase at the outset of the 1990s, reflecting a first wave of liberalisation, the share of industry then stagnated. Meanwhile, the share of services increased from 30 per cent of GDP in 1950 to 57 per cent in 2008-09, rising at an accelerating pace as the period progressed.[16]

According to Papola (2012), there was very little growth of exports during 1950-51 to 1970-71, growth rate being around 3.5 per cent per annum during these two decades. Growth rates of exports averaged to 13 per cent per annum in the 1990's and 14 per cent during 2000-2010. Another disturbing feature of the emerging trends in India's trade structure is that of an increasing trend in the import intensity of exports. A major development in India's export scenario in recent decades has been a fast growth in export of services. Increasing importance of services in exports made a significant contribution to the structural changes in the Indian economy. The period 1990-2010 has seen a rapid increase in the share of services both in GDP and exports.

The early years (1951-65) saw acceleration in industrial growth from around 3 per cent during 1939-51 to 6.5 per cent. During 1965-80 growth rate slumped to 4 per cent. Growth rate accelerated to about 8 per cent during 2000-2005 and further to 10 per cent during 2005-2010. Growth story of the manufacturing sector is characterised by the ascendancy of the organised sector over the decades. The post-reforms period has witnessed some major changes in the structure and characteristics of organised manufacturing. Agro and material based industries like textiles, food products, paper and paper products, food products and beverages have declined in importance while capital intensive industries like coke and petroleum products, motor vehicles and basic metals have sharply increased.[17]

## Conclusion

At last it can be said that economic sectors have three components: (a) agricultural sector, (b) industrial sector and (iii) service sector.

Structural change in India is a real fact. After independence contribution of agriculture in GDP was the highest but now the contribution of service sector is the highest and contribution of agricultural sector is gradually decreasing. In employment also contribution of industrial sector and service sector are increasing continuously. The numbers show that the Indian economy is going through a structural change, with the share of consumption in the economy declining, while that of investment rises.

## References

1. *History of the world (2014).* Retrieved from http://en.wikipedia.org/wiki/History_of_the_world.
2. *Economic Development (2014).* Retrieved from http://en.wikipedia.org/wiki/Economic_development.
3. *Managing the supply chain to meet customer needs (2014),* Retrieved from http://businesscasestudies.co.uk/warburtons/managing-the-supply-chain-to-meet-customer-needs/secondary-sector.html#axzz30TZmlIvK.
4. *Tertiary sector of the economy (2014).* Retrieved from http://en.wikipedia.org/wiki/Tertiary_sector_of_the_economy.
5. See http://www.wealthforumezine.net/Jargon Buster Economy 100114.html #.U2JcMztQHFw.
6. Surajit Mazumdar, *Growth and Structural Changes in Output in India since Independence: A Study Report,* Retrieved from http://isidev.nic.in/pdf/ICSSR_SM.pdf.
7. Orcan Cortuk and Nirvikar Singh (2013). *Analyzing the Structural Change and Growth Relationship in India: State-level Evidence*, Retrieved from http://economics.ucsc.edu/research/downloads/structural_ change_ growth_state_2013a.pdf.
8. *Structural change (2014).* Retrieved from http://en.wikipedia.org/wiki/Structural_change.
9. Dani Rodrik, *Structural change, fundamentals, and growth: An overview,* Retrieved from http://www.sss.ias.edu/files/pdfs/Rodrik/Research/Structural-Change-Fundamentals-and-Growth-An-Overview_revised.pdf.
10. *Sectors of the Indian economy,* Retrieved from http://www.excellup.com/notes/10_socsc_sectorsofeconomy.pdf.
11. *Rainfed agriculture in India (2014).* Retrieved from http://www.gktoday.in/rainfed-agriculture-in-india/
12. *Agricultural Biosecurity Bill 2013*, Retrieved from http://www.gktoday.in/agricultural-biosecurity-bill-2013/
13. *National Mission on Sustainable Agriculture (2014).* Retrieved from http://www.gktoday.in/national-mission-on-sustainable-agriculture/

14. *National Mission on Food Processing (2014).* Retrieved from http://www.gktoday.in/national-mission-on-food-processing/
15. T.S. Papola (2012). *Structural changes in the Indian Economy: Emerging Patterns and Implications, Institute for Studies in Industrial Development,* Retrieved from http://58.68.105.147/pdf/WP1202.pdf.
16. Barry Eichengreen and Poonam Gupta (2011). *The Service Sector as India's Road to Economic Growth,* Retrieved from http://www.nber.org/papers/w16757.pdf.
17. T.S. Papola (2012). *Structural changes in the Indian Economy: Emerging Patterns and Implications, Institute for Studies in Industrial Development,* Retrieved from http://58.68.105.147/pdf/WP1202.pdf.
18. http://www.brainyquote.com/quotes/keywords/development.html

# Chapter - 2

# Economy of South Asian Countries

*"The development of civilisation and industry in general has always shown itself so active in the destruction of forests that everything that has been done for their conservation and production is completely insignificant in comparison."*

—***Karl Marx***

## Introduction

The history of the world is the history of humanity, beginning with the Paleolithic Era. The Agricultural Revolution marked a change in human history, as humans began the systematic husbandry of plants and animals. As farming developed, grain agriculture became more sophisticated and prompted a division of labour to store food between growing seasons. Europe's Renaissance, beginning in the fourteenth century, consisted of the rediscovery of the classical world's scientific contributions, and of the economic and social rise of Europe. During this period, European powers came to dominate most of the world. The Scientific Revolution changed humanity understands of the world and led to the Industrial Revolution, a major transformation of the world's economies. After Europeans had achieved influence and control over the Americas, the imperial activities of the West turned to the lands of the East and Asia. The twenty-first century has been marked by economic globalisation, with consequent risk to interlinked economies, and by the expansion of communications with mobile phones and the Internet (source: wikipedia).[1]

Economic development ideally refers to the sustained, concerted actions of communities and policymakers that improve the standard of living and economic health of a specific locality. It can be referred to as the quantitative and qualitative changes in an existing economy. It involves development of human capital, increasing the literacy ratio, improve important infrastructure, improvement of health and safety and others areas that aims at increasing the general welfare of the citizens.[2]

According to wikipedia, rural development generally refers to the process of improving the quality of life and economic well-being of people living in relatively isolated and sparsely populated areas. It is characterised by its emphasis on locally produced economic development strategies. Education, entrepreneurship, physical infrastructure, and social infrastructure all play an important role in developing rural regions. Rural development programmes are usually top-down from the local or regional authorities, regional development agencies, NGOs, national governments or international development organisation.[3]

According to maps of india, South Asia is the southern region of the Asian continent, which comprises the sub-Himalayan countries and, for some authorities, adjoining countries to the west and east. The core countries of South Asia include Bangladesh, Bhutan, India, Maldives, Nepal, Pakistan and Sri Lanka, however, Afghanistan also included as well.

## Economic Development in India

The arrival of the East India Company in India caused a huge strain to the Indian economy and there was a two-way depletion of resources. The British would buy raw materials from India at cheaper rates and the finished goods were sold at higher than normal price in Indian market. After India got independence from colonial rule in 1947, the process of rebuilding the economy started. For this various policies and schemes were formulated. First five year plan for the development of Indian economy came into implementation in 1952. These Five Year Plans, started by Indian government, focused on the needs of the Indian economy.[4]

According to wikipedia, the economy of India is the eighth-largest in the world by nominal GDP and the third-largest by purchasing power parity. The independence-era Indian economy (from 1947 to 1991) was based on a mixed economy combining features of capitalism and socialism, resulting in an inward-looking, interventionist policies and import-substituting economy that failed to take advantage of the post-war expansion of trade. In 1991, India adopted liberal and free-market principles and liberalised its economy to international trade under the Prime Ministership of P.V. Narasimha Rao and Finance Minister Manmohan Singh. Until the liberalisation of 1991, India was largely and intentionally isolated from the world markets, to protect its economy and to achieve self-reliance.

Since liberalisation, the value of India's international trade has increased sharply. India is a founding-member of General Agreement on Tariffs and Trade since 1947 and its successor, the WTO. Since independence, India's balance of payments on its current account has been negative. Since economic liberalisation in the 1990s, precipitated by a balance of payment crisis, India's exports rose consistently. As the third-largest economy in the world in PPP terms, India is a preferred destination for FDI; during the year 2011, FDI inflow into India stood at $36.5 billion, 51.1 per cent higher than 2010 figure of $24.15 billion. The size of the middle-class population stands at 300 million and represents a growing consumer market. India's recently liberalised FDI policy (2005) allows up to a 100 per cent FDI stake in ventures. Industrial policy reforms have substantially reduced industrial licencing requirements, removed restrictions on expansion and facilitated easy access to foreign technology and foreign direct investment FDI.[5]

Indian Agriculture is one of the most significant contributors to the Indian economy. Agriculture is the only means of living for almost 60 per cent of the employed class in India. The agriculture sector of India has occupied almost 43 per cent of India's geographical area. Agriculture is still the only largest contributor to India's GDP (16 per cent) even after a decline in the same in the agriculture share of India. Agriculture also plays a significant role in the growth of socioeconomic sector in India. It is the main sector of Indian economy. It still continues to be the main sector because it provides livelihood to a majority of the people. With rapid increase in population the absolute number of people engaged in agriculture has become exceedingly large. Because of the heavy pressure of population in labour-surplus economies like India and its rapid increase the demand for food increases at a fast rate.

Agriculture provides raw materials to various industries of national importance. The Indian government also set up Ministry of Food Processing Industries to stimulate the agriculture sector of Indian economy and make it more lucrative. Agriculture sector contributed 32 per cent in 1990-91, 20 per cent during 2005-06 and around 16 per cent now. The per capita income of the agriculture sector declines to one-third of the national per capita income during the recent years. Most of the women work in agricultural sector either as workers, in household farms or as wageworkers.[6]

India was initially an agriculture based economy but after liberalisation norms of 1991 particularly, the services sector has taken a lead contributing the most to the gross domestic product. Presently the agricultural, manufacturing and service sector account for 16, 27, and 57 per cent of GDP respectively. Textile industry is a booming industry of India with India being one of the largest textile producers of the world. Chemical industry, one of the earliest of all Indian industries contributes considerably to Indian economy and has been doing so since the times of independence. In the recent times, the engineering and machinery sector has played a crucial role in boosting Indian economy and also developing other industrial sectors of the country's economy. The transportation industry of India is large and expansive. The roadways, highways, ports, aviation industry and railways, all form a part of the transportation industry. The Information Technology industry is a knowledge-based industry with skilled professionals in India. The IT–ITES industry is made up of the IT Services sector and the Business process outsourcing industry.[7]

The services sector is a vital cog in the wheel of the Indian economy. The Indian service industry has emerged as one of the largest and fastest-growing sectors on the global landscape and hence has made substantial contribution towards global output and employment. Growing at faster pace as compared to agriculture and manufacturing sectors, Indian service segment comprises of wide range of activities, such as trading, transportation and communication, financial, real estate and business services, as well as community, social and personal services.[8]

India has many long-term challenges that it has yet to fully address, including poverty, corruption, violence and discrimination against women and girls, an inefficient power generation and distribution system, ineffective enforcement of intellectual property rights, decades-long civil litigation dockets, inadequate transport and agricultural infrastructure, limited non-agricultural employment opportunities, inadequate availability of quality basic and higher education, and accommodating rural-to-urban migration.[9]

## Economic Development in Pakistan

The economy is semi-industrialised, with centres of growth along the Indus River. Major industries include textiles, chemicals, food processing (mainly sugar, salt, wheat, rice, and fruit), agriculture, fertiliser, cement, dairy and rugs. Pakistan was a very poor and predominantly agricultural country when it gained independence in 1947. According to many sources, the Pakistani government has made substantial economic reforms since 2000, and medium-term prospects for job creation and poverty reduction are the best in nearly a decade. Government revenues have greatly improved in recent years, as a result of economic growth, tax reforms, with a broadening of the tax base, and more efficient tax collection as a result of self-assessment schemes and corruption controls in the Central Board of Revenue and the privatisation of public utilities and telecommunications.

Liberalisation in the international textile trade has already yielded benefits for Pakistan's exports, and the country also expects to profit from freer trade in agriculture. Growing stability in the nation's monetary policies has contributed to a reduction in money-market interest rates, and a great expansion in the quantity of credit, changing consumption and investment patterns in the nation. Pakistan's manufacturing sector has experienced double-digit growth in recent years, from 2000 to 2007, with large-scale manufacturing growing from a minimal 1.5 per cent in 1999 to a record 19.9 per cent in 2004–05 and averaged 8.8 per cent by end of 2007. As of 2013, according to Macro Economic Insights, a research firm in Islamabad, the size of the Pakistani middle class is conservatively estimated at approximately 70 million, out of a total population of 190 million. This represents 40 per cent of the population of the country.[10]

Pakistan's principal natural resources are arable land and water. About 25 per cent of Pakistan's are accounts for about 21.2 per cent of GDP and employs about 43 per cent of the labour force. In Pakistan, the most agricultural province is Punjab where wheat and cotton are the most grown. The most important crops are wheat, sugarcane, cotton, and rice, which together account for more than 75 per cent of the value of total crop output. Pakistan's largest food crop is wheat. Pakistan is a net food exporter, except in occasional years when its harvest is adversely affected by droughts. Pakistan exports rice, cotton, fish, fruits (especially Oranges and Mangoes), and vegetables and imports vegetable oil, wheat, pulses and consumer foods.

Much of the Pakistan's agriculture output is utilised by the country's growing processed-food industry. The Food and Agriculture Organisation reported in June 2006 that in Pakistan, government initiatives are being undertaken to modernise milk collection and to improve milk and milk product storage capacity. Fishery and fishing industry plays an important role in the national economy of Pakistan. With a coastline of about 1046 km, Pakistan has enough fishery resources that remain to be fully developed. It is also a major source of export earning. About only four per cent of land is covered with forest. The forest are a main source of food, lumber, paper, fuel wood, latex, medicine as well as used for purposes of wildlife conservation and ecotourism.[11]

Agriculture is the mainstay of Pakistan's economy, employing more than 40 per cent of the population. Cotton, wheat, rice, sugarcane, fruits, vegetables, and tobacco are the chief crops, and cattle, sheep, and poultry are raised. There is also a fishing industry. Most of Pakistan's agricultural output comes from the Indus basin. Pakistan's industrial base is able to supply many of the country's needs in consumer goods and other products. The country major manufactures textiles (the biggest earner of foreign exchange), processed foods, pharmaceuticals, construction materials, paper products, and fertilizer.[12] The services sector has provided steady support to Pakistan's economic growth. It share in GDP now stands a more than 50 per cent. The good sector of Pakistan shows that share of agriculture has been declining gradually over time from 43.6 per cent in 1960-61 to 21.5 per cent of GDP in 2009-10, and share of industry has increased from 15.6 per cent in 1960-61 to 25.2 per cent of GDP in 2009-10. Whereas the share of service sector has increased from 39 per cent of GDP in 1960-61 to 53.3 per cent of GDP in 2009-10, therefore service sector is the largest contributor in the GDP of Pakistan.

The increasing growth rate of service sector is due to increasing growth in finance and insurance sector. The service sector has major contribution in value added and gross fixed capital formation. Employment share in services sector is increasing, people are moving from agriculture sector to services sector. Demography and lifestyle changes have the major contribution to increase in the growth of consumer demand of services. Although Pakistan is an agriculture country, but due to urbanisation the share of employment in agriculture sector is decreasing and people move towards the other sectors of economy for better job. The various job characteristics are used to measure the job quality such as working condition, job satisfaction and wage rate. The more highly paid employees need better working condition and some how they have choice in their working schedule.[13]

## Economic Development in Nepal

Nepal is among the poorest and least developed countries in the world, with about one-quarter of its population living below the poverty line. It has used a series of five-year plans in an attempt to make progress in economic development. Foreign aid accounts for more than half of the development budget. Government priorities over the years have been the development of transportation and communication facilities, agriculture, and industry. Agriculture remains Nepal's principal economic activity, employing 70 per cent of the population and providing 37 per cent of GDP. GDP is heavily dependent on India, particularly with regard to remittances of foreign workers. Subsequently, economic development in social services and infrastructure has not made dramatic progress.

Major towns are connected to the capital by telephone and domestic air services. The export-oriented carpet and garment industries have grown rapidly in recent years. Progress has been made in exploiting Nepal's natural resources, tourism and hydroelectricity.[14] The Nepal Economic Agriculture and Trade Activity worked to promote economic growth, reduce poverty, and improve lives. Nepal, a low-income country with high levels of poverty and modest growth rates, has been undergoing a period of social and political tension. Underlying much of the conflict was the fundamental problem of poverty. Key governance issues included deficiencies in the legal framework for and treatment of business.[15]

Although new agricultural technologies helped increase food production, there still was room for further growth. Rice is the most important cereal crop. In 1966 total rice production amounted to a little more than one million tons; by 1989 more than three million tons were produced. Other food crops included wheat, millet, barley, and coffee, but their contribution to the agricultural sector was small. Sugarcane and tobacco also showed considerable increases in production from the 1970s to the 1980s. Potatoes and oilseed production had shown moderate growth since 1980. Medicinal herbs were grown in the north on the slopes of the Himalayas, but increases in production were limited by continued environmental degradation. According to government statistics, production of milk, meat, and fruit had improved but as of the late 1980s still had not reached a point where nutritionally balanced food was available to most people.[16]

Agriculture in Nepal suffers from years of under-investment, limited research, and scant inputs, technology and services for farmers. Unless things change, Nepal may fall into deeper food insecurity and poverty. Declining resource allocation to agriculture research and development will have direct implications on attaining the objective of poverty reduction, despite investment made on infrastructure. Inputs needed to increase the land's productivity are scarce nationwide. The government's 2012 Agriculture Development Strategy Assessment Report estimated 200,000 youth, especially from rural areas, migrated abroad for employment in 2010, leaving mostly women, children and the elderly behind. Female-headed agricultural households have increased from 12 per cent in 1995 to 26 per cent in 2010. Yet only 18 per cent of women in rural households own houses or land, according to the 2011 census.[17]

Nepal's economy is expected to grow at 4.6 per cent in 2012, with the growth rate likely to be around 5.2 per cent over the forthcoming three years, according to Nepal Economic Outlook 2012. For Nepal to accelerate its growth, it needs to focus on the right things. The recent turmoil in the casino industry is an example. It is now illegal to allow Nepal's citizens to enter the eight casinos in the capital city of Kathmandu. Authorities are cracking down on casinos permitting locals to gamble.[18] Most industries are small, localised operations based on the processing of agricultural products. There are a sawmill and a meat-processing plant in Hitaura and a number of rice and oil mills in the

Tarai. Other industries include brick and tile manufacture; processing of construction materials, paper, and food grain; cigarette manufacture; cement production; and brewing of beer.[19]

Tourism is the largest industry in Nepal, and the largest source of exchange and revenue. Possessing eight of the 10 highest mountains in the world, Nepal is a hotspot destination for mountaineers, rock climbers and people seeking adventures. The Hindu and Buddhist heritage and its cold weather are also strong attractions. The major religion in Nepal is Hinduism, and the Pashupatinath Temple, the world's largest temple of Shiva which is located in Kathmandu, attracts many pilgrims and tourists.[20]

## Economic Development in Bhutan

The economy of Bhutan, one of the world's smallest and least developed countries, is based on agriculture and forestry, which provide the main livelihood for more than 60 per cent of the population. Hydropower exports to India have boosted Bhutan's overall growth, even though GDP fell in 2008 as a result of a slowdown in India, its predominant export market. Bhutan's hydropower potential and its attraction for tourists are key resources. The Bhutanese Government has made some progress in expanding the nation's productive base and improving social welfare. In 2004, Bhutan became the first country in the world to ban smoking and the selling of tobacco.[21] Bhutan's economy is mostly based on agriculture, which together with livestock keeping is the main source of livelihood for over 80 population of the population. The country hardly knows real industry, except forestry and cottage building. Most of the consumer goods and essentials are imported and its major export goods are calcium carbides, cement, wood based products, minerals and horticulture products.[22]

Agriculture has a dominant role in the economy of the country. The share of the agricultural sector in GDP declined from approximately 55 per cent in 1985 to 33 per cent in 2003. Despite this, agriculture remains the primary source of livelihood for the majority of the population. Approximately 80 per cent of the populations are involved in agriculture. Major crops cultivated are maize and rice. Forests in the nation act as the source of livestock fodder and organic materials for the purpose of development of fertility. Forests are also responsible for regulating the availability of water for agricultural purpose.

Production of cash crops such as apple, orange and cardamom have increased and have become profitable. In several areas the shifting cultivation is being replaced by the orchard cultivation. Academics expect this will increase the cultivation of cash crops.[23]

Fragmented land holding and the dominance of subsistence farming is one of the root causes of rural poverty. Moreover due to lack of sufficient irrigation facilities and limited use of mechanisation, productivity is low compared to that in other countries. Further, the lack of international markets and linkages affect the prospects of large scale exports in the country.[24] In recent years area of cultivation has increased dramatically in all parts of the country especially in valleys such as Paro, Punakha-Wangdi, Tashigang-Mongar, Chirang and in Geylegphug. Beside export-import and trade agreements, Bhutan has strong monetary links with India.

The kingdom depends on India's financial assistance, especially for the modernisation of its infrastructure. Bhutan's rugged and mountainous terrain (in addition to shortages in skilled labour and low national revenues) makes infrastructural development, such as road construction, difficult and expensive. India finances three-fifths of Bhutan's budget expenditures. Bhutan depends on India's assistance for achieving one of its primary goals: industrial modernisation.[25]

Rapid modernisation has brought about vast improvements in the living standard of the Bhutanese people. Bhutan's rich biodiversity provides the country with ample forest resources and this has brought about the development of a thriving cane and bamboo handicraft industry. Craftsmen weave a number of beautiful and intricate items out of bamboo and cane including hats, backpacks, floor mats and traditional bowls. These items are then sold to tourists or Bhutanese, supplying a secondary income source. The Bhutanese Tourism Industry was first opened in 1974. Since then it has grown to become, a major contributing factor to the Bhutanese economy creating countless employment opportunities and generating additional revenue for the government. With the industrial sector established in Pasakha, small scale industries such as cement plants, calcium and carbide, steel and Ferro silicon, Coca Cola and also wood based industries have started developing.[26]

Handicrafts, cement, food processing, wood milling, and distilling were the major industries. Most of the larger industries, established since Bhutan's economic modernisation began in the 1960s, were themselves modern and used a considerable amount of labour-saving technology. The largest industries employed no more than sixty or seventy workers. Many of the newly developing industries began making public stock offerings in the late 1980s.[27]

The Bhutan Government implemented economic reforms, beginning in 1999 and took an active role in guiding the nation's economic development. It is one of the fastest-growing economies in the region with an average annual gross domestic product growth rate of five per cent. The country's economy remains strong as a result of public- private partnership that played a significant role in economic stability of the country. At present sectors such as agriculture, live-stock, timber, tourism, telecommunication, banking, construction and hydro-electricity are expanding rapidly. The private sector plays a vital role in the agro processing industry. Agro Industries Limited was started in 1993 with financial and technical assistance from the "Danish International Development Agency". Bhutan Telecom Limited has played a major role in the country's telecommunication sector development. As of February 2007, all twenty districts in Bhutan were connected with cellular mobiles. Today, Bhutan Telecom Limited ensures its customers with cost effective and efficient service. The tradition of Bhutanese postal service can be traced back to 1962 when the first regular postal service was set up under the Department of Post and Telegraph and under the Ministry of Communications in Phuentsholing. Bhutan is already showing the results of its trade reforms and other liberalisation measures taken.[28]

## Economic Development in Sri Lanka

The main economic sectors of the country are tourism, tea export, apparel, textile, rice production and other agricultural products. Sri Lanka began to shift away from a socialist orientation in 1977. Since then, the government has been deregulating, privatising, and opening the economy to international competition. Sri Lanka's most dynamic industries now are food processing, textiles and apparel, food and beverages, telecommunications, and insurance and banking. In the recent past, the Sri Lankan Government has identified some key focal areas to address the external imbalances of the economy, especially with regard to reducing its high trade deficit.

The Central Bank of Sri Lanka is the monetary authority of Sri Lanka and was established in 1950. It is responsible for the conduct of monetary policy in the country and also has supervisory powers over the financial system. Most Sri Lankan cities and towns are connected by the Sri Lanka Railways, the state-run railway operator. The Sri Lanka Transport Board is the state-run agency responsible for operating public bus services across the island. The energy policy is governed by the Ministry of Power and Energy, while the production and retailing of electricity is carried out by the Ceylon Electricity Board. Energy is mostly generated by hydroelectric power stations in the Central Province. Tourism is one of the main industries. Major tourist attractions are focused around the islands famous beaches located in the southern and the eastern parts of the country and ancient heritage sites located in the interior of the country and resorts located in the mountainous regions of the country. The tea industry, operating under the Ministry of Public Estate Management and Development, is one of the main industries. The apparel industry mainly exports to the United States and Europe.[29]

Sri Lanka's primary form of agriculture is rice production. Rice is cultivated during Maha and Yala seasons. Tea is cultivated in the central highlands and is a major source of foreign exchange. Vegetables, fruits and oilseed crops are also cultivated in the country. The cool and salubrious climatic conditions in the hill country are ideal for temperate crops such as carrot, leek, cabbage, cauliflower, salad leaves, beet, bean, bell pepper and salad cucumber. Oilseed crops such as Groundnut, Sesame, Sunflower and Mustard are also cultivated in Sri Lanka. Agro Technology Park is one of the finest initiatives for agriculture extension, education and agro tourism implemented by the Department of Agriculture, Sri Lanka. The first A-Park was established in Kandy district.[30]

Cinnamon, cardamom, pepper, cloves, nutmeg, citronella, tobacco, cocoa, and coffee are also exported. Rice, sugarcane, grains, pulses, oilseed, fruit, and vegetables are grown for local use and consumption. Historically, industry centered chiefly on the processing of agricultural products, but textiles and garments are now Sri Lanka's biggest export.

Sri Lanka has a persistent balance of trade problem and the country is dependent on large amounts of foreign aid. The port of Colombo, on which most of the country's railroads converge, handles most of the foreign trade.[31]

In Sri Lanka, industrial production measures the output of businesses integrated in industrial sector of the economy such as manufacturing, mining, and utilities. The export oriented production of clothing (readymade garments) began in 1970s and expanded rapidly after the liberalisation of the economy in 1977. The apparel sector is the highest industrial employment generator and the highest foreign exchange earner. The most number of apparel projects operate in the Western Province. This shows that opportunities for apparel factories are available in emerging areas where enough employment is available and emerging constraint in the Western Province.[32] Sri Lanka is a large natural rubber producer and exports most of its products. It is a major supplier of high quality latex crepe and one of the world's largest manufacturers and exporter of solid tyres. Tourism is the main competitive sector in the Central Province. Sri Lanka hosts over 400,000 tourists annually. Projects of over Rs 10 million include investments in hotels, recreational complexes, etc.[33]

## Economic Development in Bangladesh

Bangladesh is a parliamentary republic with an elected parliament called the Jatiyo Sangshad. The poverty rate has declined considerably since independence, and per-capita income has doubled from 1975 levels. Bangladesh is a pioneer and founding member of SAARC. It is the world's largest contributor to United Nations peacekeeping operations. Bangladesh is a developing nation. It has seen a dramatic increase in foreign direct investment. In order to enhance economic growth, the government set up several export processing zones to attract foreign investment. The insufficient power supply constitutes an obstacle to growth. Exports of textiles and garments are the largest source of foreign exchange earnings.

Shipbuilding, pharmaceuticals and consumer goods manufacturing are important emerging industries, while the jute sector is re-emerging with increasing global demand for green fibres. Remittances from Bangladeshis working overseas, mainly in the Middle East, are another major source of foreign exchange earnings. The land is devoted mainly to rice and jute cultivation as well as fruits and other produce. The country's tea-growing regions, located in the eastern divisions of Sylhet and Chittagong, are among the major tea producing-areas of the world. Bangladesh's growth of its agricultural industries is due to its fertile deltaic land that depends on its six seasons and multiple harvests. After its independence from Pakistan, Bangladesh followed a socialist economy by nationalising all industries, proving to be a critical blunder undertaken by the Awami League government. Some of the same factors that had made East Bengal a prosperous region became disadvantages during the nineteenth and twentieth centuries. After 1975, Bangladeshi leaders began to turn their attention to developing new industrial capacity and rehabilitating its economy.[34]

It has a primarily agrarian economy. Agriculture is the single largest producing sector of the economy. A plurality of Bangladeshis earns their living from agriculture. Although rice and jute are the primary crops, wheat is assuming greater importance. Tea is grown in the northeast. Because of Bangladesh's fertile soil and normally ample water supply, rice can be grown and harvested three times a year in many areas. Rice, Wheat, Mango and jute are the primary crops, assuming greater importance. Tea is grown in the northeast. Due to a number of factors, Bangladesh's labour-intensive agriculture has achieved steady increases in food grain production despite the often unfavourable weather conditions. Food grains are cultivated primarily for subsistence. Only a small percentage of total production makes its way into commercial channels.[35]

More than three-quarters of Bangladesh's export earnings come from the garment industry in 2005. There has also been a significant growth to Bangladesh's ship building industry in the last few years. The required ships and vessels in the country are being produced by the local shipbuilders. The tourism sector in Bangladesh has experienced massive growth in recent years. The majority of growth is contributed by local tourists. It is believed to be a major tourist destination if properly advertised. Nonetheless, few government and private initiatives have been taken to attract foreign tourists. Though small in area, Bangladesh is quite rich in heritage with numerous historical and archeological sites. It has the longest natural unbroken sea beach and five World Heritage Sites. Bangladesh has the largest shopping mall in South Asia, which is 13th largest in the world. It is Bashundhara City Shopping Mall which is situated at Karwan Bazar in Dhaka.[36]

## Economic Development in Maldives

The Maldives is an island nation, and islands depend upon the ocean for their sustenance. In ancient times, the Maldives were famous for dried fish, ambergris and the cowrie shells used as currency all up and down the East African coast. Today, the Maldives is still a fishing nation, but its far better known as a beach getaway. Tourism is the largest industry in the Maldives, accounting for 28 per cent of GDP and more than 60 per cent of the Maldives' foreign exchange receipts. Fishing is the second leading sector. The economic reform programme by the government in 1989 lifted import quotas and opened some exports to the private sector. Subsequently, it has liberalised regulations to allow more foreign investment. Agriculture and manufacturing play a minor role in the economy, constrained by the limited availability of cultivable land and shortage of domestic labour. Most staple foods are imported. Industry in the Maldives consists mainly of garment production, boat building, and handicrafts.[37] Among the 1,900 islands in the Maldives, only 198 are inhabited. The population is scattered throughout the country, and the greatest concentration is on the capital island, Malé. Development of the infrastructure is mainly dependent on the tourism industry and its complementary tertiary sectors, transport, distribution, real estate, construction, and government.[38]

Agriculture is constrained by the lack of arable land. According to the World Health Organisation the Maldives' agricultural sector produces only 10 per cent of the food needed to feed its population. The country is forced to import rice, its dietary staple, from trading partners. It also imports wheat flour, sugar, dairy products, and meat and eggs. Lack of energy and mineral resources also hold back economic development in the Maldives. The islands are also highly susceptable to natural disasters like the December 2004 Asian tsunami. Fishing employs 20 per cent of the Maldivian workforce. The Maldives has an active merchant shipping fleet consisting of ten cargo ships, one container vessel and an oil tanker.

The government-owned Maldives Shipping Management Ltd is the country's largest shipping company but private companies do most of the Maldives' importing and exporting. There is some boat building and garment manufacturing in the Maldives but no heavy manufacturing. Manufacturing is constrained because the islands are so small and so geographically dispersed that logistics presents a major challenge. The tourism industry has been a boon to the Maldives' traditional handicrafts. In ancient times, the Maldives were renowned for a rope called coir, woven from coconut fibers, and coir mats still a popular Maldivian souvenir today.[39]

## Economic Development in Afghanistan

The Afghan economy has always been agricultural, despite the fact that only 12 per cent of its total land is arable and about six per cent is currently cultivated. Agriculture production is constrained by an almost total dependence on erratic winter snows and spring rains for water. Wheat and cereal production is Afghanistan's traditional agricultural mainstay. The overall agricultural production dramatically declined following four years of drought as well as the sustained fighting and instability in rural areas. The availability of land suitable for grazing has traditionally made animal husbandry an important part of the economy. There are two main types of animal husbandry: sedentary, practiced by farmers who raise both animals and crops; and nomadic, practiced by animal herders known as Kuchis.

Much of Afghanistan's livestock was removed from the country by early waves of refugees who fled to neighbouring Pakistan and Iran. The country has plenty of water reserves and suitable climate for fish farming. Fishing takes place in the lakes and rivers, particularly in the Kabul River around the Jalalabad area. Afghanistan's timber has been greatly depleted, and since the mid-1980s, only about three per cent of the land area has been forested, mainly in the east. Significant stands of trees have been destroyed by the ravages of the war. The destruction of the forests to create agricultural land, logging, forest fires, plant diseases, and insect pests are all causes of the reduction in forest coverage.[40]

Afghanistan has several major industries. The natural resources they use are natural gas, oil, copper, gold and salt. One of their most successful trades is the handmade carpets from their people. Industry is based on agriculture, and pastoral raw materials. The major industrial crops are: cotton, tobacco, madder, castor beans, and sugar beets. Sheep farming is also extremely valuable. The major sheep product exports are wool, and highly prized Karakul skins. Afghanistan is a land that is rich in natural resources.[41] As with other sectors of the economy, Afghanistan's already beleaguered industries have been devastated by over two decades of civil strife and war that left most of the countries factories and even much of the cottage industry sector inoperative.

The principal modern industry is cotton textile production, with factories at Pol e Khomri, Golbahar, Begram, Balkh, and Jabal as Saraj, just north of Charikar. Carpet making is the most important handicraft industry, but it has suffered with the flight of rug makers during the civil war and since the 2001 US-led bombing campaign. Carpet-making is centered on the north and northwest regions of the country. Afghan carpets are made of pure wool and are hand-knotted, and much of the work is done by women. Wood and stone carving have been concentrated in the northeastern provinces, while jewellery making has been done in the Kabul area. The making of leather goods has also been a handicraft industry.[42]

## Conclusion

The scope of economic development includes the process and policies by which a nation improves the economic, political, and social well-being of its people. Economic development originated in the post-war period of reconstruction initiated by the US. It typically involves improvements in a variety of indicators such as literacy rates, life expectancy, and poverty. International trade and exchange rates are a key issue in economic development. It has evolved into a professional industry of highly specialised practitioners.

South Asia is the home of some poor countries, like as Bangladesh, Nepal. Economic development of Nepal and Bhutan depends on the aid of India. Economy of Bangladesh depends on foreign aid and remittances from Bangladeshi people working in other countries. Economy of India is growing very rapidly but it is affecting by the relation with the surrounding countries. Economy of Pakistan and Afghanistan is affecting by the terrorism. Global worming is the main threat from the economy of Bangladesh and Maldives. Economy of Nepal and Bhutan depends on India. So, good socio-political relation is more important for economic development in this region.

## References


1. *History of the world (2014).* Retrieved from http://en.wikipedia.org/wiki/History_of_the_world.
2. *Economic development (2014).* Retrieved from http://www.whatiseconomics.org/economic-development
3. *Rural development (2014*). Retrieved from http://en.wikipedia.org/wiki/Rural_development.
4. *Indian Economy (2014).* Retrieved from http://www.mapsofindia.com/india-economy.html
5. *Economy of India (2014*). Retrieved from http://en.wikipedia.org/wiki/Economy_of_India.
6. *Indian agriculture -Indian economy – National income – per capita income–Agricultural income in GDP-Women in agriculture and empowerment,* Retrieved from http://tnau.ac.in/eagri/eagri50/AGRO101/lec02.pdf.
7. *Top 10 Industries that Contribute to Indian Economy,* Retrieved from http://listdose.com/top-10-industries-that-contribute-to-indian-economy/
8. *Service sector in India (2014).* Retrieved from http://www.ibef.org/industry/services.aspx.
9. See http://www.indexmundi.com/india/economy_profile.html
10. *Economy of Pakistan (2014).* Retrieved from http://en.wikipedia.org/wiki/Economy_of_Pakistan.
11. *Agriculture in Pakistan (2014).* Retrieved from http://en.wikipedia.org/wiki/Agriculture_in_Pakistan.
12. See http://www.infoplease.com/ençyclopedia/world/pakistan-economy.html
13. Ayaz Ahmed and Henna Ahsan (2011). *Contribution of Services Sector in the Economy of Pakistan,* Retrieved from http://www.pide.org.pk/pdf/Working%20Paper/WorkingPaper-79.pdf.
14. *Economy of Nepal (2014).* Retrieved from http://en.wikipedia.org/wiki/Economy_of_Nepal.
15. See http://www.chemonics.com/OurWork/OurProjects/Pages/Nepal%20Economic%20Agriculture%20and%20Trade.aspx.
16. *Agriculture in Nepal (2014).* Retrieved from http://en.wikipedia.org/wiki/Agriculture_in_Nepal.
17. *Analysis: The trouble with Nepal's agriculture,* Retrieved from http://www.irinnews.org/report/97321/analysis-the-trouble-with-nepal-s-agriculture.
18. See http://wadhwarakesh.com/what-lies-between-nepal-and-economic-growth/
19. *Nepal- Industry and trade profile*, Retrieved from http://www.britannica.com/EBchecked/topic/409152/Nepal/23646/Industry-and-trade.

20. *Tourism in Nepal (2014).* Retrieved from http://en.wikipedia.org/wiki/Tourism_in_Nepal.
21. *Economy of Bhutan (2014).* Retrieved from http://en.wikipedia.org/wiki/Economy_of_Bhutan
22. *Economy of Bhutan (2014).* Retrieved from http://www.bhutan.com/economy
23. *Agriculture in Bhutan (2014).* Retrieved from http://en.wikipedia.org/wiki/Agriculture_in_Bhutan
24. See http://www.gnhc.gov.bt/absd/?page_id=93
25. *Economy of Bhutan (2014).* Retrieved from http://dev.cushing.org/bhutan/bhutan/economy/
26. *Economy-Bhutan (2014).* Retrieved from http://www.tourism.gov.bt/about-bhutan/Economy
27. *Bhutan-Industry, Mining, Energy, and Commerce (2014).* Retrieved from http://www.mongabay.com/history/bhutan/bhutan-industry,_mining,_energy,_and_commerce.html
28. *Bhutan the Emerging Economy of South Asia*, Retrieved from http://www.bhutannewsservice.com/feature/bhutan-the-emerging-economy-of-south-asia/
29. *Economy in Sri Lanka (2014).* Retrieved from http://en.wikipedia.org/wiki/Economy_of_Sri_Lanka.
30. *Agriculture in Sri Lanka (2014).* Retrieved from http://en.wikipedia.org/wiki/Agriculture_in_Sri_Lanka
31. See http://www.infoplease.com/encyclopedia/world/sri-lanka-economy.html
32. *Key sectors for investment- Apparels,* Retrieved from http://www.invest srilanka.com/key_sectors_for_investment/apparel_overview.html
33. See http://www.nbiexpo.com/sri-lanka.
34. *Economy of Bangladesh (2014).* Retrieved from http://en.wikipedia.org/wiki/Economy_of_Bangladesh.
35. *Agriculture in Bangladesh (2014).* Retrieved from http://en.wikipedia.org/wiki/Agriculture_in_Bangladesh.
36. *Bangladesh (2014).* Retrieved from http://en.wikipedia.org/wiki/Bangladesh
37. *Economy of Maldives (2014).* Retrieved from http://en.wikipedia.org/wiki/Economy_of_the_Maldives.
38. *Economy of the Maldives (2014).* Retrieved from https://www.princeton.edu/~achaney/tmve/wiki100k/docs/Economy_of_the_Maldives.html
39. *Economy of the Maldives (2014).* Retrieved from http://www.maldive sholidays.org/economy-maldives
40. *Economy of Afghanistan (2014).* Retrieved from http://en.wikipedia.org/wiki/Economy_of_Afghanistan

41. See http://www.afghan-web.com/economy/
42. *Afghanistan- Industry,* Retrieved from http://www.nationsencyclopedia.com/Asia-and-Oceania/Afghanistan-INDUSTRY.html#b
43. http://www.brainyquote.com/quotes/keywords/development.html

# Chapter - 3

# Economy of Bangladesh

*"The financial crisis should not become an excuse to raise taxes, which would only undermine the economic growth required to regain our strength."*

— ***George W. Bush***

Bangladesh is situated in the north-eastern part of South Asia. It lies between 20° 34° and 2° 36' north latitude and 88° 1° and 92° 41' east longitude. The great Himalayas stand as the northern ramparts, while the southern frontier is guarded by the Bay of Bengal. On the west lies the expansive Gangetic plains (West Bengal) of India and on the eastern frontier lies the almost impassable forest of Myanmar (Arakan Province) and India (Tripura and Assam hills). These picturesque geographical boundaries delineate out a low lying plain of about 147,570 sq.km. Mighty rivers the Padma, Jamuna, Meghna, Karnaphuli and others flow through Bangladesh.

The history of Bangladesh has been one of extremes, of turmoil and peace, prosperity and destitution. It has thrived under the glow of cultural splendour and suffered under the ravages of war. The seeds of independence were sown through the Language Movement of 1952 to recognise Bangla as a state language. Ultimately the then East Pakistan emerged as a sovereign and independent state of Bangladesh in 1971 after nine month-long war of Liberation (starting on 26 March 1971) in which three million people courted martyrdom.[1]

The trading relationship between India and Bangladesh is currently of special interest in both countries for a number of reasons.

- There are urgent and longstanding concerns in Bangladesh arising from the perennial, large bilateral trade deficit with

India, and from the large volumes of informal imports from India across the land border which avoid Bangladesh import duties. These concerns have been particularly acute on the Bangladesh side in the context of discussions between the two governments of the possibility of a bilateral free trade agreement along the lines of the India-Sri Lanka FTA.

- Even though India's trading relationship with Bangladesh is much less significant for it than it is for Bangladesh, closer economic integration with Bangladesh is nevertheless seen as a very important way of reducing the economic and political isolation of the seven Indian eastern and north-eastern states from the rest of the country.
- Both countries have long shared common objectives for closer economic integration within the South Asia region, and these have recently been reemphasised by signing on to SAFTA, which takes effect from January 2006.[2]

As Bangladesh has grown and developed in the four decades since its independence in 1971, Bangladeshi society and the US -Bangladesh relationship have been transformed. As Bangladesh nears middle-income status, a relationship once based on aid, humanitarian help, and remittances now rests on a foundation of trade and investment. Infrastructure-aviation, energy, rail, healthcare, water-raises people's quality of life, demonstrates government accountability, and enables greater efficiency and economic growth. US companies provide many of the leading infrastructure products and services, and they are committed local players that provide quality, promote corporate social responsibility, transfer technology, and invest in the community.[3]

## Situation of the Economy

The rate of growth of GDP in Bangladesh has picked up in recent years. During the period 1980–1990, it grew at an average annual rate of 3.7 per cent, barely exceeding the population growth rate; but subsequently, during the period 1999–2004, it exceeded an average annual rate of five per cent, to reach about $54 billion in the fiscal year 2003-2004. There were only modest changes in the relative shares of consumption and savings in GDP in recent years. In 1991, consumption accounted for nearly 86 per cent of GDP, but fell to 82 per cent in

2004, while the share of savings in GDP rose from 12 per cent to 8 per cent over this period. Changes in the sectoral distribution of GDP indicate that Bangladesh's economy has undergone important structural transformations over the past three decades. At independence in 1971, agriculture was the dominant sector, accounting for over half of total GDP.[4]

In the years to come, some of Bangladesh's major objectives in building and maintaining its foreign relations will be to promote multilateralism, regional cooperation and security, combating terrorism, increasing remittances, mobilising international support for debt reduction, market expansion, and promotion of trade. It will need the support of the major powers in pursuing these goals and objectives. It is important that the Bangladesh Government's foreign policy is geared towards a comprehensive policy framework that accommodates financial support and foreign assistance in boosting agricultural productivity, training for civil servants, improving the infrastructure, combating corruption and terrorism, and expanding employment and labour productivity.[5]

## Agriculture

Bangladesh is primarily an agrarian economy. Agriculture is the single largest producing sector of economy since it comprises about 30 per cent of the country's GDP and employing around 60 per cent of the total labour force. Meeting the nation's food requirements remains the key-objective of the government and in recent years there has been substantial increase in grain production. Due to calamities like flood, loss of food and cash crops is a recurring phenomenon which disrupts the continuing progress of the entire economy. Agricultural holdings in Bangladesh are generally small.[6] Rice is the staple food in the everyday diet of Bangladeshis. Jute, often called the "golden fibre" of Bengal, is the main export-earner for Bangladeshi agriculture, as Bangladesh remains the world's second-largest producer of jute (after India) and the world's largest exporter of fiber. Bangladesh also produces tea leaves, mainly for export, although the export of this product contributes only one per cent of the country's hard currency earnings.

Flood, riverbank erosion, cyclone, and storm surge have severe impacts on fisheries, with moderate effects on poverty and economic growth. These shocks damage aquaculture infrastructure and cause fish loss, leading to loss of livelihoods of poor fishers and decreasing the nutrition status of the rural poor. Frequent cyclone warnings lead fishers to stay at home for longer periods, lowering their income. In addition, drought, salinity intrusion, and erratic rainfall affect the fisheries sector moderately. Severe impacts of flood, drought, cyclone, and storm surge, as well as sea level rise and salinity intrusion, will severely affect the poverty of this livelihood group.[7]

Farmers are more interested to produce some few crops like: rice, because of less risk. And for this reason other cash crops and non-rice crops are in risk because of non-production. Rice uses four or more times more water than crops like wheat and maize, and the lack of adequate water will be a major impediment to future agricultural productivity.[8] The government continues to support the agricultural sector through a number of policy interventions, with the ultimate view to promoting food self-sufficiency as envisaged in the Fifth Five Year Plan (1997-2002). However, the non-crop sector, which includes livestock and fisheries, seems to have performed much better, on account of private sector initiatives.

Bangladesh is in the process of a transition from a predominantly agrarian economy to an industrial and service economy. The private sector is playing an increasingly active role in the economic life of the country, while the public sector concentrates more on the physical and social infrastructure.[9] Most Bangladeshis earn their living from agriculture. Although rice and jute are the primary crops, maize and vegetables are assuming greater importance. Due to the expansion of irrigation networks, some wheat producers have switched to cultivation of maize which is used mostly as poultry feed. Tea is grown in the northeast. Because of Bangladesh's fertile soil and normally ample water supply, rice can be grown and harvested three times a year in many areas. Due to a number of factors, Bangladesh's labour-intensive agriculture has achieved steady increases in food grain production despite the often unfavourable weather conditions. These include better flood control and irrigation, a generally more efficient use of fertilisers, and the establishment of better distribution and rural credit networks.[10]

## Industry

Bangladesh today is a country with a thriving economy in primary, manufacturing and tertiary sectors. As a developing country, which gained independence a few decades ago, in 1971, it has come a long way from a predominantly agrarian and a labour intensive manufacturing economy to its present state of a diversified economy and now has industries, many of which effectively compete with regional and worldwide players. In this process, the defining role of foreign investors has been a key element. The Foreign Investors' Chamber of Commerce and Industry, started off in Bangladesh as the Agrabad Chamber of Commerce based on Chittagong, where most of the foreign industries and business houses were then located. In 1987, the Chamber changed to its present name and its offices moved to Dhaka.[11]

More than 78 per cent of Bangladesh's export earnings come from the garment industry. The ready-made garments sector has a greater potential than any other sector in terms of employment and foreign exchange earnings to reduce poverty and make a contribution to the national economy. Working conditions in this vital sector are poor. Bangladesh's ready-made garments factories fall short on 'social compliance.[12]

The country's clothing industry has the advantage of scale. It has 5,000 factories, compared with 2,500 in Indonesia and 2,000 in Vietnam. Its labour costs less than any of its Asian rivals, even a near tripling in the minimum wage, to $100 a month, as garment workers are demanding from the government, would not change this. And unlike clothes put together in China, India and Sri Lanka, those stitched in Bangladesh enjoy duty-free access to the European Union. Such is the growth in demand for cheap wear that Bangladesh's clothing industry is forecast to quadruple in size over the next 20 years. It already employs four millions, mostly women, in a country with 31 millions households. Unless productivity raises sharply, millions more women will be drawn from their homes into the workplace, a drastic change in a conservative society.[13]

## Tourism

Ministry of Civil Aviation and Tourism was a ministry under central government before independence. After independence of Bangladesh in 1971 matters relating to communication and tourism were vested with the Ministry of Commerce. In 1972, Civil Aviation Division was created and brought under the Ministry of Shipping, Inland Water

Transport and Civil Aviation. However, an independent Ministry of Civil Aviation and Tourism was created in August 1975.

Bangladesh's tourist attractions include, historical and monuments, resorts, beaches, picnic spots, forests and tribal people, wildlife of various species. Bangladesh offers ample opportunities to tourists for angling, water skiing, river cruising, hiking, rowing, yachting, sea bathing as well as bringing one in close touch with pristine nature. In the south-eastern part, which is the Chittagong division, there are natural and hilly areas like Chittagong Hill Tracts, along with sandy sea beaches. The most notable beach, in Cox's Bazar, is a contender for the title of longest unbroken sandy sea beach in the world.

The historically and architecturally important sixty domed mosque in Bagerhat is a notable site. In the north-eastern part, Sylhet division, there is a green carpet of tea plants on small hillocks. Natural reserved forests are great attractions. Migratory birds in winter, particularly in the haor areas, are also very attractive in this area. The World Travel and Tourism Council reported in 2013 that the travel and tourism industry in Bangladesh directly generated 1,281,500 jobs in 2012 or 1.8 per cent of the country's total employment, which ranked Bangladesh 157 out of 178 countries worldwide.[14] Cox's Bazar is a seaside town; a fishing port and district headquarter. St. Martin's Island is a small island in the northeastern part of the Bay of Bengal, about nine kilometers south of the tip of the Cox's Bazar. Bandarban is a district in South-Eastern Bangladesh, and a part of the Chittagong Division and Chittagong Hill Tracts. Dhaka Division is an administrative division in Bangladesh. Dhaka is the largest and capital city of Bangladesh.[15]

Although there are opportunities of developing tourism attractions and facilities across the country, at present only a handful tourism spots are available for visits by tourists. These limited facilities are concentrated in some places, like Dhaka, Chittagong and Sylhet Divisions. In Chittagong Division, the site seeing facilities are mainly located at Cox's Bazar, Rangamati, Khagrachari and Bandarban districts. Mainamati at Comilla is an important archaeological site and Lalbagh Fort in Dhaka is a great historic site. In Sylhet Division, the major tourist attractions are located mainly at Jaflong, Madhabkunda, Tea gardens and the Shrines of Harzat Shah Jalal and Shah Poran.

Some renowned attractions in Rajshahi Division are Kantaji's Temple, Swapnapuri, Ramsagor and Rajbari at Dinajpur, Paharpur at Noagaon, and Mahasthangarh at Bogra. In Khulna Division, some attractions are Shatgombuj Mosque at Bagerhat and Sundarban, the largest mangrove forest in the world, is located in the southern part of Khulna Division along the Bay of Bengal.[16] Bandarban district is the hub of natural resources and beauties. The nature remains unchanged here still now. There are a great number of mountains, lake, waterfalls and forests at Bandarban which has no alternative or similarities in any part of the world.[17]

## Export-Import

Trade is an integral part of the total developmental effort and national growth of all economies including Bangladesh. It particularly plays a central role in the development plan of Bangladesh where foreign exchange scarcity constitutes a critical bottleneck. The export sector performed rather well throughout the 1990s. This sector achieved a growth rate of 37.04 per cent in the FY 1994-95. During the twelve years, 1991-92 to 2002-2003, Bangladesh experienced negative export growth (-7.44 per cent) only in FY 2001- 2002. The terrorist incident of September 11, 2001 in USA and subsequent events may be blamed for this unexpected suffering of the export sector in the particular fiscal year. Readymade garments and knitwear are the main contributors to the export earnings of Bangladesh. Their contributions are, respectively, 52.20 per cent and 24.37 per cent of total export earnings in FY 2001-2002 and 49.75 per cent and 25.26 per cent in FY 2002-2003.

The export growth of Bangladesh has occurred due to both price and volume increases over the years. The export earnings also continuously increased over the years with increased import payments. Though import payments are always higher than the export earnings in absolute terms, the percentage of Bangladesh's export to imports is improving gradually and in recent years has been quite impressive. The contribution of the export sector to Bangladesh's GDP has been gradually increasing over the years. European Union dominates over any other regions for Bangladesh's exports. Bangladesh exported more than 50 per cent of its total exports to EU in 2002-03 and this region's imports from Bangladesh have been continuously increasing over the years. The American region, Asian region and the Middle East occupy the second, third and fourth positions respectively for the direction of Bangladesh's exports.[18]

Bangladesh's export boom for in the 1990s particularly the rapid expansion of the readymade garment exports under the umbrella of the Multi-Fibre Arrangement and under the WTO Agreement on Textiles and Clothing (ATC). Bangladesh's business environment generally compares favourably with other Asian countries and USA, Canada as well as some European countries particularly England, Germany and France. The past decade's boom in exports–particularly the apparel sector is very significant to country's economic growth, but the recent GDP growth has not led to significant improvements in the living standards of most people and the social factors are still challenging.[19]

## Mineral Resources

Modern urbanisation, industrialisation, transportation and communication systems are the achievements of worldwide sustainable mineral resource development and their proper utilisation in various sectors. Sustainable mineral resources have played, and are still playing a vital role in shaping the modern civilised industrial world. This means that the sustainable socio-economic infrastructure of any country is an indication of its richness in natural resources, its technological know how, its ability to explore and exploit mineral resources, and, finally, its wisdom in utilising those resources properly in the development activities of the nation.[20]

Natural Gas is Bangladesh's most important source of commercial energy. It meets 70 per cent of the country's commercial energy requirement. Other sources of primary energy are imported petroleum products and coal. The construction work of Barapukuria Coal Mine project has been started in 1994. It has a proven reserve of 303 million metric tons and is expected to he commissioned in 2000-2001. The Madhyapara Hard Rock project is expected to produce 1.65 million tons of hard rock annually after its commissioning in the year 2000. The government has invited foreign investments to expedite exploration, production and development of natural gas and petroleum. Incentives for foreign investors have been offered in the National Petroleum Policy adopted recently.

Some multinational companies have already started work in different exploration blocks of the country after signing production sharing contracts with the government.[21] There are 22 discovered gas fields in Bangladesh of various sizes. The total reserve of 20 gas fields is about 26 Tcf (trillion cubic feet). Gas in most of the fields is dry, in a few fields it is wet, with considerable amounts of condensate, e.g. at Beanibazar (16 bbl/mmcfg), Jalalabad (15 bbl/mmcfg), and Kailashtila (13 bbl/mmcfg). Currently, natural gas accounts for more than 70 per cent of the total commercial energy consumption and the major part of the future energy demand would be met from it. The only oilfield of the country has been discovered at Haripur in 1986. It has an estimated in-place oil reserve of about 10 million barrels, with a recoverable reserve of about six million barrels.[22]

After gaining independence in 1971, energy exploration activities increased among both national and international companies. The part of OGDC that was in operation in Bangladesh was reorganised as the Bangladesh Mineral Oil and Gas Corporation (Petrobangla) and continued its predecessor's exploration efforts. In 1974, the Bangladesh Petroleum Act was enacted to facilitate international participation in the exploration and extraction of Bangladesh's oil and gas. In 1985, all of Bangladesh's mineral extraction and management were merged under the new Bangladesh Oil Gas and Minerals Corporation, once again short named Petrobangla, which since then is in charge of managing all of Bangladesh's oil and gas exploration, development, transmission, distribution and conversion, as well as the development and marketing of Bangladesh's other minerals. Between 1974 and 1993, some 23 onshore/ offshore exploration blocks were delineated.

The first National Energy Policy was introduced in 1996 with the purpose to ensure proper exploration, production, distribution and rational use of energy sources to meet the growing energy demand of different zones, consuming sectors and consumers groups on a sustainable basis. In 2005, natural gas production amounted to 494 billion cubic feet, of which about 48 per cent were consumed for the purpose of power generation, about 32 per cent for fertiliser production, and the remaining 20 per cent were consumed for other industrial, commercial and domestic purposes.[23]

## Fishing

More than 80 per cent of the animal protein in the Bangladeshi diet comes from fish. Fish accounted for six per cent of GDP in the fiscal year of 1970, nearly 50 per cent more than modern industrial manufacturing at that time. Most commercial fishermen are low-caste Hindus who eke out the barest subsistence working under primitive and dangerous conditions. The World Bank and the Asian Development Bank financed projects to develop shrimp aquaculture in the 1980s. Much of the emphasis was on construction of modern hatcheries. Private investors were also initiating similar projects to increase capacity and to introduce modern technology that would increase average yields. The Food and Agriculture Organisation of the United Nations has provided assistance to the shrimp and fishing industry in meeting fish safety and quality control standards based on the Hazard Analysis Critical Control Point approach. Training for the fishing industry of Bangladesh, as well as for merchant shipping and related maritime industries is provided by the Bangladesh Marine Fisheries Academy.[24]

Otter fishing is a centuries-old tradition in Bangladesh, where fishermen have been using trained otters to lure fish into their nets–a rare technique passed on from father to son that relies on coordination between man and otter. Fishing is usually done at night, and the otters can help fishermen catch as many as 26 pounds of fish, crabs and shrimp. But the partnership between man and otter is on the verge of extinction. It's already died out in other parts of Asia as fish populations decline, wildlife experts say. Short-haired otters are an endangered species in Bangladesh and experts say that otter fishing may play a key role in their conservation.[25]

Like other river deltas; Bangladesh is a very fertile place. There are no rocks, stones, boulders or pebbles. It's all silt and mud washed down from the Himalayan Mountains over millions of years. The water is teaming with fish, which (along with lentils) provides most of the protein for people. Weighted throw nets are one of the most common fishing tools. The weights are sewn in around the edges. As soon as they hit the water, they sink fast, trapping fish below between the muddy bottom and the net. The kid who is spear fishing has to use some science to hit his underwater mark. Kids make them out of bamboo with one way trap doors. The kids get together to splash the water and force the fish to try to escape into another rice paddy.[26]

Although the media portrays Bangladesh as poor, dirty and full of doom and gloom, it is home to the happiest people in the world, according to a study done by the London School of Economics.

With an existence that depends primarily on subsistence agriculture and fishing, maybe the Bengali people are too busy working to worry about the stresses of everyday life that are often spoken of in the developed world.[27]

## Foreign Remittances

**Foreign remittance** can be defined as 'the purchase and sale of freely convertible foreign currencies as admissible under Exchange Control Regulations of the country'. A looser translation is the sending of money home while working in a foreign country. Thousands of people are currently working and living in a country that is not their home, and sending funds regularly back to their families in their home country. There are two types of remittances:

- **Foreign Outward Remittance:** The sending country, where the wage earner is located. The sender uses a bank or foreign exchange company to send money to foreign country. Many of the receiving banks have established remittance relationships with currency houses and banks in other countries to better facilitate the flow of remittances into the country; and
- **Foreign Inward Remittance:** The receiving country, where the beneficiary resides. The bank receives the money that has been sent from the sending person in the country in which the money has been earned.[28]

Remittance has become a major contributor to the Bangladeshi economy. As the emigrant workers from Bangladesh gradually increased over the years, the amount of annual remittance to the country significantly rose. According to World Bank, Bangladesh is now one of the largest recipients of remittance with almost $14.5 billion as of June 2013. In 1974, Wage Earners' Scheme was initiated in order to help the Non-resident Bangladeshis remit their earnings home through legal channels. The scheme soon became popular among the Bangladeshis working abroad. Some $11.8 million was remitted to Bangladesh in the fiscal year of 1974-75. Remittance is sent formally through various ways such as demand draft, traveller's check, telegraphic transfer, postal order, direct transfer, Automatic Teller Machine etc.[29]

The export of manpower is one of the most significant foreign currency earning sectors. It contributes national economy in a large measure by increasing foreign exchange reserve, per capita income and employment opportunities. The remittance which has sent by the migrant workers is the 11 per cent of the total GDP (Gross Domestic Product). Beside this, these remittances are seven times higher than the amount which has got the government of Bangladesh as foreign aid and 13 times higher than the amount which got the government of Bangladesh as foreign investment. There are approximately 90 lakh Bangladeshi workers working in 155 countries in the world.[30] Bangladesh received its highest-ever annual remittance of about US$14.5 on in the just out fiscal year as expatriate Bangladeshis sent home hard-earned money through formal channels. The remittance grew by 12 per cent over the same period last fiscal year when it was $12.8 bn, registering 10 per cent growth from $11.6 on of fiscal 2010-11.

The mobile banking is gradually gaining popularity in the country due to its easy transaction procedure, facilitating rural people as well as the readymade garments workers to avail of the comparatively new services. Most of the workers of Bangladesh migrated abroad are working in the Middle East: Saudi Arabia, UAE, Qatar, Oman, Bahrain and many other countries. There is hardly a country where Bangladeshi workers are not present. The remittance inflow crossed the double-digit mark in 2009, buoyed by a record outflow of migrants during 2007 and 2008 in the wake of a construction boom in the Gulf States. After 2008, the outflow of new migrants slowed down due to demand fall. But it rose again last year, enabling Bangladesh to emerge as the eighth largest remittance earning country, according to a World Bank survey. The growth in remittances, the second biggest foreign currency earning sector after exports, give a much needed cushion to the government to face a rising pressure on the country's balance of payments.[31]

Cash remittances to Bangladesh from its global Diaspora of migrant workers are the country's second-largest source of foreign exchange behind the garment industry. A report in the Dhaka Tribune newspaper pointed out that the number of Bangladeshi workers overseas peaked in 2008–when about 875,000 workers went abroad and has been in general decline ever since. The following year, the number plunged to 475,000. In 2013, only about 389,000 Bangladeshis migrated for work out of the country. The export of workers had fallen due to the global recession, noting that the recruitment of Bangladeshi workers to Kuwait and the UAE virtually stopped, and was substantially reduced in Oman, Saudi Arabia, and Malaysia. But, remittances from workers abroad are crucial to the impoverished, overcrowded South Asian country–billions of dollars of remittances in the past few decades have helped push up Dhaka's foreign exchange reserves above $18 billion, Reuters reported.

Bangladesh, a state of some 160 million people, has an estimated nine million migrant workers in the Middle East, Europe, North America and elsewhere; they sent a total of $14.5 billion in remittances during the 2012-2013 fiscal year. In order to boost remittances, the Bangladesh central bank suggested a comprehensive effort to increase the skills of migrants and to improve incentives for such workers overseas to remit funds back home for the purposes of investments.[32] Economists say exports, remittances and foreign reserves have come to form a growth triangle that helped Bangladesh pull a large part of its population out of poverty and help it achieve UN targets two years in advance.[33]

## Service Sector

The Economy of Bangladesh is classified into three sectors. Of these, the average contribution of service sector, industry sector, agriculture sector to the GDP are 49.33 per cent, 28.42 per cent and 22.42 per cent respectively. So, the service sectors contribute most of the development of national economy.[34]

The service sector constitutes a significant share of gross domestic product in most of the developing countries in South Asia, Africa and the Caribbean region since these countries have an important stake in the Doha Round of negotiation on services liberalisation. In the era of global economic integration, competitiveness plays a vital role in the success of international trade. In addition, the competitive environment of domestic markets facilitates higher economic growth and can help in reducing poverty. Competition in the services sector can play a fundamental role in ensuring the competitiveness of an economy.

Economic development inevitably triggers a structural change in the composition of output in favour of services. One of the striking features of the Bangladesh's growth performance during the last decade has been the strength of the services sector. Services sector in Bangladesh is the largest sector, and it is the area where local firms have larger participation and are better able to compete, as compared with the manufacturing sector. Demand for many services is highly income-elastic, i.e. as people grow richer, their consumption of services such as tourism, education and health, expands more rapidly than their demand for manufactures and agricultural products.[35]

The World Bank is helping Bangladesh address its main growth areas through a mix of analytic work, technical assistance, and lending. Urbanisation has been rapid and largely imbalanced. A quarter of the population now lives in urban areas, while in 1960 the number was just five per cent. Fifty per cent of GDP is spent on urban activities. Urbanisation has been skewed toward Dhaka, making it among the fastest growing metropolises in the world. Bangladesh is one of the most closed economies in the world. Opening up trade has to be one of the pillars of future growth. Growth dividends from trade openness will depend upon concomitant investment climate reforms to boost competitiveness of domestic firms. Despite the impressive improvements, many problems plague the education system. Its quality is weak with a huge rural/urban gap and not relevant to market needs. Tertiary education and vocation studies have been largely neglected.[36]

Bangladesh is a third world country with an under developed banking system, particularly in terms of the services and customer care provided by the government run banks. Managed by the Bangladesh Krishi Bank, a specialised agricultural banking institution, lending to farmers and fishermen dramatically expanded. The number of rural bank branches doubled between 1977 and 1985, to more than 3,330. One major exception to the management problems of Bangladeshi banks was the Grameen Bank, begun as a government project in 1976 and established in 1983 as an independent bank. In the late 1980s, the bank continued to provide financial resources to the poor on reasonable terms and to generate productive self-employment without external assistance. Its customers were landless persons who took small loans for all types of economic activities, including housing.[37]

## Conclusion

The rate of growth of GDP in Bangladesh has picked up in recent years. It is primarily an agrarian economy. Agriculture is the single largest producing sector of economy since it comprises about 30 per cent of the country's GDP and employing around 60 per cent of the total labour force. Flood, riverbank erosion, cyclone, and storm surge have severe impacts on fisheries, with moderate effects on poverty and economic growth. After independence of Bangladesh in 1971 matters relating to communication and tourism were vested with the Ministry of Commerce. Bangladesh's tourist attractions include, historical and monuments, resorts, beaches, picnic spots, forests and tribal people, wildlife of various species.

The contribution of the export sector to Bangladesh's GDP has been gradually increasing over the years. European Union dominates over any other regions for Bangladesh's exports. Natural Gas is Bangladesh's most important source of commercial energy. It meets 70 per cent of the country's commercial energy requirement. Other sources of primary energy are imported petroleum products and coal. More than 80 per cent of the animal protein in the Bangladeshi diet comes from fish. Fish accounted for six per cent of GDP in the fiscal year of 1970, nearly 50 per cent more than modern industrial manufacturing at that time. Remittance has become a major contributor to the Bangladeshi economy. As the emigrant workers from Bangladesh gradually increased over the years, the amount of annual remittance to the country significantly rose. The export of manpower is one of the most significant foreign currency earning sectors.

## References

1. *Ministry of civil aviation and tourism*, Retrieved from http://www.mocat.gov.bd/tourism.php
2. *India-Bangladesh Bilateral Trade and Potential Free Trade Agreement, Bangladesh Development Series*, Paper No: 13, 2006, The World Bank Office, Dhaka, Retrieved from http://siteresources.worldbank.org/INTBANGLADESH/Resources/Trade.pdf
3. *The United States and Bangladesh Toward the Future: Policy Recommendations to Strengthen the U.S.-Bangladesh Commercial Relationship*, Retrieved from https://www.uschamber.com/sites/default/files/legacy/international/files/020706_Bangladesh_Report_fin.
4. Nurun N. Rahman, *Policy Reforms and Trade Liberalisation in Bangladesh*, Retrieved from http://www.unctad.info/upload/TAB/docs/TechCooperation/bangladesh_study.pdf
5. Lt.Gen Mollah Fazle Akbar, *Foreign Policy of Bangladesh*, Retrieved from http://www.bei-bd.org/images/publication/whc50c59b33459fb.pdf
6. *Agriculture of Bangladesh,* Retrieved from http://www.discoverybangladesh.com/meetbangladesh/agriculture.html

7. Timothy S. Thomas et al. *Agriculture and Adaptation in Bangladesh: Current and Projected Impacts of Climate Change*, 2013, IFPRI Discussion Paper 01281.df
8. See http://www.shaon84.com/pennpaper/writings/e_e_challenges_in_agricultural_sector_in_bangladesh_web_edition.pdf
9. *Sectoral Information & Summary,* Retrieved from http://www.ibfb.org/index.php?option=com_content&view=article&id=23&Itemid=56
10. *Agriculture Sector of Bangladesh*, Retrieved from http://www.assignment point.com/science/zoology/agriculture-sector-of-bangladesh.html
11. See http://www.ficci.org.bd/ficci-home.asp
12. Ferdous Ahamad, *Improving Social compliance in Bangladesh's Ready-made Garment Industry*, Retrieved from http://www.nla.gov.au/openpublish/index.php/lmd/article/viewFile/2269/3148.
13. *Bangladesh's clothing industry,* Retrieved from http://www.economist.com/news/business/21588393-workers-continue-die-unsafe-factories-industry-keeps-booming-bursting-seams.
14. *Tourism of Bangladesh (2014),* Retrieved from http://en.wikipedia.org/wiki/Tourism_in_Bangladesh.
15. *Ibid.*
16. Md. Lutfur Rahman et al. An Overview of Present Status and Future Prospects of the Tourism Sector in Bangladesh, *Journal of Bangladesh Institute of Planners*, Vol. 3, December 2010, pp. 65-75.
17. Nushrat Nahida Afroz and Md Hasanuzzaman (2012), *Problems and Prospects of Tourism in Bangladesh Bandarban,* Retrieved from https://globaljournals.org/GJMBR_Volume12/4-Problems-and-Prospects-of-Tourism.pdf
18. Mohammad Mafizur Rahman, *The Foreign Trade of Bangladesh: Its Composition, Performance, Trend, and Policy*, Retrieved from https://eprints.usq.edu.au/4193/1/Rahman_JBS_v9n2.pdf
19. Dr Laila Arjuman Ara and M. Masudur Rahman, *The Competitiveness and Future Challenges of Bangladesh in International Trade,* Retrieved from http://www.wto.aoyama.ac.jp/file/090126laila_paper.pdf
20. See http://sp.lyellcollection.org/content/250/1/127.abstract.
21. *Bangladesh: Mineral Resources*, Retrieved from http://www.discovery bangladesh.com/meetbangladesh/mineral_resources.html
22. *Mineral Resources of Bangladesh*, Retrieved from http://www.studymode.com/essays/Mineral-Resources-Of-Bangladesh-1041537.html
23. Bernhard G. Gunter (2008), *Mineral Extraction in Bangladesh: Some Fundamental Reform Suggestions,* Retrieved from http://www.bangladesh studies.org/files/WPS_no3.pdf

24. Fishing in Bangladesh (2014), Retrieved from http://en.wikipedia.org/wiki/Fishing_in_Bangladesh.
25. See http://time.com/40632/bangladesh-otters-fishermen/
26. See http://www.sciencetoymaker.org/bangladesh/food.htm
27. Jessica Morelock, Fishing in Bangladesh, Retrieved from http://traveltips.usatoday.com/fishing-bangladesh-100250.html
28. *Foreign remittance (2014),* Retrieved from http://www.foreignremittance.com/what-is-foreign-remittance/
29. *Remittances to Bangladesh,* Retrieved from http://en.wikipedia.org/wiki/Remittance_to_Bangladesh.
30. Sheikh Abdur Rahim and Md. Asraful Alam, Foreign Remittance Income in Bangladesh: Opportunities and Challenges, *Asian Business Review,* Volume 2, Numebr 2/2013 (Issue 4), Retrieved from http://oaji.net/articles/800-1398828786.pdf
31. Jebun Nesa Alo (2013). Remittance records 12 per cent growth in FY13, Retrieved from http://www.dhakatribune.com/economy/2013/jul/03/remittance-inflow-breaks-record.
32. Palash Ghosh (2014), *Taka To Dhaka: Cash Remittances From Bangladeshi Migrant Workers Keep Declining,* Retrieved from http://www.ibtimes.com/taka-dhaka-cash-remittances-bangladeshi-migrant-workers-keep-declining-1556317
33. See http://bdnews24.com/bangladesh/2013/06/25/bangladesh-grows—on-remittances-exports
34. *Mohammad Shahidul Islam, Md. Musa, Rajib Kanti Das (2012), The Comparative Growth of Service Sectors in Bangladesh,* Retrieved from http://www.iiste.org/Journals/index.php/RJFA/article/view/2138
35. *Evolution of Service Sector in Bangladesh: An Overview*, Retrieved from http://www.cuts-citee.org/pdf/bp08-wto-5.pdf
36. See http://web.worldbank.org/WBSITE/EXTERNAL/COUNTRIES/SOUTHASIAEXT/EXTSARREGTOPMACECOGRO/0,,contentMDK:20592479~menuPK:579404~pagePK:34004173~piPK:34003707~theSitePK:579398,00.html
37. *Banking in Bangladesh (2014),* Retrieved from http://en.wikipedia.org/wiki/Banking_in_Bangladesh.

# Chapter - 4

# Economy of Nepal

*"There are a few things that people all around the world need to admit to themselves. Trade restraints slow economic growth, the euro is not a reserve currency, and scoreless sports ties are boring."*

—*P. J. O'Rourke*

Nepal is well known as the land of Everest, the highest peak in the world. It is situated in the lap of the Himalayas and landlocked between India and China. It lies between the latitudes of 26°22' N to 30' 27° N and longitudes of 80° 4° E to 88° 12° E. The elevation of the country ranges from 60 m above the sea level to the highest global altitude, Mount Everest, of 8848 m, all within a distance of 150 km. This vast sudden variation in its altitude gives a country a climatic condition, which ranges from sub-tropical to that of the arctic. According to the census of 2001, the population of Nepal stands at 23.2 million which comprises of 11.59 million males and 11.63 million females population. The annual population growth rate in the 90s was 2.27 per cent whereas in the 80s it was 2.1 per cent. The rural-urban split scenario of both 1991 and 2001 census show a higher share of population in the rural areas. The rural population in 2001 is 85.77 per cent as compared to 14.23 per cent in the urban areas. The main spoken language in Nepal is Nepali which is also the official language. This is the mother language of more than 50 per cent of the population. This language is followed by Maithali which is nearly 11 per cent and Bhojpuri which is spoken by nearly seven per cent.[1]

Nepal is a landlocked country on the southern slope of the Himalayas, located between China in the north and India in east, south and west- two huge countries with vibrant economies. Politically, it has been designated as a Federal Democratic Republic since May 2008. It has been in transition since the decade-long conflict that ended in 2006, focusing its efforts in achieving sustainable peace, economic growth, employment generation, inclusive development, poverty alleviation, food security, and a reliable electricity supply. The government and private sector institutions have been addressing issues such as reforming the financial sector, strengthening the private sector's capacity, streamlining the private sector's development agenda, finding solutions to double-digit growth issues, and increasing industrialisation based on trade competitiveness.[2]

Nepal has eight of the world's ten highest mountain peaks, including Mt. Everest at 8,848 m (29,000 ft.). The country is a tourist destination for hikers and mountain climbers, as well as devout Buddhists who visit Lumbini, the birthplace of Siddhartha Gautama, the Supreme Buddha. Since 2007, tourism has grown, helped by greater peace and stability following the official end of the 10-year insurgency and rising incomes of Indian and Chinese travellers. Figures from the Department of Immigration showed a 24.6 per cent increase in air arrivals between January and August 2011 over the same period in 2010, with arrivals of Indian travellers growing by 46.3 per cent and Chinese travellers by 60 per cent. In 2011, Nepal celebrated its "Year of Tourism."[3]

Nepal is divides into three regions, i.e. *Himalayan region, Hilly region* and *Terai region*. Terai region is located on the bottom part of Nepal. Terai is usually known as the *grain house of Nepal* since most the crops that are sold throughout Nepal are farmed from Terai region. The land area of Terai region is also very plain i.e. it is most suitable for growing crops and other food items. The Terai is a region of grasslands, savannas and forests between the foots of the Hilly region. It covers about 17 per cent of the total area of Nepal. The Terai stretches from the international border with India in the Far-Western region to the Eastern region. It is located at an altitude of 67-300 m (220-980 ft.). The Terai region consists of many small and seasonal rovers, most of them which originate straight from the Himalayan regions.[4]

## Economy of Nepal

Nepal is one of the least developed countries in the world. It is sandwiched between India and China, the two fastest growing economies. It is landlocked. In terms of human development indicators, Nepal ranks 140 from the top and 38 from the bottom. The average citizen of Nepal earns US $ 230 per year. Culturally, Nepal is primarily a feudalistic society. Various forms of discriminatory practices perpetuated in the political, social and economic life of the people have constrained improvement in human development and people's livelihood. Nepal started late in modern development with the beginning of democracy in 1951. Ushering in of democracy heralded a new era of politico-economic were awakening and realisation of the need for major reforms in the feudal agrarian structure in order to enhance people's access to land and equitable distribution of livelihood opportunities.

Like many other developing countries during those times, Nepal pursued an inward looking and state-led development strategy. Consequently, a number of enterprises were established in the public sector. The most modern components of industry and trade sectors were controlled by the state through licensing and quotas. Industries were protected through high tariff walls. Politically, the country was governed by an autocratic party-less Panchayat system, introduced in 1960 following the royal coup d'etat against a nascent parliamentary form of government. Lack of accountability and transparency in governance led to rampant rent-seeking practices. The unprecedented rise in the magnitude of budgetary deficit fuelled current account deficits. This resulted in huge BOP deficit precipitating a serious foreign exchange crisis.[5]

The 2006 peace process was preceded by the realignment of political forces that culminated which an alliance between the SPA and the CPN-M against the king. The king's dismissal of the prime minister on 1st February 2005 changed the perception of the political parties and the CPN-M towards each other. The SPA joined the alliance because it was increasingly vulnerable to repression and attacks by the CPN-M. The CPN-M entered the alliance out of recognition that they lacked substantive presence in urban areas and thus the futility of trying to capture Kathmandu militarily. These developments, however, were only possible after the CPN-M had overcome internal divisions towards peace negotiations. In general, Maoist ideology was opposed to an exit strategy through negotiation because a class struggle could not be concluded with a compromise. The three sets of meetings of the 2001 peace process confirm the dominance of political and military issues. While the talks of 30 August 2001 focused on introducing the negotiation teams, the talks of 13 and 14 September 2001 were substantive.[6]

Some 75 per cent of Nepal's people engage in agriculture, which contributes about 40 per cent of the GDP. In the Terai, the main agricultural region, rice is the chief crop; other food crops include pulses, wheat, barley, sugarcane, and oilseeds. Jute, tobacco, cotton, indigo, and opium are also grown in the Terai, whose forests provide sal wood and commercially valuable bamboo and rattan. Transportation and communication difficulties have hindered the growth of industry and trade. Biratnagar and Birganj, in the Terai, are the main manufacturing towns, and Kathmandu also has some industry. There are rice, jute, sugar, and oilseed mills; other products include carpets, textiles, cigarettes, and building materials. Wood and metal handicrafts are also important. Tourism, a chief source of foreign exchange (along with international aid and Gurkha pensions), was hurt during the conflict with the country's Maoist rebels. Carpets, clothing, leather and jute goods, and grain are exported; imports include gold, machinery and equipment, petroleum products, and fertiliser.[7]

The Gross Domestic Product (GDP) in Nepal expanded 3.65 per cent in 2013 from the previous year. GDP Annual Growth Rate in Nepal averaged 4.34 per cent from 1994 until 2013, reaching an all time high of 8.60 per cent in 1994 and a record low of 0.16 per cent in 2002. GDP Annual Growth Rate in Nepal is reported by the Central Bureau of Statistics, Nepal.[8] Nepal's economic growth rate remained 3.6 per cent in the last one year against the prediction of 5.5 per cent as Nepal performed poorly in the overall economic front.[9]

## Agriculture

Agriculture continues to provide a broad base to the Nepalese economy. Nearly four-fifths of all Nepalese households are essentially farm households, who derive nearly half of income from agricultural sources consisting of farm income and agricultural wage income. Engaging two-thirds of labour force, this sector alone contributes some one-third to the GDP. As such, the growth originating in agriculture holds high potential to have relatively wider impact on poverty reduction and inclusiveness. Smallholders and marginal farms pre-dominate

Nepalese agriculture with the average holding size of 0.8 ha. Landless farmers are gradually leaving agriculture as it is hard to eke out livelihood there without holding land asset. Nepal's agriculture is overwhelmed by subsistence family farms. Seventy-eight per cent farm holdings have been reported to be producing mainly for home consumption. The proportion of holdings that produce mainly for sale is not even 1 per cent, while little over 21 per cent farm families use their farm produce almost equally for both sale and home consumption.[10]

Agriculture remains Nepal's principal economic activity, employing over 73 per cent of the population and providing about one-third per cent of GDP. Only about 25 per cent of the total area is cultivable; another 33 per cent is forested; most of the rest is mountainous. Rice and wheat are the main food crops. The lowland Tarai region produces an agricultural surplus, part of which supplies the food-deficient hill areas. Because of Nepal's dependence on agriculture, the magnitude of the annual monsoon rain strongly influences economic growth.[11]

Agriculture is the principal source of food, income, and employment for the majority, particularly the poorest. Growth in agriculture is crucial for reducing poverty, and preliminary findings from the National Living Standards Survey indicate that despite the insurgency, the sector has made a significant contribution to poverty reduction. A mountainous terrain and poorly developed road network restrict access to markets, constraining agricultural growth and diversification into higher value added and non-farm activities. Tenancy restrictions, high land fragmentation, absentee landlordism, and unequal distribution pose key challenges to tenure security and, in turn, private investment.[12]

As the agriculture sector is the key sector of the economy, determining economic growth and employment, the standard of living of the majority of the population depends on its development. Despite investment in irrigation and agricultural development projects, agriculture production is still largely determined by favourable weather condition.[13]

## Industry

During the 1950s and 1960s, Kathmandu received aid commitments from Moscow and Beijing. During the 1960s, Soviet and Chinese aid also supported development of a few government-owned industries. Most of the industries established used agricultural products such as jute, sugar, and tea as raw materials. Among the modern industries were large manufacturing plants, including many public sector operations. The major manufacturing industries produced jute, sugar, cigarettes, beer, matches, shoes, chemicals, cement, and bricks. The Nepal Companies Act of 1936 provided for the incorporation of industrial enterprises on joint stock principle with limited liability. The most important mineral resources exploited were limestone for cement, clay, garnet, magnetite and talc. Crude magnetite production declined from a high of approximately 63,200 tons in 1986 to approximately 28,000 tons in 1989; it was projected to decline further to 25,000 tons in 1990.[14]

The jute industry, centred in Biratnagar, is an important earner of foreign exchange. Sugar factories are located in Biratnagar, Birganj, and Bhairahawa. There are sawmill and meat-processing plant in Hitaura and a number of rice and oil mills in the Tarai. In general, there are more industrial enterprises in the private than in the public sector, although most of these are cottage industries. The main areas of manufacturing concentration are Biratnagar, the Birganj–Hitaura corridor, and the Kathmandu Valley. Transport facilities in Nepal are very limited; few independent nations in the world of comparable size have such little road mileage and so few motor vehicles. Construction of new roads has been undertaken since the 1970s with aid from India, China, Great Britain, and the United States. The meagre road-transport facilities are supplemented by only a few railway and air-transport links. Increased use of road transport has reduced the significance of the two narrow-gauge railroads that run from Amlekhganj to Raxaul (India) and from Janakpur to Jaynagar (India).[15]

## Service Sector

The service industry has emerged as one of the major contributors to world GDP, providing more than 70 per cent in developed countries and around 50 per cent in developing countries. Like many other countries, the Government of Nepal is increasing its emphasis on the services sector, considering its importance to the Nepalese economy in terms of its contribution to GDP, employment, international trade and balance of payments.[16] Nepal Telecom (NT) became the largest contributor to income tax in fiscal year 2011/12, paying ₹ 6,015 million.

Given the sluggish performance of the manufacturing sector, the service sector has dominated the top-10 list of largest contributors to income tax, according to a confidential source. With the manufacturing sector slowing down consistently, its contribution to Nepal's gross domestic product has been hovering between 6.7 per cent and 6.9 per cent over the last five years. The service sector's contribution to GDP stood at 49.5 per cent during both fiscal years 2011 and 2012, while 50.6 per cent contribution is projected for 2013.[17]

## Export-Import

Adoption of liberal economic policy in 1991 has played a positive role in the expansion and diversification of foreign trade of the country. Encouraging trend is clearly visible in the areas of foreign trade and payments as a result of the implementation of foreign trade policy and reforms initiated in the exchange regime. The programmes that are implemented over the years for the promotion of exportable goods, quality improvement, and market management are continued for the further expansion of foreign trade and to enhance its competitiveness. Trade deficit during 1999/2000 had increased by 6.7 per cent to ₹ 55,343.8 million as compared with that of 1998/99. During this period, total trade deficit went up as a result of 14.8 per cent rise in deficit with other countries apart from India.

Woollen carpets and readymade garments have been occupying major place in exports to countries other than India since last few years. Among the imported items, classified finished products, transport and mechanical equipment, mineral fuels, food items, and chemicals and medicines had a share of 83.2 per cent of the total imports of ₹ 106,966.8 million in FY 1999/2000. C. Though Nepal is one of the countries with the highest potential of hydropower energy, but this potential has not been utilised fully for the economic development of the country.

## Poverty and Unemployment

Nepal ranks among the world's poorest countries, with a per capita income of around $490 in 2009. In 2008, it was estimated that 25 per cent of the population was below the poverty line. An isolated, agrarian society until the mid-twentieth century, Nepal entered the modern era in 1951 without schools, hospitals, roads, telecommunications, electric power, industry, or a civil service. The country has made progress toward sustainable economic growth since the 1950s and is committed to a program of economic liberalisation.[18] Nepal is one of the world's poorest countries, and is struggling to overcome the legacy of a 10-year Maoist insurrection. Until Nepal became a republic in May 2008, it had been ruled by monarchs or a ruling family for most of its modern history in relative isolation. But political instability has plagued Nepal since the end of the civil war. Politicians have yet to agree on a new constitution.[19]

Overall, people who tend to remain poor are households of agricultural wage earners, those who are landless or have small land holdings, those with illiterate household heads, and those living in large households. In terms of different caste and ethnic groups, Hill and Terai Dalits represent the poorest segment of the population, despite a decline in poverty. Nepal has also improved some of its human development indicators: infant and child mortality rate decreased, albeit with large regional variations. Child malnutrition and maternal morality remain high and the prospects of achieving these Millennium Development Goals are unclear.[20]

The 2013 report of multidimensional poverty index prepared by Oxford University reveals that Nepal is able to reduce poverty in a considerable size. It is a composite index of three dimensions of poverty–health, education each with two indicators (nutrition, child mortality and years of schooling, school attendance) and living standard with six indicators (cooking fuel, sanitation, water, electricity, floor and asset). The percentage of people under deprivation is the outcome of equal weight of all dimensions and their respective indicators. It is used to identify a person as multi-dimensionally poor if he or she is deprived in at least one-third of the dimensions.[21]

As a signatory of the Millennium Declaration in September 2000; the Government of Nepal is committed to achieving the MDGs by 2015. The MDGs set quantitative targets for poverty reduction, and improvement in health, education, gender equality, the environment and other aspects of human development. The paucity of data makes it difficult to assess the performances so far made by Nepal on the MDGs.[22]

There are many causes of unemployment in Nepal. Nepal is an agro-based country. Firstly many people are employed in agriculture, but nowadays it is a trend of leaving agriculture is increasing. People feel that agriculture is not economically beneficial. They go to towns to look for good job but they can't get any job easily and become unemployed. Secondly, some educated people are extremely traditional. They think that educated people should not start simple job they stay at home being jobless. Thirdly, most of the students in Nepal are getting general education. They do not have apt knowledge and skill of technical and practical education. Fourthly, the job opportunity in Nepal is very limited.[23]

Because of a lack of domestic job opportunities and increasing aspirations to earn much in little time, many individuals are started seeking employment abroad, primarily in countries like India, Malaysia, and the Gulf states. As most illiterates are generally employed in menial and low-paying work, it is certain that although they are employed, they do not earn much and therefore, their families are forced to survive in poor living conditions. When people are educated, they can find well-paying white-collar jobs inside the country and they generally do not have to get involved in jobs they consider disrespectful and can choose to go abroad.[24] In Nepal, people from low-opportunity areas have always moved to areas where jobs are aplenty. Also, a dearth of jobs means quitting one to find another has not been a luxury available to Nepali workers.

## Mineral Resources

In Nepal, the notion of providing energy even to meet basic needs has been a big challenge mainly because of poor infrastructure development and lack of fund for investment in the generation and management of energy sources. Even after four decades of modern periodic planning, the country still suffers from the dogma of inefficient use of biomass energy sources. Import is the only method to meet the demand for petroleum products, the supply of which has increased by almost eight-fold since 1975 in value.

Between 1995 and 2000 there was a considerable increase in the supply of liquefied petroleum gas because of recent trend to replace the use of kerosene, electricity and fuel wood in urban and semi-urban areas. A total reserve of 300 million cu. m of methane associated with ground water and distributed over an area of 26 sq. km is the only natural biogenic gas identified in the country. Evidence on existence of natural biogenic gas in other sedimentary basin of the country has not been so far established. The feasibility study conducted in 1996/97 for utilisation of biogenic natural gas in the Kathmandu Valley indicated that the use of methane is viable for both domestic and industrial purposes. Coal consumption is met mainly through imports, which amounts to about 250,000 short tons per year. There are few lignite occurrences in Nepal and the maximum production capacity of these mines is estimated at about 20,000 short tons per year at present.[25]

A number of the councils and commissions formed by His Majesty's Government of Nepal are existent in the country with an objective to bring the coordination among the sectoral plan and to ensure that the activity are undertaken in consistent with the broader perspective of the government on development and policies. Relevant councils and commission with fossil fuel energy resources development are National Development Council, Environment Protection Council and National Planning Commission. The Ministry of Industry, Commerce and Supplies is the line ministry for formulation of legislation for the exploration and development of fossil fuel resources, as well as for the marketing and distribution of their products.

The Department of Mines and Geology created in 1976 to avoid overlapping activities between Bureau of Mines and Nepal Geological Survey. The Nepal Oil Corporation established as regulated public enterprises by HMG/N in 1971 currently operates under the Ministry of Industry, Commerce and Supplies after amalgamation of the three Ministries namely, Industry, Commerce and Supplies. Nepal Oil Corporation Ltd. was established in 1971 by His Majesty's Government of Nepal (HMG/N). Its primary objectives are to import petroleum products and distribute throughout the Kingdom of Nepal at the most reasonable prices.[26]

Population pressure on natural resources is increasing. Overpopulation is already straining the "carrying capacity" of the middle hill areas, particularly the Kathmandu Valley, resulting in the depletion of forest cover for crops, fuel and fodder, and contributing to erosion and flooding. Water supplies within the Kathmandu Valley are not considered safe for consumption, and disease outbreaks are not uncommon. Although steep mountain terrain makes exploitation difficult, mineral surveys have found small deposits of limestone, magnesite, zinc, copper, iron, mica, lead, and cobalt.[27]

## Foreign Remittances

The World Bank's new report 'Migration and Remittance Factbook 2011' says Nepal is among the top five countries with remittance amounting to 23 per cent of the GDP. Tajikistan, Tonga, Lesotho and Moldova are ranked ahead of Nepal. Among the least developed countries, Nepal is placed second behind Bangladesh. According to UNDP's 'Human Development Report 2010', remittance was one of the factors behind Nepal's remarkable success in human development in the last 40 years. Nepal emerged one of the world's fastest movers in Human Development Index since 1970, coming in third among 135 countries studied.

According to the report, remittance inflow to Nepal is estimated to reach US$ 3.5 billion in 2010. Nepal received payments worth US$ 2.98 billion in 2009. The World Bank's latest report says remittance flows are expected to reach US$ 440 billion by the end of 2010. The World Bank estimates that after recovering by the end of this year, remittances to developing countries will rise further in 2011 and 2012, possibly exceeding US$ 370 billion in two years' time. The top remittance sending countries in 2009 were the US, Saudi Arabia, Switzerland, Russia and Germany. Worldwide, the top recipient countries in 2010 are India, China, Mexico, the Philippines and France.[28]

Nepal is third among the countries receiving the highest proportion of remittance in terms of gross domestic product with the country receiving remittance worth 25 per cent of GDP in 2012, according to a report made public by the World Bank. African country Lesotho had also received remittance of 25 per cent of GDP in 2012. Nepal was fifth in the list in 2011.[29] Remittances now contribute around $3.5 bn a year to Nepal's annual income, up from just $50 m in the mid-1990s, and equivalent to almost a quarter of GDP. According to World Bank figures, extreme poverty has declined from almost 70 per cent to 25 per cent in the last 15 years, and the extra billions arriving direct to Nepalese households during this period are undoubtedly part of the story, along with large-scale state investment in social sectors and infrastructure.[30]

## Transport

Kathmandu valley comprises agglomerate with Kathmandu Metropolitan City at its core together with the cities of Patan, Kirtipur,

Thimi, and Bhaktapur. According to the 2011 national census, the metropolitan city has 975,453 inhabitants and the agglomerate has a population of more than 2.5 million. Roads are narrow and traffic congestion is a major and worsening problem. In addition to around 5,300 public transport vehicles including buses, micro and mini buses, tempos and taxis currently registered the number of privately-owned cars and especially motorbikes are growing fast. There are nearly half a million motorbikes accounting for most of the increase in registration of new vehicles in recent years.[31]

In the last four decades total of 15308 Kms. roads have been constructed in Nepal. Out of those there are 4522 Kms. Black toped surfaced, 3646 Kms. graveled and 7141 Kms. roads are muddy. In the same period 44 airports have also been constructed. Out of 75 districts of the Kingdom the headquarters or districts are connected with road. As the development of railways, waterways and ropeways is negligible and the feasibility of its expansion in a mentionable manner has been also found negligible it has been found that we have to depend in the road and air transportation mainly for the social and economic development of Nepal.[32]

Nepal's total road network and density are low and only 43 per cent of the population has access to all-weather roads. More than 60 per cent of the network is concentrated in the lowland (Terai) areas of the country. In 2007, the network consisted of 17,282 km of roads. The poor condition of the road network hampers the delivery of social services in the remote hill and mountainous districts and affects the country's economic development. High transport costs and the lack of connectivity are major impediments to Nepal's development. With 42 domestic and one international airport, civil aviation plays a vital role in linking the hilly and mountainous parts of the Kingdom. Most of them are green field without modern navigation systems. Domestic Airports are crucial to the growth of trade and tourism in the country as villages in hills and mountains are inaccessible by roads.

The country has the total physical railway line of the 57 km. Nepal Railways Company, a government agency owns the 53-kilometer narrow-gauge rail line, which is composed of two sections -32-kilometer section between Jaynagar in India to Janakpur in Nepal, and a 21-kilometer portion from Janakpur to Bijalpura. Janakpur to Bijalpura network is not operational at present.[33] Nepal has also realised the importance of railways and thus started exploring the possibility of developing it. Nepal has an ambitious goal of running East-West Railway linking to Kathmandu. The government's highly ambitious modern electric railway project is to cost about $12 billion (NRs 8 trillion). The plan is to construct a 1318-km project including Mechi/Kakarvitta-Mahakali/Gaddachuki (945 km) and Kathmandu-Pokhara (185 km) sections.[34]

## Conclusion

Nepal is a landlocked country on the southern slope of the Himalayas. Politically, it has been designated as a Federal Democratic Republic since May 2008. Nepal is divides into three regions, i.e. Himalayan region, Hilly region and Terai region. Terai region is located on the bottom part. Nepal is one of the least developed countries in the world. Some 75 per cent of Nepal's people engage in agriculture, which contributes about 40 per cent of the GDP. Agriculture continues to provide a broad base to the Nepalese economy. Agriculture is the principal source of food, income, and employment for the majority, particularly the poorest. During the 1950s and 1960s, Kathmandu received aid commitments from Moscow and Beijing.

During the 1960s, Soviet and Chinese aid also supported development of a few government-owned industries. The major manufacturing industries produced jute, sugar, cigarettes, beer, matches, shoes, chemicals, cement, and bricks. The jute industry, centred in Biratnagar, is an important earner of foreign exchange. Sugar factories are located in Biratnagar, Birganj, and Bhairahawa. In 2008, it was estimated that 25 per cent of the population was below the poverty line. In Nepal, the notion of providing energy even to meet basic needs has been a big challenge mainly because of poor infrastructure development and lack of fund for investment in the generation and management of energy sources.

Population pressure on natural resources is increasing. Nepal is third among the countries receiving the highest proportion of remittance in terms of gross domestic product with the country receiving remittance worth 25 per cent of GDP in 2012. Kathmandu valley comprises agglomerate with Kathmandu Metropolitan City at its core together with the cities of Patan, Kirtipur, Thimi and Bhaktapur.

## References


1. *Energy Country Analysis Brief: Nepal, February,* 2002, Retrieved from http://www.sari-energy.org/Publications/eia/Nepal.pdf
2. *About Nepal: Introduction,* Retrieved from http://www.investnepal.gov.np/portal/index.php?p1=content&p2=5#.U6_UWjtQHFw
3. *Nepal economy,* Retrieved from http://globaledge.msu.edu/countries/nepal/economy.
4. *Terai Region of Nepal (2011),* Retrieved from http://supnepal.blogspot.in/2011/02/terai-region-of-nepal.html
5. Dilli Raj Khanal et al. (2005), *Understanding Reforms in Nepal*, Retrieved from http://internationalbudget.org/wp-content/uploads/Understanding-Reforms-in-Nepal-Political-Economy-and-Institutional-Perspective.pdf
6. Achim Wennmann, *Socio-Economic Inequalities and Peace in Nepal*, Retrieved from http://graduateinstitute.ch/files/live/sites/iheid/files/sites/ccdp/shared/6305/CCDP-Working-Paper-2-Nepal.pdf
7. *Nepal economy,* Retrieved from http://www.infoplease.com/encyclopedia/world/nepal-economy.html
8. *Nepal GDP Annual Growth Rate,* Retrieved from http://www.trading economics.com/nepal/gdp-growth-annual.
9. *Nepal's growth rate stuck at 3.6pc: Economic Survey,* Retrieved from http://www.nepalnews.com/archive/2013/jul/jul12/news12.php
10. Madhab Karkee (2008), *Nepal economy growth assessment-Agriculture*, Retrieved from http://pdf.usaid.gov/pdf_docs/PNADN016.pdf
11. *Nepal economy,* Retrieved from http://globaledge.msu.edu/countries/nepal/economy.
12. *Nepal: Priorities for Agriculture and Rural Development,* Retrieved from http://web.worldbank.org/WBSITE/EXTERNAL/COUNTRIES/SOUTHASIAEXT/EXTSAREGTOPAGRI/0,,content MDK: 20273771~menu PK:548215~pagePK:34004173~pi PK:34003707~theSitePK:452766,00.html
13. See http://www.fao.org/sd/wpdirect/WPre0110.htm
14. *Industries (2013),* Retrieved from http://countrystudies.us/nepal/44.htm
15. *Industry and trade*, Retrieved from http://www.britannica.com/EBchecked/topic/409152/Nepal/23646/Industry-and-trade.
16. *National services policy review: Nepal,* Retrieved from http://unctad.org/en/docs/ditctncd20103_en.pdf
17. *Service sector tops income tax payers,* Retrieved from http://www.myrepublica.com/portal/index.php?action=news_details&news_id=67175
18. *Nepal economy,* Retrieved from http://globaledge.msu.edu/countries/nepal/economy.

19. *Nepal profile,* Retrieved from http://www.bbc.co.uk/news/world-south-asia-12511455
20. *Poverty in Nepal*, Retrieved from http://web.worldbank.org/WBSITE/EXTERNAL/COUNTRIES/SOUTHASIAEXT/EXTSAREGTOPPOVRED/0, contentMDK:20574069~menuPK:493447~pagePK:34004173~piPK:34003707~theSitePK:493441,00.html
21. See http://www.thehimalayantimes.com/fullNews.php?headline=Poverty+reduction+&NewsID=373096
22. *Nepal: Poverty Reduction Strategy Paper Progress Report (2007),* Retrieved from http://planipolis.iiep.unesco.org/upload/Nepal/PRSP/Nepal%20PRSP%20Progress%20report.pd
23. *Unemployment in Nepal (2011),* Retrieved from http://nepal-madhu.blogspot.in/2011/01/unemployment-in-nepal.html
24. *Educated, unemployed and mobile*, Retrieved from http://www.ekantipur.com/the-kathmandu-post/2013/09/28/free-the-words/educated-unemployed-and-mobile/254166.html
25. *Energy Country Analysis Brief: Nepal, February, 2002*, Retrieved from http://www.sari-energy.org/Publications/eia/Nepal.pdf
26. *Ibid.*
27. *Nepal economy*, Retrieved from http://globaledge.msu.edu/countries/nepal/economy.
28. *Nepal among top 5 countries*, Retrieved from http://www.ekantipur.com/the-kathmandu-post/2010/11/09/money/nepal-among-top-5-countries/214646/
29. See http://www.karobardaily.com/news/2013/10/nepal-third-in-receiving-remittance-in-terms-of-gdp
30. *Remittances are not the only reason young Nepalese decide to migrate*, Retrieved from http://www.theguardian.com/global-development/poverty-matters/2012/jul/05/money-not-only-motivation-nepalese-migrants.
31. *Gender and Public Transport: Kathmandu, Nepal*, Retrieved from http://www.worldbank.org/content/dam/Worldbank/document/SAR/nepal/Gender-and-Public-Transport-in-Nepal-Report.pdf
32. *National transport policy,* Retrieved from http://www.dor.gov.np/documents/National_Transport_Policy_2058.pdf
33. *Nepal transport sector*, Retrieved from http://web.worldbank.org/WBSITE/EXTERNAL/COUNTRIES/SOUTHASIAEXT/EXTSARREGTOPTRANSPORT/0,,contentMDK:20560914~menu PK:869038~pagePK:34004173~piPK:34003707~theSitePK:579598,00.html
34. See http://www.thehimalayantimes.com/fullNews.php?headline=Railways+for+Nepal+&NewsID=323186.

# Chapter - 5

# Economy of Bhutan

*"Economic growth may one day turn out to be a curse rather than a good, and under no conditions can it either lead into freedom or constitute a proof for its existence."*

***—Hannah Arendt***

Bhutan is a small Himalayan constitutional monarchy that made the transition from absolute monarchy to parliamentary democracy in March 2008. It has one of the world's smallest and least-developed economies. Until a few decades ago, the country was still largely agrarian, with few roads, little electricity, and no modern hospitals. Rugged terrain makes the development of infrastructure difficult. Recent interregional economic cooperation, particularly involving trade with Bangladesh and India, is helping to encourage economic growth. Connections to global markets are limited and dominated significantly by India.[1]

Geographically; the country is made up of extremely diverse terrains. The northern region of the country consists of an arc of eastern Himalayan alpine shrub and meadows reaching up to high mountain peaks of over 7,000 m above sea level. The Black Mountains in the central region form a watershed between two major river systems. Central and southern Bhutan is dominated by forests; most of the population lives in the central highlands. The climate varies with the altitude, from sub-tropical in the south to temperate in the highlands, with a polar-type climate in certain areas, with year-round snow.

Gross National Happiness was first used in 1972 by Bhutan's former King Jigme Singye Wangchuck. The King made a decision to preserve Buddhist values and to retain a balanced relationship with the natural environment. Instead of measuring development on the basis of economic growth alone, GNH broadens the concept of development and includes the following four pillars:

1. The promotion of equitable and sustainable socioeconomic development;
2. The preservation and promotion of cultural values;
3. The conservation of the natural environment; and
4. The promotion of good governance.[2]

## Economy of Bhutan

The economy of Bhutan, one of the world's smallest and least developed countries, is based on agriculture and forestry, which provide the main livelihood for more than 60 per cent of the population. Agriculture consists largely of subsistence and animal husbandry. Rugged mountains dominate the terrain and make the building of roads and other infrastructure difficult and expensive. The economy, one of the world's smallest and least developed, is based on hydroelectricity, tourism, agriculture, and forestry. Rugged terrain makes it difficult to develop roads and other infrastructure.

Despite this constraint, hydroelectricity and construction continue to be the two major industries of growth for the country. As these two economic sectors contribute to increased productivity, Bhutan's development prospects are positive. The Tala hydroelectric project, completed March 2007, has bolstered government revenue and exports, and will continue to do so for the next several years.[3] Bhutan's hydropower potential and its attraction for tourists are key resources. The Bhutanese Government has made some progress in expanding the nation's productive base and improving social welfare. Model education, social, and environment programmes are underway with support from multilateral development organisations.[4]

In May 2003, the Bilateral Free Trade Agreement between Bangladesh and Bhutan was re-signed. Bangladesh is Bhutan's second largest trade partner, after India. In January 2004, as a member of the South Asian Association for Regional Cooperation, Bhutan also joined the South Asian Free Trade Agreement. In February 2004 Bhutan joined the Bangladesh, India, Myanmar, Singapore, and Thailand Economic

Cooperation Forum. Bhutan has applied for membership in the World Trade Organisation and is in the process of developing clear legal and regulatory systems designed to promote business development.[5]

The biggest impetus to the economic growth is still provided by foreign aid and large-scale hydropower projects. Real GDP growth increased to 21.4 per cent in 2007 as compared to 8.5 per cent in 2006 mainly on account of the commissioning of the Tala Hydroelectric Project. The small base of the national economy also makes it possible for a single large industrial activity to boost growth substantially.[6] Although Bhutan has made sustained progress toward attaining the MDGs and is well on track to reach most of the targets by 2015, challenges remain, especially in rural areas, where poverty prevalence stands at 30.9 per cent (and in some areas as high as 52.9 per cent), compared to about 1.7 per cent among the urban population. Reducing food poverty, enhancing gender equity, improving skilled birth attendance to reduce maternal mortality, curtailing the spread of HIV/AIDS, and addressing youth unemployment are the major areas of concern.[7]

## Agriculture

The government has focused on sustainable forest management. In the 1960s, Bhutan sought to develop its forests as a source of revenue by promoting the lumber trade. Timber extraction increased significantly in the 1980s. The government then decided to shift its forest priority away from revenue generation towards environmental protection to align it with the country's general development philosophy. The National Forest Policy of 1991 implemented restrictions on tree felling, created new afforestation programmes and declared all non-private forest land to be government-owned forest reserves in order to mitigate the adverse effects of commercial logging. In 1995, the National Assembly decreed that 60 per cent of the country would remain under forest cover in perpetuity.[8]

Bhutan plans to become the first country in the world to turn its agriculture completely organic, banning the sales of pesticides and herbicides and relying on its own animals and farm waste for fertilisers. Bhutan's future depends largely on how it responds to interlinked development challenges like climate change, and food and energy security. In the west, organic food growing is widely thought to reduce the size of crops because they become more susceptible to pests. But this is being challenged in Bhutan and some regions of Asia, where smallholders are developing new techniques to grow more and are not losing soil quality.

In Paro, a largely farming district in south-west Bhutan, farmers are already struggling to grow enough to feed their families and local government officials say they have to distribute fertiliser and pesticides in larger quantities to help people grow more.[9] The agricultural sector provided 38.5 per cent of GDP in 1997, a significant decline from the 55 per cent in 1985. The 1997 GDP consisted of a total production of 18.1 per cent crops, 11.4 per cent of economic activity in the forestry sector, and 9 per cent livestock production. Of the 970,000 people who were employed in Bhutan in 1998 (using a population estimate of 2 million) 93.8 per cent were engaged in agricultural activities. There were 160,000 hectares of arable land under permanent crops in 1998, compared to the 1980 level of 122,000. In 1998 only 40,000 hectares of this land was irrigated, an improvement upon the 1980 level of 26,000 hectares.[10]

## Industry

The manufacturing sector is the major contributor to national revenue. With the industrial sector established in Pasakha, small scale industries such as cement plants, calcium and carbide, steel and Ferro silicon, Coca Cola and also wood-based industries have started developing. As a result of the recent economic development, Bhutan has one of the highest per capita incomes in South Asia at US$1,321. However, despite this high level of growth and development, efforts stringent regaliations have been enacted in order to protect Bhutan's natural environment. Bhutan's rich biodiversity provides the country with ample forest resources and this has brought about the development of a thriving cane and bamboo handicraft industry. Craftsmen weave a number of beautiful and intricate items out of bamboo and cane including hats, backpacks, floor mats and traditional bowls. These items are then sold to tourists or Bhutanese, supplying a secondary income source.[11]

## Transport

Transport in Bhutan comprises approximately 8,000 kilometres (5,000 mi) of roads and four airports, out of which three are operational and interconnected. Paro Airport is the only airport that serves international flights. As part of Bhutan's infrastructure and modernisation programmes, its road system has been under development since the 1960s. The single runway at Paro Airport is located in a steep-sided valley with restricted VFR approaches. During the monsoon season, flights are often delayed by cloud cover. Drukair is the national carrier, connecting Paro to Kolkata and Delhi in India, Bangkok in Thailand, Dhaka in Bangladesh and Kathmandu in Nepal.[12]

The country's primary road is the East-West highway, known locally as the Lateral Road, which was constructed starting in 1962. The road starts in Phuentsholing on the southwestern Indian border and terminates in Trashigang in the Far East, with spurs to other main centres such as Paro, Thimphu, and Punakha. The Lateral Road is built to a standard width of only 2.5 meters yet must support traffic in both directions. Safety barriers, road markings, and signage are sparse. Traffic proceeds at a slow speed, typically around 15 km/h, to minimise head-on collisions. As of 2013, Bhutan had no railways.[13]

## Banking

The nation's commercial bank The Bank of Bhutan was established in 1968 as a joint venture with the Chartered Bank of India, Australia and China, which owned 25 per cent of the bank. In 1970, this share was transferred to the State Bank of India. Since its establishment, the Bank of Bhutan's board of directors has been composed of key officials from the economic ministries and departments and two officials from the Indian banks. The bank was restructured in 1971. The Bhutan Development Finance Corporation, upon its establishment in 1988, took over the administration of rural financial assistance from the Royal Monetary Authority.

Loans were granted for improving farmland, acquiring livestock, and meeting short-term, seasonal requirements. Non-bank financial institutions also were set up as part of the economic modernisation process. Insurance was offered by the Royal Insurance Corporation of Bhutan, which was established in 1975 with its headquarters in Phuntsholing. Starting in 1980, individuals could invest their savings in the newly established Unit Trust of Bhutan.[14] Unit Trust of Bhutan, an undertaking of the Royal Government was incorporated on its Memorandum and Articles of Association under the Rules and regulations of Bhutan with an initial capital of Nu.2.5 million, contributed by the Royal Government and the Royal Insurance Corporation of Bhutan.[15]

## Minerals

Accordingly, Bhutan's policies on mining and quarrying consider inter-generational equity. This is important since minerals constitute vital raw materials for the mineral based manufacturing industries and are a major resource for economic development of a country. The management of mineral resources has to be closely integrated with the overall strategy for development and long-term national goals. Only about 33 per cent of the country has been geologically mapped and prospected in 1:50,000 scale. There is potential for further discovery of minerals in the unexplored parts of the country. From the past exploration it has been found that the country is endowed with rocks, industrial minerals like limestone, dolomite, gypsum, quartzite, graphite, talc etc and metallic minerals like tungsten, lead-zinc and copper.[16]

Minerals are valuable natural resources but are finite and non-renewable. Accordingly, Bhutan's policies on mining and quarrying consider inter-generational equity. This is important since minerals constitute vital raw materials for the mineral-based manufacturing industries and are a major resource for economic development of a country. The Department of Geology and Mines has the primary responsibility of geological mapping and exploring for additional mineral deposits and the management of mineral resources of the country. In addition, the department has been mandated to conduct geological investigations for slope stability and foundation, undertake risk assessments from Glacial Lake Outburst Floods, monitor glaciers and glacial lakes and carry out seismic studies.[17]

In Bhutan, the Geological Survey of India (GSI), Bhutan Unit, commenced the geological investigation of mineral deposits in the year 1962. Since then minerals such as gypsum, limestone, marble, coal, graphite, dolomite, iron ore, slate, quartzite, copper, tungsten, granite, lead zinc, soapstone etc were explored and mapped. The Geological Survey of Bhutan was established in 1981 and later it became Department of Geology and Mines (DGM). Initially core drilling to prove the mineral deposits was done by GSI and then later by DGM,

Cement Corporation of India Limited, and Associated Cement Company Limited. Based on the report of proved or measured deposit Final Mine Feasibility Study, Environmental Management Plan and Environmental Impact Assessments reports are prepared in order to obtain a mining concession.[18]

According to the Division of Geology and Mines, most industrial minerals mining was by privately owned companies operating in the southern part of the country. Mining of dolomite was by Chundu Enterprise at Khagrikhola and Pugli and Bhutan Mining Enterprise at Pugli, all in the Samchi District of southwestern Bhutan; by Tashi Commercial Corp. at Kalesore and Singye Dolomite Industries at Duarpani in the Samdrup-Mongar and the Shemgang Districts of southeastern Bhutan. Mining of gypsum was by the References Cited state-owned Shumar Gypsum at Khothakpa near Pemagatsel in southeastern Bhutan. Mining of marble was by Bhutan Marble and Minerals at Gidakhom in the Thimphu Valley. Mining of slate was by the state-owned Sha Slate Mine at Sha Bhel.[19]

## Electricity

Due to its fast flowing, glacier-fed rivers, Bhutan have enormous potential to produce hydroelectricity. With the construction of several major dams, the power sector has undeniably been the biggest contributor to the Bhutanese exchequer. The Chukha Hydro Power Corporation, the Tala Hydro Power Corporation, the Baso Chu Hydro Power Corporation and the Kurichu Hydro Power Corporation, under the umbrella of Druk Green Power Corporation, are some of the existing mega projects in the country. The 1500 MW of power they generate, most of which is exported to our neighbouring country India, barely scratches the surface of Bhutan's untapped hydroelectric potential. With its abundant water resources, Bhutan still has the capacity to generate another 30,000 MW of electricity. However, the government is preceding cautiously with new construction projects in order to minimise the impact upon the surrounding areas.[20]

Bank of Bhutan was established as the public sector commercial bank and until the establishment of the Royal Monetary Authority of Bhutan; it rendered the function of the Central Bank in Bhutan. The Royal Monetary Authority of Bhutan is the Central Bank of Bhutan, which was established in 1982 and is responsible for the regulating the financial sector and formulating the monetary policies in Bhutan. Bank of Bhutan started with only 20 account holders and currently has about 150,000 accounts. The bank was established with a paid-up capital of Nu 2.5 million. From 2004 until 2007, the market share of Bank of Bhutan was about 35 per cent and it is expected to increase further.[21]

The main development challenges faced by Bhutan's power sector in the mid-1990s were identified as (i) the institutional weakness of the sector, and (ii) its inability to assume the role of key growth driver in promoting the country's economic development through power exports and providing access to electricity for rural consumers. The sector also suffered from poor cost recovery and dependence on donor financing for new investments. The government's development strategy during 1994–2009 recognised the central role of the power sector in promoting (i) economic development and poverty alleviation by exploiting the abundant hydropower potential for increasing the government's fiscal revenues from power exports, (ii) balanced regional growth through access to electricity for rural communities, and (iii) industrial investments based on cheap and reliable supply of electricity.

Bhutan is the only country in South Asia with surplus power generation capacity and a power sector that contributes a significant share to its national economy. The Asian Development Bank has been a major development partner in Bhutan's power sector. It has provided financial assistance through concessionary loans for the expansion of the rural power distribution network. It also played a catalytic role in structuring and financing Bhutan's first public–private partnership transaction in the export-oriented hydropower sector.[22]

## Poverty and Unemployment

Bhutan is a least developed country and its economy is essentially an agrarian one with 79 per cent of the people dependent on agriculture and livestock rearing for their livelihood. Bhutan embarked on its first development initiative with the inception of the first five-year plan in 1961. Prior to this, a vast majority of Bhutanese lived rugged lives of isolation. Bhutan has undergone major transformation and there has been remarkable improvement in all aspects of the lives of Bhutanese people.[23]

About 23 per cent of the Bhutanese population lives below the national poverty line of about Nu 1,100 per person per month. This is according to the Bhutan Living Standard Survey which was conducted by the National Statistics Bureau from March to May, 2007. Poverty in urban areas at 1.7 per cent is significantly lower than in rural areas, which is estimated at around 31 per cent. Poverty rates are found to be high in Zhemgang, Samtse, Monggar, Lhuentse, and Samdrup Jongkhar. The poverty line, the minimum acceptable standard of per capita consumption needed to assure a minimum standard of living, was obtained using the Cost of Basic Needs approach, a commonly used methodology in many countries for constructing the poverty line. The Royal Government of Bhutan has initiated a Poverty Reduction Strategy Paper process as a part of the broader ongoing efforts to combat poverty. The main objective of it is to strengthen the strategic framework for poverty reduction, improve donor coordination, and build support for new initiatives in public expenditure management (annual plans and two years rolling budget introduced from financial year 2003-04) and poverty monitoring and assessment system.[24]

In education, the overall literacy rate is estimated at 56 per cent. Thimphu has the highest literacy rate at 72 per cent while Gasa has the least at 40 per cent. The country's unemployment rate is estimated at 3.7 per cent. The survey says high unemployment rates are prominent in the age group 15 to 24 years, especially in urban areas. Among the estimated 274,000 employed persons in Bhutan, two-thirds are employed in the agriculture sector, three out of twenty works in industry, three out of twenty work in the services sector, and one out of forty works in other enterprises. In urban areas, 80 per cent of women who give birth over a period of one year before the survey began delivered in hospitals or clinics. But in rural areas only 45 per cent delivered in hospitals or clinics. More than 70 per cent of all women who gave birth during the same period are below 35 years. About two-thirds of households in the country own dwellings. In urban areas, only one in five households has their own house. In urban areas 97 per cent of the population has access to electricity while in rural areas only 56 per cent have access to electricity.[25]

## Migration

In most rural areas, the impact of rural-urban migration is rapid deterioration of rural economy caused due to low agricultural production which leads to high cost. Rural-urban migration gives rise to problems such as increased crime rate, pollution, congestion, loosening of family bonds, and loss of traditional way of life, cultural practices and values. This happens mainly due to inundated influx of youth into the cities. This process of flow from rural areas leaves only the older and aged members to form the labour force and fend for them.[26] Net migration in Bhutan was last measured at 10,000 in 2012, according to the World Bank. Net migration is the net total of migrants during the period, that is, the total number of immigrants less the annual number of emigrants, including both citizens and non-citizens.[27]

## Tourism

Tourism in Bhutan began in 1974, when the Government of Bhutan, in an effort to raise revenue and to promote the country's unique culture and traditions to the outside world, opened its isolated country to foreigners. In 1974, 287 tourists visited Bhutan. Despite being open to foreigners, the government is acutely aware of the environmental impact tourists can have on Bhutan's unique and virtually unspoiled landscape and culture. Therefore, they have restricted the level of tourist activity from the start, preferring higher quality tourism.

Until 1991, the Bhutan Tourism Corporation, a quasi-autonomous and self-financing body, implemented the government's tourism policy. The most important centres for tourism are capital Thimphu, and in the western city of Paro, near India. Taktshang, a cliff side monastery overlooking the Paro Valley, is one of the country's attractions. This temple is incredibly sacred to Buddhists. Housed inside the temple is a cave in which the Buddhist Deity who brought Buddhism to Bhutan fasted for 90 days as he battled the demons that inhabited this valley, in order to spread Buddhism.[28]

The royal government has always been aware that an unrestricted flow of tourists can have negative impacts on Bhutan's pristine environment and its rich and unique culture. The government adopted a policy of "high value-low volume" tourism, controlling the type and quantity of tourism right from the start. Until 1991 the Bhutan Tourism Corporation, a quasi-autonomous and self-financing body, implemented the government's tourism policy. All tourists, up to that time came as guests of Bhutan Tourism Corporation, which in turn operated the tour organisation, transport services and nearly all the hotels and accommodation facilities. The government privatised tourism in

October 1991 to encourage increased private sector participation in the tourism sector. Today there are more than 75 licenced tour operators in the country. Bhutan's main tourism attractions are its traditional culture and way of life, its religious festivals, historic monuments and its pristine environment. It has received much international acclaim for its cautious approach to development that places a high priority on conserving the nation's natural and cultural heritage. Protecting nature and culture is part of the Bhutanese value system and is an important aspect of the traditional way of life in Bhutan, and the tourism policy reflects this concerns.[29]

The tourism industry has become a major service industry generating foreign exchange and creating employment opportunities. There are important spin-off benefits in the form of small scale enterprises, income for rural families, and employment for the hundreds of young job seekers. Tourism has positively strengthened Bhutan image in the world as a small country with big ambitions for its environment and culture. In some ways, it has also provided the incentives to promote some of Bhutan's local cultures that are unique to small remote settlements.[30]

## Foreign Remittances

Bhutan needs more remittance, probably more than anything in the past. Remittance helps to back up and sustain the general spending in daily life. Bhutan is not a country which sends a lot of people to international labour market, therefore no question of getting larger revenue as remittance. With low capacity of absorbing a large volume of tourist and low investment on developmental projects by the citizens, remittance if any, can be of risk to melt down to Indian rupees. Kuensel on December 21 reflected on the contribution of remittance to GDP and development infrastructures, and Bhutan is definitely losing it.

Remittance to Bhutan by the diaspora shall be purely based on mutual understanding of government and people. It is the responsibility of government to put in place a conducive investment climate in development projects by the Bhutanese themselves or at least give leverage to the local government to accept donations and charity funds.[31]

## Conclusion

The economy of Bhutan is based on agriculture and forestry, which provide the main livelihood for more than 60 per cent of the population. Agriculture consists largely of subsistence and animal husbandry. In May 2003, the Bilateral Free Trade Agreement between Bangladesh and Bhutan was re-signed. Bangladesh is Bhutan's second largest trade partner, after India. The government has focused on sustainable forest management. The National Forest Policy of 1991 implemented restrictions on tree felling, created new afforestation programmes and declared all non-private forest land to be government-owned forest reserves in order to mitigate the adverse effects of commercial logging.

Bhutan's future depends largely on how it responds to interlinked development challenges like climate change, and food and energy security. With the industrial sector established in Pasakha, small scale industries such as cement plants, calcium and carbide, steel and Ferro silicon, Coca Cola and also wood-based industries have started developing. Transport in Bhutan comprises approximately 8,000 kilometres (5,000 mi) of roads and four airports, out of which three are operational and interconnected. Paro Airport is the only airport that serves international flights. The nation's commercial bank The Bank of Bhutan was established in 1968 as a joint venture with the Chartered Bank of India, Australia and China, which owned 25 per cent of the bank. From the past exploration it has been found that the country is endowed with rocks, industrial minerals like limestone, dolomite, gypsum, quartzite, graphite, talc etc and metallic minerals like tungsten, lead-zinc and copper. Due to its fast flowing, glacier-fed rivers, Bhutan have enormous potential to produce hydroelectricity.

The Royal Government of Bhutan has initiated a Poverty Reduction Strategy Paper process as a part of the broader ongoing efforts to combat poverty. Tourism in Bhutan began in 1974, when the Government of Bhutan, in an effort to raise revenue and to promote the country's unique culture and traditions to the outside world, opened its isolated country to foreigners. The most important centres for tourism are capital Thimphu, and in the western city of Paro, near India. Taktshang, a cliff side monastery overlooking the Paro Valley, is one of the country's attractions.

## References


1. *Bhutan Economy (2014),* Retrieved from http://www.heritage.org/index/country/bhutan.
2. *Bhutan's success in conservation,* Retrieved from http://www.developmentprogress.org/sites/developmentprogress.org/files/bhutan_report_-_master.pdf
3. *Bhutan Economy,* Retrieved from http://globaledge.msu.edu/countries/bhutan/economy.
4. *Economy of Bhutan (2014),* Retrieved from http://en.wikipedia.org/wiki/Economy_of_Bhutan.
5. *Ibid.*
6. *Economic development policy of Kingdom of Bhutan 2010,* Retrieved from http://www.gnhc.gov.bt/wp-content/uploads/2012/04/EDP.pdf
7. *Bhutan: Rural economy advancement,* Retrieved from http://www.undp.org/content/dam/undp/library/Poverty%20Reduction/MDG%20Strategies/Bhutan(2011nov)_web.pdf
8. *Bhutan's success in conservation,* Retrieved from http://www.developmentprogress.org/sites/developmentprogress.org/files/bhutan_report_-_master.pdf
9. *Bhutan set to plough lone furrow as world's first wholly organic country,* Retrieved from http://www.theguardian.com/global-development/poverty-matters/2013/feb/11/bhutan-first-wholly-organic-country.
10. See http://www.nationsencyclopedia.com/economies/Asia-and-the-Pacific/Bhutan-AGRICULTURE.html
11. *Economy: Tourism Council of Bhutan*, Retrieved from http://www.tourism.gov.bt/about-bhutan/Economy.
12. *Transport in Bhutan (2014)*, Retrieved from http://en.wikipedia.org/wiki/Transport_in_Bhutan.
13. *Transportation system in Bhutan,* Retrieved from http://www.tinyhimalayan.com/about-bhutan/transportation-system-in-bhutan/
14. *Banking in Bhutan*, Retrieved from http://en.wikipedia.org/wiki/Banking_in_Bhutan.
15. See http://www.bnb.bt/history.html
16. *Economic development policy of Kingdom of Bhutan 2010*, Retrieved from http://www.gnhc.gov.bt/wp-content/uploads/2012/04/EDP.pdf
17. *Mines sector*, Retrieved from http://www.asiatradehub.com/bhutan/mines.asp
18. *Mining Has Great Economic Potential for Bhutan,* Retrieved from http://www.thebhutanese.bt/mining-has-great-economic-potential-for-bhutan/
19. John C. Wu, *The mineral industry of Bhutan*, Retrieved from http://minerals.usgs.gov/minerals/pubs/country/1997/9304097.pdf

20. *Economy: Tourism Council of Bhutan*, Retrieved from http://www.tourism.gov.bt/about-bhutan/Economy.
21. See http://www.bob.bt/about-us/
22. *Bhutan: Energy Sector*, Retrieved from http://www.oecd.org/countries/bhutan/47177609.pdf
23. *Poverty and Inequality in Bhutan*, Retrieved from http://www.nsb.gov.bt/publication/files/pub10ks2884sy.pdf
24. *Bhutan: Poverty Reduction Strategy Paper (2004*), Retrieved from http://planipolis.iiep.unesco.org/upload/Bhutan/PRSP/Bhutan%20PRSP.pdf
25. *23 per cent Bhutanese live below national poverty line*, Retrieved from http://www.bbs.com.bt/Bhutan%20Living%20Standard%20Survey.html
26. See http://jr.sherubtse.edu.bt/index.php/ISPD2012/article/view/74/97
27. See http://www.tradingeconomics.com/bhutan/net-migration-wb-data.html
28. *Tourism in Bhutan (2013),* Retrieved from http://en.wikipedia.org/wiki/Tourism_in_Bhutan.
29. Tandi Dorji, *Sustainability of tourism in Bhutan*, Retrieved from http://www.mtnforum.org/sites/default/files/publication/files/6471.pdf
30. *Tourism in Bhutan*, Retrieved from http://www.chhundu.com.bt/tourism-in-bhutan.
31. *Remittance to Bhutan*, Retrieved from http://apfanews.com/opinion/remittance-to-bhutan.html.

# Chapter - 6

# Economy of Sri Lanka

*"If you ask an economist what's driven economic growth, it's been major advances in things that mattered-the mechanisation of farming, mass manufacturing, things like that. The problem is, our society is not organised around doing that."*

***—Larry Page***

## Introduction

Sri Lanka is an island nation located in the Indian Ocean, just off the southeastern coast of India. Despite its modest size, Sri Lanka has a population of about 20 million people, almost equal to the population of Texas. The island is rich in natural resources and has a diverse economy based on agriculture, mining, fishing, manufacturing, and tourism. On becoming an independent nation in 1948 Sri Lanka seemed to be headed for a future as a stable and prosperous democracy. Located between 5 and 10 degrees latitude north of the equator, Sri Lanka has a tropical climate dominated by two monsoon seasons.

The summer monsoon lasts from mid-May to October, when winds from the southwest bring rain from the Indian Ocean to the southern and western parts of the island. During the winter monsoon, from December through March, winds from the northeast bring rain from the Bay of Bengal to northern and eastern regions. All over South Asia (including today's countries of India, Sri Lanka, Myanmar, Pakistan, and Bangladesh), resistance to British rule grew rapidly after the end of World War I in 1919. In Sri Lanka, which was comparatively small, stable, and well governed under British rule, the country's first democratic election was held in 1931. A movement toward economic self-determination leading to full independence was spearheaded by Sri Lanka's greatest modern leader, Don Stephen Senanayake (1884-1952). When Sri Lanka became independent on February 4, 1948, Senanayake became the country's first prime minister.[1]

Sri Lanka is a country famous for hospitality, tourism and well being people from the past. Once Marco Polo has told in 1293 A.D., 'this for its actual size is better circumstanced than any other island in the world. The island produces more beautiful and valuable rubies than found in any other place in the world. In this island there is a very high mountain where the tomb of Adam, our first parent, is supposed to be found.'[2]

## Economy of Sri Lanka

With an economy worth \$64 billion (2012 IMF estimate) (\$170 billion PPP estimate), and a per capita GDP of about \$7900 (PPP), Sri Lanka has mostly had strong growth rates in recent years. In GDP per capita terms, it is ahead of other countries in the South Asian region. The main economic sectors of the country are tourism, tea export, apparel, textile, rice production and other agricultural products. In addition to these economic sectors, overseas employment contributes highly in foreign exchange, 90 per cent of expatriate Sri Lankans reside in the Middle East. The Central Bank of Sri Lanka is the monetary authority of Sri Lanka and was established in 1950. The Central Bank is responsible for the conduct of monetary policy in the country and also has supervisory powers over the financial system.[3]

Sri Lanka is a developing economy based largely on agriculture, services, and light industry. Agriculture accounts for approximately 21 per cent of the gross domestic product and employs 38 per cent of the workforce. Agricultural output is divided between cash crops from plantation agriculture and food crops from subsistence agriculture. Cash crops (namely tea, rubber, and coconuts) are largely grown on plantations. Rice is the principal food crop and the main livelihood for over 70 per cent of Sri Lanka's rural population. The country is endowed with many natural resources. It has an equatorial climate with a high average rainfall.

The land is fertile and suitable for growing a variety of crops, and one-third of the land is arable. Foreign trade is an important segment of the Sri Lankan economy. Major imports include petroleum, consumables, machinery and capital equipment, motor vehicles, and various manufactured goods. Sri Lanka is a mixed economy, in which both the private sector and the state sector engage in the production process. Foreign investments are encouraged and several free zones have been established. The Sri Lankan economy has since become highly diversified; it has rapidly growing manufacturing and service sectors, agricultural activities have been modernised, and the country is nearly self-sufficient in rice production.[4]

Growth in gross domestic product rebounded to 7.3 per cent in 2013. The recovery reflected domestic demand strengthening and a pickup in exports and tourism. Faster growth in wholesale and retail trade, hotels and restaurants, transport, banking, insurance, and real estate lifted performance in the large service sector to 6.4 per cent from 4.6 per cent a year earlier, providing the impetus for the rebound. Industry grew by 9.9 per cent, slightly less than a year earlier, as slower growth in mining and quarrying and in construction offset a pickup in manufacturing and utilities.[5]

## Agriculture

Agriculture is the most important sector of the Sri Lankan economy. Even though its contribution to the gross domestic product declined substantially during the past three decades (from 30 per cent in 1970 to 21 per cent in 2000), it is the most important source of employment for the majority of workforce. The major plantation crops of tea, rubber, and coconuts continue to figure prominently in the economy; however, the contribution of these commercial crops to gross domestic product declined from 11.5 per cent in 1970 to five per cent in 2000. Tea, the prominent crop of the plantation sector, grows in many parts of the wet zone, and in particular in the central hill country.[6]

The agricultural sector of the country produces mainly rice, coconut and grain, largely for domestic consumption and occasionally for export. The tea industry which has existed since 1867 is not usually regarded as part of the agricultural sector, which is mainly focused on export rather than domestic use in the country. Around eighty different varieties of fruits and vegetables are grown in Sri Lanka's varied agro-climatic areas. The cool and salubrious climatic conditions in the hill country are ideal for temperate crops such as carrot, leek, cabbage, cauliflower, salad leaves, beet, bean, bell pepper and salad cucumber. The well demarcated low country and dry wet areas are suitable for a variety of tropical fruits and vegetables ranging from green chilli, red onion, pumpkin, bitter gourd, melon, sweet and sour banana types, queen pineapple, papaya, mango, lemon and gherkins etc.

Oilseed crops such as Groundnut, Sesame, Sunflower and Mustard are also cultivated in Sri Lanka. Groundnut is grown mainly in Moneragala, Hambantota, Kurunegala, Anuradhapura, Badulla, Ratnapura and Puttalam districts. Though groundnut is an oil crop, it has a demand as a snack and confectionery in Sri Lanka.[7] The wide variation in temperature, rainfall, topography and soils in the country has provided a wide variation of ecosystems resulting in a rich diversity of plant species which the Sri Lankan farmers have been able to maintain over thousands of years. Sri Lankan food crop diversity has been enriched by introduction of several crop plants of economic importance since historical times. The introduced types, depending on the time and the area also exhibit secondary genetic diversity.

Sri Lanka is rich with around 60 varieties of underutilised crops. Most of these underutilised species have lost their significance among the present generation due to many reasons such as urbanisation and changing food habits. There is no organised or proper cultivation of these crop species. Most of these underutilised plant species are fruit crops and they are found in wild or in home gardens, which are 100 $m^2$ to 1000 $m^2$ in extent and are commonly found in many rural areas. As altitude increases, the extent of home gardens becomes smaller with greater diversity of plant species and lesser diversity within the species. Very little inventory work has been so far done on the state of diversity of crops in home gardens.[8]

## Industry

The design, manufacture and export of textiles and apparel products is one of the biggest industries and one which plays a key role in advancing the country's economy. The apparel industry employs about 15 per cent of the country's workforce, accounting for about half of the country's total exports, and Sri Lanka is among the top apparel-producing countries in the world relative to its population. Over the next few decades, the apparel industry grew to represent Sri Lanka's number one export. The United States is the main importer of textile goods, accounting for 76 per cent of total exports from Sri Lanka.

As of 2009, Sri Lanka ranked 12th among apparel exporters to the United States in terms of value.[9]

Sri Lanka's apparel export industry is the most significant and dynamic contributor for Sri Lanka's economy. The industry has enjoyed epic growth levels over the past four decades and is today Sri Lanka's primary foreign exchange earner accounting to 40 per cent of the total exports and 52 per cent of industrial products exports. This industry, entirely privately owned has successfully exploited the opportunities in the international market. Around 350 garment factories are operating in different parts of Sri Lanka and around 16 textile and fabric manufacturing units are in operation which plays a key role in the advancement of the apparel industry.[10] Over the past two decades since its arrival into mainstream export production the country has strategically developed a skill base in research, design and innovation accounting for top quality manufacturers. Sri Lanka's major producers service some of the biggest apparel brands in the world such as Nike, Victoria's Secret, Ann Taylor and Marks and Spencer.[11]

Sri Lanka's garment exports have been largely governed by the Multi-fibre Arrangement since 1978. It is a system of export restrictions imposed by developed countries on textiles and garment exports originating in developing countries to protect the garment industry in developed countries. The Uruguay Round Agreement on Textiles and Clothing of WTO succeeded MFA in 1995. According to the new rules, the sector is to be fully integrated into normal rules of WTO by phasing out MFA in four phases by 2005. Sri Lanka has already fulfilled its commitments under Phase I and Phase II of the elimination of MFA phasing out procedures. The government submitted to the Textiles Monitoring Body of WTO in 1996 and 1998 lists of items on which Sri Lanka is ready to accept the removal of quota. The third phase of integration became effective on January 2002.[12]

Sri Lanka is the largest supplier of brown fibre to the world with annual exports of fibre of more than 100,000 MT. Also famous for its value added coir products such as coir twine, brushes, brooms, coir mats, rugs and geotextiles. Sri Lanka also produces a range of rubberized coir-based horticulture products such as coir pots, baskets, basket liners, seed trays, hanging baskets, weed control mats and coir poles. Sri Lanka is the world's largest exporter of coir fibre. Its coir industry is in urgent need for infrastructure upgrading for it to sustain its coir supremacy.

New technology infusion to coir sector can greatly enhance coir appeal in the competitive global marketplace.[13]

The history of Sri Lanka's rubber industry began way back in 1876 with the planting of rubber trees while took place in Henerathgoda. While the latex coming out from the rubber tree is used in the manufacture of various rubber products, even the timber is used, in treated form for producing furniture and other timber based products. The rubber industry generates employment to a vast number of people mainly from rural areas, where the estates are. This trend continues with Sri Lanka exporting about 20-30 per cent of the rubber production in raw form while 70-80 per cent is used by the domestic industries. Value of rubber industry exports has been growing steadily from approx. US$ 135 mn in 1995 to more than US$ 284 Mn in 2004 and increasing to US$ 483 in 2009. Out of this value, rubber products export value consists of around 80 per cent.[14] Sabaragamuwa and Western provinces record 87 per cent of the total number of rubber industries in the country. All large and small-scale industries and 80 per cent of medium-scale rubber industries can provide employment for trained personnel in rubber technology. Within a relatively short period, this industry has become a reputable major world supplier of quality rubber products.[15]

## Banking Sector

The banking sector in Sri Lanka is monitored by the Bank Supervision Department of the Central Bank of Sri Lanka under the Banking Act, Monetary Law Act and the Exchange Control Act. The Sri Lankan banking industry was changed during the late 1980s with the introduction of automation by private banking corporations. In 1986, Sampath Bank opened, offering customers access to their account from any branch, instant money transfers within cities and access to automated teller machines. The Institute of Bankers of Sri Lanka, established under Act of Parliament No. 26 of 1979, is the apex body governing the banking education.[16]

The Financial system consists of financial institutions, markets, instruments and infrastructure, which facilitate payments and settlements associated with real sector transactions. This sector responds to changes in both internal and external factors. The stability of the financial system depends on such changes and the responses of participants in the financial system to those changes.[17] The Sri Lankan banking and financial services industry is vibrant and market driven and hence as a consumer are at an advantage. The Sri Lankan banking industry is known to have high interest rates ranging six per cent to 20 per cent (both saving and borrowing). The advantage of this scenario is, as an individual will earn more by saving money in LKR denominated accounts.[18] The Sri Lankan banking sector is concentrated and dominated by public-sector banks. About half of sector assets are with the public sector, including the three largest banks.

## Transport

Transport in Sri Lanka is based mainly on the road network which is centred on Sri Lanka's capital, Colombo. There is also a railway network, but it is largely a legacy of British colonial rule and today only handles a small fraction of the country's transport needs.[19] Roads are the backbone of the transport sector in the country. They are vital for the movement of people and goods and play an important role in integrating the country, facilitating economic growth, and ultimately reducing poverty. National roads carry over 70 per cent of the traffic in Sri Lanka. While Sri Lanka Railways played a dominant role in the country's transport sector until 1928, its share in passenger and freight transportation has reduced to about eight per cent and five per cent respectively.

Sri Lanka has several large ports such as Colombo, Galle, Trincomalee, and Kankasanthurai, as well as harbours. The Port of Colombo, the country's premier commercial port, is one of the better performing ports in Asia. It handles both conventional cargo as well as containers, and has been acknowledged as one of the most economical ports in the region.[20]

With over a 100 years history of bus transportation in Sri Lanka, there are at present approx. 23,000 buses active around the country of which approx.18,000 buses are of the private sector. For healthy competition among operators in the bus service, the National Transport Commission has introduced the coordinated bus services and rotated time table system.[21] The SLTB was reconstituted by Sri Lanka Transport Board Act No. 25 of 2005 and is the successor to the Ceylon Transport Board (1958-1978), Sri Lanka Central Transport Board and Regional Boards (1978-2005), Peoplised Transport Service (1990-1997) and the Regional Transport Companies (1997-2005).[22]

Transportation in Sri Lanka is based mainly on the road network which is centered on Sri Lanka's capital, Colombo. There is also a railway network, but it is largely a legacy of British colonial rule and is less appropriate for the modern transport requirements of the country. There are navigable waterways, harbours and airports, including an international airport, located in Katunayake, 22 miles north of Colombo. The highways and roadways around the capital are in very good condition and are being upgraded.[23]

## Tourism

Tourism is a very popular industry in the entire world. Today tourism is a fast developing industry even in Sri Lanka. There are many picturesque waterfalls and mountains, golden sandy beaches, forests, botanical gardens and wildlife sanctuaries that are frequented by tourists. Historical places such as Anuradhapura, Polonnaruwa, Yapahuwa, Dambulla, Dambadeniya and Sigiriya attract tourists from various parts of the world to visit Sri Lanka. Sri Lankan people can also learn languages and improve their knowledge about different cultures, food, lifestyles and many more things around the world via tourism.[24]

Major tourist attractions are focused around the islands famous beaches located in the southern and the eastern parts of the country and ancient heritage sites located in the interior of the country and resorts located in the mountainous regions of the country. Due to precious stones such as rubies and sapphires being frequently found and mined in Ratnapura and its surrounding areas, they are a major tourist attraction.

Sri Lankan government with the intention of developing tourism industry in the North and East had launched certain development projects to achieve its vision to transform tourism industry in the country as the largest foreign exchange earner benefiting the stakeholders of tourism and the people of Sri Lanka. World Bank offered its fullest support in this regard and certain areas were totally unreachable due to the war which was there for the last three decades. Certain performance targets were revised after the eradication of the terrorism problem and subsequent restoration of peace and order in the country.[25]

Sri Lanka has an inherent advantage of having a highly diversified tourism product which could be pitched against any other well established tourism destination in the world. It has beaches like Maldives or Mauritius, ancient heritage sites like Egypt or Greece, Rain forests like Congo or Amazon, art and culture like India or Thailand, waterfalls like Zambia or Canada, wildlife like Kenya or South Africa, natural beauty like Switzerland or Myanmar, gemstones like Madagascar or Burma, spices like India or Indonesia and festivals like China or Brazil.[26]

## Mineral Resources

Sri Lanka has a variety of industrial minerals, which include ball clay, kaolin, and other clays; calcite; dolomite; feldspar; gemstones; graphite; limestone; mica; mineral sands; phosphate rock; quartz and silica sand. The mineral industry produced cement, gemstones and jewellery, nonmetallic mineral products, and petroleum products. The country produced no metals or crude oil, and it imported petroleum for refining. The development of mineral resources is the responsibility of the Geological Survey and Mines Bureau and is governed by the Mines and Minerals Act No. 33 of 1992 and the Mining (Licensing) Regulations No. 1 of 1993.

The mining of graphite, mineral sands, phosphate rock, and salt was performed by state-owned companies. A crude oil refinery was operated by state-owned Ceylon Petroleum Corp. Sri Lanka, which faced a potential cement shortage owing to increased demand, imported cement from Indonesia, Malaysia, and Pakistan. Sri Lanka's cement industry continued to draw investment from abroad. Holcim Ltd. of Switzerland planned to expand the grinding capacity of its cement plants and to construct a new cement plant of undetermined production capacity. The government decided to reactivate the Kankesanthurai cement plant after the region was determined to have substantial limestone deposits sufficient for 100 years at a production rate of 3,500 metric tons per day.

Sri Lanka's gemstone deposits contain a wide range of gemstones and semiprecious stones. The majority of the deposits are secondary alluvial gravels, and the dominant gem mineral is corundum in the form of geuda, rubies, and sapphires. Sri Lanka's production of graphite was steady at about 3,500 t in 2011. The country's two major producers were Bogala Graphite Lanka plc and Kahatagaha Graphite Lanka Ltd., which had a combined production capacity of 11,000 t/yr. The black mineral sands of Pulmoddai beach which is located 52 kilometers north of Trincomalee, have heavy mineral concentrates of 50-60 per cent and were considered to be some of the world's richest mineral sand deposits. The resource of heavy minerals at Pulmoddai beach was estimated to be 12.5 million metric tons containing 65 per cent limonite, 10 per cent rutile, 10 per cent zircon, and minor amounts of garnet and monazite.[27]

## Poverty and Unemployment

The national poverty head count for Sri Lanka, which declined from 26.1 per cent in 1990/91 to 15.2 per cent in 2006/07. The poverty has decreased by 42 per cent during that period. But the gap in poverty incidence between sectors widened from 1990/91 to 2006/07. Urban and rural poverty declined by 59 per cent and 47 per cent respectively, while the inverse trend shows in estate sector, which increased by about 56 per cent over the last 15 years. A higher variation can be observed in poverty incidence between districts. All the districts other than Nuwara-Eliya achieved their goals to reduce poverty over the period of last 15 years. Extraordinary Nuwara-Eliya district increased poverty by about 68 per cent over the two interim periods 1990/91 to 2006/07. It is noticed that the real total expenditure per month in estate sector with a low non-food proportion remains much closer to the poverty line. It is revealed that that nearly 73 per cent population of the estate sector falls into poorest 40 per cent population of the country.[28]

According to the World Bank, 42 per cent of Sri Lanka's population lives on under US$2 a day in 2005 compared with six per cent living under US$1 a day. This is evidence that while acute poverty is no longer an issue, poverty still remains widespread and continues to be a challenging problem. In 2008, it was reported that tens of thousands of men from impoverished villages were joining the Armed Forces and Police Service to escape rural poverty, as the wages offered by the security services significantly raise the standard of living for soldiers and their families.[29]

Life is slowly returning to normal in northern Sri Lanka, but three years after a decades-long conflict was officially declared over, jobs and housing are the prevailing concerns of returnees. Most of the estimated 448,000 people displaced before or during 2008 by fighting between government forces and rebels wanting an independent Tamil state have returned to the Northern Province, according to the latest figures from the UN Office for the Coordination of Humanitarian Affairs. Some 13,000 are still living in temporary camps, mostly from areas infested with landmines, which may take a decade or more to clear due to lack of funding. There are no official unemployment figures for the region but experts say joblessness, especially among returnees, is likely to be widespread because work is scarce. An estimated 40,000 war widows are particularly hard hit and need more targeted programmes.[30]

Sri Lanka is a country full of resources and with free education; the literacy rate is higher than other SAARC countries such as India, Pakistan and Bangladesh.[31] Unemployment has become a burning problem in Sri Lanka today. The number of unemployed is increasing day by day. According to a statement of the central Bank the number is around 700,000 and of this 55 per cent are females. Around 80 per cent of the unemployed are in the rural sector. Unemployment is highest among the age group of 20-30 years.[32] The high unemployment rate has been attributed to skills mismatch, to queuing for public sector jobs, and to stringent job security regulations.[33]

The overall rate of unemployment has decreased from double digit levels of the 1970s to a moderate level of 4.5 per cent at the end of last year. However, unemployment among those who had GCE Advanced Level or above was more than double at 10.8 per cent. Graduate unemployment is high and female graduate unemployment is higher than that of males. The highest unemployment rate was reported from the G.C.E (A/L) and above group which was about 10.8 per cent. The problem of unemployment is more acute for educated females than educated males.

Educated female unemployment was about twice that for educated males: 14.5 per cent for females compared to 7.5 per cent for males. The overall rate of unemployment too was higher for females at 7.3 per cent compared to 2.9 per cent for males. It is clear that unemployment was higher among females than males in all age groups. The problem of unemployment has been a much studied subject, especially since the youth insurgency of 1971. The reasons for the emergence of a huge unemployment problem in the 1970s were primarily due to the surge in population in the 1950s and 1960s, when the rates of annual average increase in population were 2.8 and 2.6 per cent. This increase in population resulted in a large influx into the labour force in the next decades. Coupled with the large numbers seeking employment was the fact that with the expansion of secondary and tertiary education those seeking employment were educated youth. Their aspirations were for white collar and executive jobs that they deemed their right on the basis of their educational qualifications.[34]

Sri Lanka has a significant chronic unemployment problem. Depending on time period and the definition of unemployment it varies from the low teens to over twenty per cent. Nearly all of this unemployment is concentrated among young people who are looking for their first job. Unemployment duration is very long with typical spells lasting four years or more. Although past authors have blamed unemployment on over education, a closer examination shows that once sex, sector and age are controlled for the relation between education and unemployment disappears for urban youth and is significantly weakened for rural youth.[35]

## Export-Import

India and Sri Lanka have agreed to take steps to double their bilateral trade to $10 billion in the next three years. Recognising that India is Sri Lanka's leading trade partner and that bilateral trade between the two countries has now reached $5 billion, it was agreed that the potential which remains to expand bilateral trade further to the tune of $10 billion would be exploited in the next three years. India has emerged as Sri Lanka's foremost development partner in public investment strategy through the provision of assistance and credit totaling $1.75 billion. Indian projects include the construction of 50,000 houses in the former conflict affected areas in the north and east and also in the central hill plantation areas.

India's major exports to Sri Lanka include automobiles, mineral fuel, pharmaceuticals and iron and steel, while imports include natural rubber, poultry feed, copper and paper and paper products.[36] Sri Lanka recorded a trade deficit of 682.20 USD Million in April of 2014. Balance of Trade in Sri Lanka averaged -427.26 USD Million from 2003 until 2014, reaching an all time high of -50.10 USD Million in May of 2003 and a record low of -1100.70 USD Million in November of 2011.

Balance of Trade in Sri Lanka is reported by the Central Bank of Sri Lanka.[37]

## Foreign Remittance

Sri Lanka is a comparatively small open market economy with a large expatriate labour force that sends substantial remittances to the country. In 2007, remittances were around 11 per cent of GDP. As in many other developing nations, Sri Lanka's official records show that remittances have grown dramatically over the past decade. Nevertheless, the role remittances plays in development as well as the growth effect of this unconditional migrant assistance are under-researched and needs more development policy-oriented attention. In the meantime, the protracted civil war has elevated the importance of this injection of foreign exchange into the national economy.

Over the last 30 years, ever since the introduction of outward-oriented liberalised trade policies in 1977, Sri Lanka has continuously recorded more worker remittances than foreign direct investment. This is evidenced by the fact that Sri Lanka's recent remittances have exceeded foreign direct investment inflows by six to seven times. Remittances have great potential to generate a positive impact on development and poverty reduction. It is important to note that remittances can reduce the probability of food-based and capability-based poverty among underprivileged entities at the receiving end. This applies to both rural and conflict affected areas of the country.[38]

*Foreign* Employment Promotion and Welfare Minister Dilan Perera expect *Sri Lankan* migrant worker *remittances* to surge over US $7 billion. International labour migration from Sri Lanka has grown during the last several decades and has become a part of the country's economic, social, political fabric in the development process. For Sri Lanka, migrants' remittances are one of the main sources of foreign exchange earning and national income. In January 2010, USD 289.8 million was received from Sri Lankan migrant workers, recording a growth of 12.3 per cent over 2009.

Over the past years, foreign employment has generated substantial inflows of remittances (USD 2,947 million in 2008), and relieved local unemployment pressures and provided employment opportunities for both skilled and unskilled Sri Lankans. According to Sri Lanka Bureau of Foreign Employment, foreign employment placements have grown by 8.2 per cent in the last year and stands at 230,963 persons. Estimated annual outflow of migrant workers is approximately 250,000 people.[39]

## Conclusion

Sri Lanka is a developing economy based largely on agriculture, services, and light industry. Agriculture accounts for approximately 21 per cent of the gross domestic product and employs 38 per cent of the workforce. It is the most important sector of the Sri Lankan economy. The design, manufacture and export of textiles and apparel products is one of the biggest industries and one which plays a key role in advancing the country's economy. The banking sector in Sri Lanka is monitored by the Bank Supervision Department of the Central Bank of Sri Lanka under the Banking Act, Monetary Law Act and the Exchange Control Act. Transport in Sri Lanka is based mainly on the road network which is centred on Sri Lanka's capital, Colombo.

Tourism is a very popular industry in the entire world. Today tourism is a fast developing industry even in Sri Lanka. There are many picturesque waterfalls and mountains, golden sandy beaches, forests, botanical gardens and wildlife sanctuaries that are frequented by tourists. Sri Lanka has a variety of industrial minerals, which include ball clay, kaolin, and other clays; calcite; dolomite; feldspar; gemstones; graphite; limestone; mica; mineral sands; phosphate rock; quartz; and silica sand. Sri Lanka has a significant chronic unemployment problem. Depending on time period and the definition of unemployment it varies from the low teens to over twenty per cent. Sri Lanka is a comparatively small open market economy with a large expatriate labour force that sends substantial remittances to the country. In 2007, remittances were around 11 per cent of GDP.

## References

1. *Sri Lanka: An introductory essay*, Retrieved from http://asiasociety.org/countries/sri-lanka-introductory-essay.
2. *The Tourism Industry in Sri Lanka Tourism Essay*, Read more: http://www.ukessays.com/essays/tourism/the-tourism-industry-in-sri-lanka-tourism-essay.php#ixzz36DJ7EKCT.
3. *Economy of Sri Lanka (2014)*, Retrieved from http://en.wikipedia.org/wiki/Economy_of_Sri_Lanka.

4. *Sri Lanka: overview of economy,* Retrieved from http://www.nation sencyclopedia.com/economies/Asia-and-the-Pacific/Sri-Lanka-OVERVIEW-OF-ECONOMY.html
5. See http://www.adb.org/countries/sri-lanka/economy.
6. *Sri Lanka-Agriculture,* Retrieved from http://www.nation sencyclopedia.com/economies/Asia-and-the-Pacific/Sri-Lanka-AGRICULTURE.html
7. *Agriculture in Sri Lanka,* Retrieved from http://en.wikipedia.org/wiki/Agriculture_in_Sri_Lanka.
8. *Country report on the state of plant genetic resources for food and agriculture,* Retrieved from http://www.fao.org/docrep/013/i1500e/SriLanka.pdf
9. *Apparel industry of Sri Lanka*, Retrieved from http://en.wikipedia.org/wiki/Apparel_industry_of_Sri_Lanka.
10. See http://www.srilankabusiness.com/find-sri-lankan-suppliers/product-profiles/apparel-and-accessories.
11. See http://www.masfabricpark.com/textile_apparel_industry.html
12. Rupa Dheerasinghe, *Garment Industry in Sri Lanka Challenges, Prospects and Strategies*.
13. *Sri Lanka Must Vigorously Promote Coir and Coir based Products Globally*, Retrieved from http://dbsjeyaraj.com/dbsj/archives/7820
14. *Rubber and Rubber Based Products*, Retrieved from http://www.srilankaexpo.com/index.php/products-a-services/industrial-products/rubber-and-rubber-products.
15. See http://www.dailymirror.lk/business/features/35612-status-of-sri-lankan-nr-based-industry-.html
16. *Banking sector in Sri Lanka,* Retrieved from http://en.wikipedia.org/wiki/Banking_in_Sri_Lanka.
17. *Central Bank of Sri Lanka*, Retrieved from http://www.cbsl.gov.lk/htm/english/08_stat/s_6.html
18. See http://workinsrilanka.lk/living/banking-and-financial-services-industry-in-sri-lanka/
19. *Transport in Sri Lanka*, Retrieved from http://en.wikipedia.org/wiki/Transport_in_Sri_Lanka.
20. *Sri Lanka Transport Sector*, Retrieved from http://web.worldbank.org/WBSITE/EXTERNAL/COUNTRIES/SOUTHASIAEXT/EXTSARREGTOPTRANSPORT/0,,contentMDK:20699037~menuPK:869140~pagePK:34004173~piPK:34003707~theSitePK:579598,00.html
21. See http://www.ntc.gov.lk/sub_pgs/projects_1.html
22. See http://www.gic.gov.lk/gic/index.php?option=com_info&id=650&task=info&lang=en

23. *Transportation in Sri Lanka*, Retrieved from https://www.princeton.edu~achaney/tmve/wiki100k/docs/Transport_in_Sri_Lanka.html
24. *Tourism in Sri Lanka*, Retrieved from http://www.sundayobserver.lk/2012/01/15/jun03.asp
25. *Development of Tourism in Sri Lanka Tourism Essay*, Read more: http://www.ukessays.com/essays/tourism/development-of-tourism-in-sri-lanka-tourism-essay.php#ixzz36DJWHXr6
26. *Sri Lanka has one of the best tourism products in the world*, Retrieved from http://www.sundaytimes.lk/120513/BusinessTimes/bt07.html
27. Chin S. kuo, *The minerals industry in Sri Lanka*, Retrieved from http://minerals.usgs.gov/minerals/pubs/country/2011/myb3-2011-ce.pdf
28. *Poverty in Sri Lanka*, Retrieved from http://www.statistics.gov.lk/poverty/reportnew-Final.pdf
29. *Poverty in Sri Lanka*, Retrieved from http://en.wikipedia.org/wiki/Poverty_in_Sri_Lanka.
30. *Sri Lanka: Legacy of war - unemployment and homelessness*, Retrieved from http://www.irinnews.org/report/95488/sri-lanka-legacy-of-war-unemployment-and-homelessness.
31. *Unemployment Problem in Sri Lanka,* Retrieved from https://www.tigweb.org/youth-media/panorama/article.html?ContentID=2841
32. *Unemployment problems in Sri Lanka,* Retrieved from http://jayanath.wordpress.com/2008/07/06/unemployment-problem-in-sri-lanka/
33. Martín Rama, *The Sri Lankan Unemployment Problem Revisited,* Retrieved from http://elibrary.worldbank.org/doi/pdf/10.1596/1813-9450-2227
34. *Unemployment, unemployed and the unemployable,* Retrieved from http://www.sundaytimes.lk/110501/Columns/eco.html
35. William T. Dickens, *Kevin Lang, An Analysis of the Nature of Unemployment in Sri Lanka,* Retrieved from http://www.nber.org/papers/w3777
36. *The Times of India (June 29, 2013),* India, Sri Lanka target $10bn bilateral trade in next 3 years, Retrieved from.
37. *Sri Lanka Balance of Trade*, Retrieved from http://www.tradingeconomics.com/sri-lanka/balance-of-trade.
38. H.M.P. Sanjeewanie, *Remittances and impact on development and poverty reduction*, Retrieved from http://www.sundaytimes.lk/090301/Financial Times/ft311.html
39. See http://www.colomboprocess.org/index.php?option=com_content&view=article&id=60&Itemid=65.

# Chapter - 7

# Economy of Pakistan

*"Electricity is an example of a general purpose technology, like the steam engine before it. General purpose technologies drive most economic growth, because they unleash cascades of complementary innovations, like lightbulbs and, yes, factory redesign."*

***—Erik Brynjolfsson***

## Introduction

Pakistan is a sovereign country in South Asia. With a population exceeding 180 million people, it is the sixth most populous country and with an area covering 796,095 km$^2$ (307,374 sq mi). It is the 36th largest country in the world in terms of area. Pakistan has a 1,046-kilometre (650 mi) coastline along the Arabian Sea and the Gulf of Oman in the south and is bordered by India to the east, Afghanistan to the west and north, Iran to the southwest and China in the far northeast. It is separated from Tajikistan by Afghanistan's narrow Wakhan Corridor in the north, and also shares a marine border with Oman.

Pakistan is a federal parliamentary republic consisting of four provinces and four federal territories. The post-independence history of Pakistan has been characterised by periods of military rule, political instability and conflicts with neighbouring India. Pakistan is a federation of four provinces: Punjab, Sindh, Khyber Pakhtunkhwa and Balochistan, as well as the Islamabad Capital Territory and the Federally Administered Tribal Areas in the northwest, which include the Frontier Regions. The government of Pakistan exercises de facto jurisdiction over the western parts of the disputed Kashmir region organised into the separate political entities Azad Kashmir and Gilgit–Baltistan.

The country continues to face challenging, including overpopulation, terrorism, poverty, illiteracy and corruption but regardless of that it ranks among the countries with the most income equality.

Prior to independence in 1947, the land that is now Pakistan was ruled in different periods by local kings and numerous imperial powers. The ancient history of the region comprising present-day Pakistan also includes some of the oldest empires of Indian Subcontinent and some of its major civilisations. On 12 March 1949, the first constituent assembly of Pakistan passed the Objectives Resolution which was proposed by the first Prime Minister Liaquat Ali Khan, proclaimed that the future constitution of Pakistan would not be modeled entirely on a European pattern, but on the ideology and democratic faith of Islam.[1]

## Economy of Pakistan

In 1947, Pakistan had 30 million people with per capita income of 100$. Agriculture accounted for almost 50 per cent of economic output with hardly any manufacturing, as all industries were located in India. It was unable to feed 30 million people and was dependent on PL-480 imports from the USA. From thereon, Pakistan has come a long way. Today with 170 million people, per capita income in 2008 was 1000$ which was ten times more. Pakistan is the third largest exporter of rice in the world and producing enough food grains to feed its people. three million tons of rice is exported every year which is surplus to requirements. Pakistan is also one of the five major textile producing countries in the world.[2]

Pakistan's economy continued to face challenges like energy shortages, floods and rains, poor law and order situation, and a host of other structural impediments that have held back investment and growth in the country. Deterioration in the power sector is the main constraint on growth. Power outages have shaved off annual GDP growth two per cent. GDP growth has been stuck at a level, which is half of the level of Pakistan's long-term trend potential of about 6.5 per cent per annum. Agriculture Sector accounts 21.4 per cent of GDP. The performance of the agriculture sector remained weak due to unfavourable weather conditions, which resulted in lower production of cotton and rice.[3]

The economy on an average grew since 2008-09 at 2.94 per cent. During FY12 and FY13 the power shortage became so severe that it wiped out two per cent from GDP. Agriculture, Manufacturing as well as Services sector performed below their capacity. Though economy has the growth trajectory of more than six per cent, but the worst energy crises, bleeding public sector enterprises, economic mismanagement and menace of informal economy hemorrhaged the system. The other challenges to the macroeconomic environment emanated from the external front. After remaining in primarily surplus driven by inflows under Coalition Support Fund, strong remittances and a lower trade deficit were turned current account into deficit of US$ 1.4 billion in July-April 2012-13.

The economy received nominal support from farms income particularly from minor crop and livestock whereas the major crops particularly cotton and rice missed the target but to some extent compensated by the better crops of and wheat.[4] More than two-thirds of Pakistanis live in rural areas, of which about 68 per cent are employed in agriculture (40 per cent of total labour force). The agriculture sector accounts for about 22 per cent of the national GDP and has enjoyed steady growth for almost three decades, substantially contributing to poverty reduction during the 1970s and 80s.[5]

## Agriculture

Pakistan is blessed with a variety of climatic and geographic regimes which are suitable to grow almost all kinds of food, fiber and cash crops including fruits and vegetables. Wheat and rice are the main staple food crops while cotton and sugarcane are the main cash/ industrial crops and the economy of the country is purely dependant on them. The major crops include wheat, rice, maize, millets, sorghum, sugarcane, pulses, cotton, and oilseeds. Pakistan is home to the aromatic long grain 'Basmati rice' grown in the plains of north Punjab. Some of the best varieties of fruits are grown in Pakistan includes mangos, oranges, apples, peaches, plums, apricots, cherries, grapes, pears, pomegranate, guava, melons and dates. A wide variety of vegetables are also produced in Pakistan.[6] Pakistan's principal natural resources are arable land and water. About 25 per cent of Pakistan's total land area is under cultivation and is watered by one of the largest irrigation systems in the world. Pakistan irrigates three times more acres than

Russia. Agriculture accounts for about 23 per cent of GDP and employs about 44 per cent of the labour force.[7]

Pakistan's total land area is about 803,940 square kilometers. About 48 million hectares, or 60 per cent, is often classified as unusable for forestry or agriculture consists mostly of deserts, mountain slopes, and urban settlements. Since independence, the amount of cultivated land has increased by more than one-third. This expansion is largely the result of improvements in the irrigation system that makes water available to additional plots. Substantial amounts of farmland have been lost to urbanisation and water logging, but losses are more than compensated for by additions of new land. In the early 1990s, more irrigation projects were needed to increase the area of cultivated land. In the early 1990s, irrigation from the Indus River and its tributaries constituted the world's largest contiguous irrigation system, capable of watering over 16 million hectares. The system includes three major storage reservoirs and numerous barrages, headworks, canals, and distribution channels.[8]

Pakistan is one of the world's largest producers of raw cotton. The size of the annual cotton crop (the bulk of it grown in Punjab province) is a crucial barometer of the health of the overall economy, as it determines the availability and cost of the main raw material for the yarn-spinning industry, much of which is concentrated around the southern port city of Karachi. Pakistan is a major rice exporter and annually exports about 2 million tons, or about 10 per cent of world trade. About 25 per cent of exports are Pakistan's famous fragrant Basmati rice. Rice is Pakistan's second leading source of export earnings. Tobacco is grown mainly in the North-West Frontier Province and Punjab and is an important cash crop.

Yields in Pakistan are about twice those for neighbouring countries largely due to the extension services provided by the industry. Minor crops account for only five per cent of total cultivated area; these include oilseeds (sunflower, soybean), chilies, potatoes, and onions. Pakistan's fishing industry is relatively modest, but has shown strong growth in recent years. The domestic market is quite small, with per capita annual consumption of approximately 2 kilograms. Livestock accounts for 40 per cent of the agricultural sector and 9 per cent of the total GDP. Principal products are milk, beef, mutton, poultry, and wool.

Forests cover an area of 4.2 million hectares or about five per cent of the total area of Pakistan. The principal forest products are timber, principally for house construction, furniture, and firewood.[9]

Agriculture holds great significance for Pakistan. From start, Pakistan had large potential of agriculture and at the time of independence Pakistan was mainly agricultural centred country. Industrialisation is the period of social and economic change that transforms a country from an agrarian society to an industrial one. As the time proceeded Pakistan turned into more diversified country as industrialisation took place. Though the share of agriculture has reduced considerably since its birth but the development of industries had not removed the agricultural presence in Pakistan.[10]

As far as fisheries sector, Pakistan has a coastal line about 1,050-km and has been famous for fishing in the region. Pakistan sell abroad good quality seafood's to various countries namely, China, Thailand, UAE and other gulf countries. Fresh, chilled or frozen fish comprise around 69 per cent and shrimps around 21 per cent of total exports. Pakistan is endowed with vast aquatic resources; however the fisheries sector only constitutes one percent to the GDP. The government aims to increase this share as fisheries can play an important role in the growth of the state economy by helping to reduce poverty and increase food security.[11]

## Industry

Pakistan has huge potential for the technology industry, which includes software development and electronics manufacturing. Pakistan Aeronautical Complex recently started manufacturing of Tablet PCs, E-book readers and notebooks in collaboration with INNAVTEK of China. Software development also has a huge potential, which is being utilised as a result of numerous projects initiated by the Government of Pakistan. Major reserves of copper and gold in Balochistan's Reko Diq area have been discovered in early 2006. The Reko Diq mining area has proven estimated reserves of two billion tons of copper and 20 million ounces of gold.

According to the current market price, the value of the deposits has been estimated at about $65 billion, which would generate thousands of jobs. Khyber Pakhtunkhwa Province accounts for at least

78 per cent of the marble production in Pakistan. Pakistan is home to some of the finest and purest grades of marble, granite and slate found in the world. Much of the grades A Marble that is exported out of European countries like Italy actually have their origins in Pakistan which previously lacked fine polishing and processing machinery.[12]

The Automotive industry has been an active and growing field for a long time, however not as much established to figure in the prominent list of the top automotive industries, having a stable annual production 100-170 thousands only. Despite significant production volumes, transfer of technology and localisation of vehicle components remains low, and only a few car models are assembled in the country while customers have a very small variety of vehicles to choose from. According to Ministry of Industries, Pakistan produced its first vehicle in 1953, at the National Motors Limited, established in Karachi to assemble Bedford Trucks. Subsequently buses, light trucks and cars were assembled in the same plant. The industry was highly regulated until the early 1990s.[13]

Textile is a flexible woven material consisting of a network of natural or artificial fibers often referred to as thread or yarn. Yarn is produced by spinning raw fibers of wool, flax, cotton, or other material to produce long strands. Textiles are formed by weaving, knitting, crocheting, knotting, or pressing fibers together. Textiles have an assortment of uses, the most common of which are for clothing and containers such as bags and baskets. In the household, they are used in carpeting, upholstered furnishings, window shades, towels, covering for tables, beds, and other flat surfaces, and in art. In the workplace, they are used in industrial and scientific processes such as filtering. Miscellaneous uses include flags, backpacks, tents, nets, cleaning devices such as handkerchiefs and rags, transportation devices such as balloons, kites, sails, and parachutes, in addition to strengthening in composite materials such as fiberglass and industrial geotextiles. Children can learn using textiles to make collages, sew, quilt, and toys.[14]

The Textile industry is the largest manufacturing industry. It has traditionally, after agriculture, been the only industry that has generated huge employment for both skilled and unskilled labour. The textile industry continues to be the second largest employment generating sector. Pakistan is the eighth largest exporter of textile products in Asia.

The Textile Industry is dominated by Punjab. Nearly three per cent of United States imports regarding clothing and other form of textiles are covered by Pakistan.[15] The industry consists of large-scale organised sector and a highly fragmented cottage / small-scale sector. The various sectors that are a part of the textile value chain are: Spinning, most of the spinning industry operates in an organised manner with in-house weaving, dying and finishing facilities. Weaving comprises of small and medium sized entities. The processing sector, comprising dyeing, printing and finishing sub-sectors, only a part of this sector is operating in an organised state, able to process large quantities while the rest of the units operate as small and medium sized units.

Pakistan is the world's fourth largest producer and third largest consumer of cotton. The Textile and Clothing Industry has been the main driver of the economy for the last 50 years in terms of foreign currency earnings and jobs creation. The Textile and Clothing trade has increased; from US$ 212 Billion in 1990 to US$ 612.1 Billion in 2008.The clothing trade is growing at a faster rate. Pakistan exported textiles worth $7.19 Billion and clothing worth $3.9 Billion in 2008. The year 2009 was dismal period. The industry was confronted with problems of multiple natures. The global economic crisis in Oct. 2007 had impacted the trade badly. Weaker demand in the developed economies limited the expansion of global trade.[16]

The textile industry of the country organised itself in 1957 and soon it became the premier industry of the country. Now-a-days, the textile industry is the mainstay of Pakistan's economy. Besides, the spinning industry, being the sole consumer of cotton, sustains the largest cash crop. Pakistan is the fourth largest producer of cotton yarn and cloth in the world and ranks second in export of yarn and third in export of cloth. The country's cotton production reached an all-time high level of 14.81 million bales of cotton on April 31, 2012 by breaking the previous high record of 14.31 million bales in 2004-05. Textile sector developed in a rapid rate. Thanks to abundance of basic inputs like cotton, and cheap and skilled labour.

In Pakistan, cotton picking is done by manual methods, which must be done when more than 50 per cent bolls are opened. One of the prime reasons of contamination of Pakistani cotton is this method of picking up. Contamination of raw cotton can take place at every step i.e. from the farm picking to the ginning stage.[17] The global recession which has hit the global textile really hard is not the only cause for concern. Serious internal issues also affected Pakistan's textile industry very badly. The high cost of production resulting from an instant rise in the energy costs has been the primary cause of concern for the industry.[18]

## Banking

Banking in Pakistan first formally started in Pakistan during the period of British colonialism in the South Asia. After independence from British Raj in 1947, and the emergence of Pakistan as a country in the globe, the scope of banking in Pakistan has been increasing and expanding continuously. Pakistan's oldest bank is the State Bank of Pakistan, which is also the central bank of the nation. Before independence on August 14, 1947, the Reserve Bank of India was the central bank of what is now Pakistan. After independence, Muhammad Ali Jinnah took actions to establish a central bank in Pakistan which resulted in the new founding of the State Bank of Pakistan, with its headquarters to be based in Karachi.[19]

Islamic Banking and finance growth has generated considerable interest in the financial world in recent years. The concept of Islamic banking has received encouraging response from different corners of the globe as one discovers its ideological dimensions and practical significance. Given its ability to offer innovative financial solutions for basic financial needs in under-served markets especially in the Muslim worlds to complex financial requirement of the modern times, it is seen as a socially responsible and ethical banking model with considerable growth potential.[20]

Islamic Banking Industry in Pakistan has been growing at a fast pace ever since its re-launch in 2001. Starting from almost scratch the Islamic banking industry now represents 10 per cent of overall banking system with 19 banking institutions offering Islamic banking products and services. State Bank of Pakistan initiated three-prong strategy in 2001 and facilitated setting up of (i) Islamic Banks, (ii) Islamic Banking subsidiaries of commercial banks and (iii) dedicated Islamic banking branches by the conventional commercial banks. During the period, SBP has issued detailed licensing criteria, instructions and guidelines for Shariah compliance, instructions for Profit and Loss Distribution and Pool Management and also adopted few IFSB prudential and AAOIFI Shariah standards.[21]

Demand for Islamic banking services is strong. Since 2002, the industry has grown at an impressive rate. Promotion and advocacy of Islamic banking services really took off in 2002, even though has toyed with the idea since 1979. Today, the scope for further expansion is vast and the inert demand potential for Islamic banking services needs to be tapped into quickly through active education drives for the population and training of bank staff. In Pakistan, Islamic banking really started in the late 70s. Serious efforts were undertaken to transform the economy into one that was Islamic.

The efforts of the late 70s laid the foundation for modern Islamic banking. However, the real growth of Islamic banking kicked off in Pakistan after 2002. This was the time when the State Bank of Pakistan changed its approach to the promotion of Islamic banking. The first full-fledged commercial Islamic bank license was issued in 2002. Before this time, while there were Islamic financial institutions, they were not popular. Inadequate information about Islamic banking products and services were important factors for a lack of growth of Islamic banking. Today, there are five fully fledged Islamic banks and 13 conventional banks with Islamic banking windows.[22]

## Tourism

Pakistan's tourism industry was in its heyday during the 1970s when the country received unprecedented amounts of foreign tourists, thanks to the Hippie trail. The main destinations of choice for these tourists were Khyber Pass, Peshawar, Karachi, Lahore, Swat and Rawalpindi. The country's attraction range are from the ruin of the Indus Valley Civilisation such as Mohenjo-Daro, Harappa and Taxila, to the Himalayan hill stations, which attract those interested in winter sports. Pakistan is home to several mountain peaks over 7000 m. The north part of Pakistan has many old fortresses, ancient architecture and the Hunza and Chitral valley, home to small pre-Islamic Animist Kalasha community.

The romance of the historic Khyber Pakhtunkhwa province is timeless and legendary; Punjab province has the site of Alexander's battle on the Jhelum River and the historic city Lahore, Pakistan's cultural capital, with many examples of Mughal architecture such as

Badshahi Masjid, Shalimar Gardens, Tomb of Jahangir and the Lahore Fort.[23] Nanga Parbat is second highest mountain peak of Pakistan and ninth highest mountain in the world. It is also known as Killer Mountain due to its difficult climb. Killing of these climbers will prove a setback to Pakistan's already embattled tourism industry that otherwise could have flourished given the favourable and tourist friendly environment. Post 9/11,wave of terrorism and suicide attacks in the whole country in general and in Khyber Pakhtunkhwa in particular has badly affected all the areas, tourism industry was among the worst hit. Sectarian and ethnic violence in Gilgit Baltistan has also contributed in worsening law and order situation and decline of tourism.[24]

Pakistan, tourism can be a massive source of earning as the country possesses top-class tourist attractions from the stunning Himalayan peaks, beautiful lakes, scenic valleys, rich culture, centuries-old civilisations, vast deserts, golden beaches of Makran to all the other natural and man-made attractions. Although security of foreign tourists is a major concern of the government, once they are issued visas, there should not be any extra hurdles in their way to visit places of tourist interest for which they have paid thousands of dollars on air travel and other ground arrangements.

By developing tourism industry, other businesses such as hotels, restaurants, transport, handicrafts, shopping, local recreational spots and local entrepreneurs get simultaneously boosted and it create thousands of new jobs for unskilled and skilled workforce. A targeted investment strategy by the government, coupled with a sound tourism development policy can do very well help in addressing these challenges and capitalising on this untapped potential.[25]

## Transport

Transportation in Pakistan is extensive and varied but still in its developing stages and serving a population of over 170 million people. Construction of new airports, roads, and railway are providing a massive employment boost in Pakistan. Rail services are provided by the state-run Pakistan Railways, under the supervision of the Ministry of Railways. Pakistan Railways provides an important mode of transportation, catering to the large-scale movement of people and freight. During the 1990s, Pakistan began an ongoing project to rebuild all National Highways of Pakistan throughout the country specifically to important financial, cargo and textile centres. The construction of motorways began in the early 1990s with the idea building a world class road network and to reduce the load off the heavily used national highways throughout the country.[26]

Road transport is the backbone of Pakistan's transport system. The 9,574 km long National Highway and Motorway network-which is 3.65 per cent of the total road network-carries 80 per cent of Pakistan's total traffic. Port traffic grows at 8 per cent annually in recent years. Two major ports, Port Karachi and Port Qasim, handle 95 per cent of all international trade. Pakistan Railways has a broad gauge system (with a small network of meter gauge in the South East). The network consists of the main North–South corridor, connecting the Karachi ports to the primary production and population centres in Pakistan. There are 36 operational airports. Karachi is Pakistan's main airport but significant levels of both domestic and international cargo are also handled at Islamabad and Lahore.[27]

Construction of new airports, roads, and railway lines has led to an employment boost in the country. Much of Pakistan's road network (National Highways) and railway network were built before 1947, mainly during the British Raj. In recent years, new national highways have been built, with the addition of motorways which has accelerated trade and logistics within the country. Airports and seaports have been built within the last 30 years with the addition of foreign and domestic funding.[28]

## Minerals

Pakistan is endowed with extensive geological potential. The country possesses extensive reserves of mineral deposits such as coal copper, gold, limestone etc. Exploration by government agencies as well as by multinational mining companies and various regional geological surveys, conducted in the recent past have confirmed the great potential in the metallic minerals like copper, gold, silver, platinum, chromites, iron, lead and zinc. Regarding industrial minerals, there is a vast potential of multi-coloured granite, marble and other dimensional stones of high quality for export purposes. Currently about 52 minerals are under exploitation but on a small scale. The major production is of coal, rock salt, and other industrial and construction minerals. At this time, the value addition in the mineral sector is mainly concentrated in five principal minerals, namely, limestone, coal, gypsum, sulphur, crude oil, and natural gas.[29]

Quartz is mined from Balochistan and so is chromite. Gold, silver and copper have also been discovered in Balochistan. Balochistan also has the largest supply of natural gas which is supplied throughout the country. Khewra salt mines the world's largest deposit of rock salt is situated in the plains of Punjab. Marble in various shades and colours has been mined too. Pakistan is particularly famous for its onyx productions. Iron ores and fireclay have also been discovered along with other non-metallic minerals. Thar region of Sindh has vast deposits of coal and crude oil has been found in Sindh as well.[30]

Recently, it surfaced that significant deposits of natural gas reserves in the heart of Kohat city in Khyber Pakhtunkhwa were discovered by the state-run Oil and Gas Development Company Limited. The province of Balochistan is enviably rich in this regard, many surveys have identified the geological conditions for the existence of antimony and gold in the Punjgore and Kharan districts but the larger focus this post will direct towards are the new zones and districts where such minerals have been found, projects promulgated for them and their utilisation. Reko Diq is a small town in Chagai District, Balochistan, in the view of development expert Syed Fazl-e-Haider, contains under its sands some 12.3 million tons of copper and 20.9 million ounces of gold. The copper-gold deposits at there are believed to be even bigger than those of Sarcheshmeh in Iran and Escondida in Chile.[31]

## Poverty and Unemployment

Poverty in Pakistan has fallen dramatically independent bodies supported estimates of a considerable fall in the statistic by the 2007-08 fiscal years, when it was estimated that 17.2 per cent of the total population lived below the poverty line. At the time of partition and independence in 1947, Pakistan inherited the most backward parts of South Asia with only one university, one Textile Mill and one Jute Factory. The country has made tremendous progress and its per capita GNP remains the highest in South Asia.

The Khyber Pakhtunkhwa of Pakistan was one of the most backward regions of the South Asia. Despite this, tremendous progress has been made in many areas. The gender discriminatory practices in

Pakistani society also shape the distribution of poverty in the country. Traditional gender roles in Pakistan define the woman's place as in the home and not in the workplace, and define the man as the breadwinner. Consequently, the society invests far less in women than men. Environmental problems, such as erosion, use of agro-chemicals, deforestation etc. contributes to rising poverty. Increasing pollution contributes to increasing risk of toxicity, and poor industrial standards in the country contribute to rising pollution.[32]

Pakistan is an agriculture country blessed with four seasons with the land enriched with natural resources; the land of Baluchistan is full of minerals and resources. It is the country having more than 97 per cent Muslims following Islamic rules, Zakat is included in five pillars of Islam, which apparently shows that Pakistan have the well distributed wealth, but the ground reality is exactly opposite. The poverty level in Pakistan is increasing day by day and more than 40 per cent people within the country are living their lives below the poverty line on average they are earning less than ₹ 125, the cost of petrol is increasing day by day which affects the rate of other prices as well.[33] In recent years, to help the poor, schemes like the Pakistan Poverty Alleviation Fund, Tameer-e-Watan Programme, Benazir Income Support Programme, Pakistan Bait-ul-Maal, subsidies on food, Employees Old Age Benefit Scheme and Workers Welfare Fund have been launched.[34]

As many as 58.7 million people are living in multidimensional poverty with 46 per cent of rural population and 18 per cent of urban households falling below the poverty line. The report titled *'Clustered Deprivation'* is prepared by the Sustainable Development Policy Institute (SDPI) with the financial and technical assistance of United Nation Development Programme. The SDPI measures poverty on the basis of five dimensions–education, health, water supply and sanitation, household assets/amenities and satisfaction to service delivery. Further, a person taking less than 2,350 calories per day and earning less than $1.25 per day according to the United Nations standard has also been regarded as living below the poverty threshold. The highest incidence of poverty prevails in Balochistan with 52 per cent of the households living under the poverty line, followed by 32 per cent, 33 per cent and 19 per cent respectively in Khyber Pakhtunkhwa (K-P), Sindh and Punjab. The southeast part of Sindh is the poorest region, while central Sindh is relatively less poor and southwest Sindh the least poor region of the province. Out of 27 districts, the inhabitants of 18 districts are facing severe poverty conditions.[35]

The economic difficulties of the 1990s have worsened the poverty problem. The spiral of political instabilities and external shocks actually started in 1988 and further deteriorated with the onslaught of natural calamities in 1992-93. A severe economic crisis has plagued the country since then. Deflationary Structural Adjustment Policies have compounded the difficulties. Slow economic growth, drastic cuts in the Public Sector Development Programme, stagnant investment, downsizing in the government departments, ban on new positions and huge inflow of returning expatriates are some contributing factors in the rise of unemployment and poverty today. There are no jobs to accommodate the labour force growing at 3.3 per cent annually.[36]

Generally in South Asia, labour markets continued to suffer from high rates of informal, agricultural employment where jobs are poorly paid and unprotected. Domestic problems and political unrest dampened growth, whereas GDP grew in India, Sri Lanka and Bangladesh. India's unemployment report has also been predicted to stay constant at 3.8 per cent. Compared to 20122s numbers (5.04 per cent for Pakistan and 3.58 per cent for India), unemployment has increased in both countries. In South-East Asia and the Pacific, employment expanded by 1.6 per cent in 2013 and is projected to outpace growth in the working age population in the coming years.[37]

The Government of Pakistan has endorsed the Millennium Development Goals and has set the target of halving poverty from its 1990/91 level of 26.1 per cent to 13 per cent by 2015. This commitment of government has been fully reflected in its MTDF (2005-10), PRSP-II (2009-10) and Vision 2030. MTDF and PRSP targets have been aligned with the MDGs. The poverty related goal has been measured in Pakistan by three indicators: reduction in headcount ratio, reduction in the proportion of underweight children of age five and reduction in the proportion of population below minimum level of dietary energy consumption.[38]

## Electricity

Pakistan is blessed with many natural resources for the past few years and has been facing the problem of load-shedding due to the electricity demand being more than the production capacity of the national power grid.[39] Pakistan produces about 81 per cent of its electricity through oil and gas which costs about 9.4 billion dollars. To put it in other terms, that is about 53 per cent of total exports and is the biggest cost on our import bill.[40] Pakistan has been facing severe energy shortage for the last few years, both of electric power and natural gas, which are two major sources of energy for industry, domestic supply and transport sectors.

The shortage of natural gas which is widely used in four sectors i.e. domestic supply, industry, power generation and transport, in descending order, has been caused by fast depleting gas reserves and rapidly increasing demand. During 2011-12, Pakistan's total energy availability was 66.015 million tons of oil equivalent (mtoe), of which 45.251 mtoe (i.e. 68.54 per cent) was indigenous production while 20.764 mtoe (31.46 per cent) was imported. The ongoing energy crisis is a serious challenge which would require very serious and sustained effort on the part of the government to save the economy and provide relief to the suffering population. If Pakistan chooses to rely on imported oil, gas and coal to meet its energy demand, it would be a constant burden on the country's foreign exchange reserves, and due to continuously increasing price of energy, export surplus would become progressively more uncompetitive, goods for local consumption would become costlier, some industries could face closure/bankruptcy and the country could face economic stress on a wide scale. There is an urgent need for a quicker switch over of energy systems from conventional to renewable that are sustainable and can meet the present and projected energy demand of the country.[41]

Pakistan's energy crisis resulted primarily from the failure of a strategy which was driven by short-term considerations and misguided notions about the role of the private sector and how it should be engaged. Until the mid-1980s, the Water and Power Development Authority and Karachi Electric Supply Company, the two public sector organisations responsible for the generation, transmission, and distribution of electricity did a reasonably good job. Faced with the power shortages in the early 1990s and due to delays in exploitation of hydro power potential in the country, the 1994 energy policy opened up the power generation industry to the private sector. There were two serious flaws with that policy.[42]

The origins of Pakistan's energy crisis can be traced back to the 1990s. A major energy crisis was actually averted in the 1970s, when the government launched the massive Mangla and Tarbela dams, leading to a short-lived period of robust hydro-driven energy generation that ably responded to demand. After a period of strong economic growth in the 1980s, energy demand soared, and supply and infrastructure could not keep up. The government sought to ramp up generation but was unable to satisfy demand. Pakistan's acute energy crisis is posing a serious predicament for its feeble economy and volatile national security environment.

The country's energy problems are deep and complex, being rooted more in shortages of governance and political will than of pure supply. This stems from (a) the absence of a comprehensive and integrated energy strategy, resulting in interagency turf wars and a lack of coordination, (b) insufficient revenue to support energy generation and infrastructure, owing to low liquidity in Pakistan's struggling economy and high rates of tax default, and (c) the leadership's unwillingness to implement politically unpopular changes to address the situation.[43]

At present, less than 45 per cent of Pakistan's population has no access to electricity. The nation is currently facing a 5000 MW power supply shortage-the most severe energy crisis to ever hit the country. Currently, approximately 60 per cent of power generation is derived from fossil fuels (primarily oil and gas) followed by hydroelectricity (35 per cent) and nuclear energy (2.84 per cent). The electricity production sector is a miscellaneous industry of hydro, thermal and nuclear power plants. The main technical causes of the shortfall in the ability of energy crisis in Pakistan are: (a) Insufficient installed generating capacity; (b) Transmission system unable to transmit the load imposed; (c) Grid stations and related equipment unable to carry the load imposed; and (d) Substantial distribution system of power supply.[44]

## Export-Import

In Pakistan's scenario, despite of having a significant openness to international trade, the country encounters low diversification in production and exports. This makes it vulnerable to adverse fluctuations and shocks in world markets, as is evident, for instance, in the terms of trade fluctuations and the volatility in its economic performance. Before examining Pakistan's long run terms of trade pattern and probing the loss in terms of GDP the country had to bear owing to deterioration in its terms of trade in detail, it is essential to conceptualise certain associated terminologies and comprehend the correlation that exists between them.[45]

Since 1947 the pattern of Pakistan's trade has changed dramatically. Exporting almost solely agricultural goods and minerals in the early 1950s, Pakistan rapidly became an exporter of manufactured goods. Although these largely involved the first stages of processing of agricultural goods-converting raw cotton into yam and hides into tanned leather, for example-the rapid rise of manufactured goods as a share of total exports is rather remarkable given Pakistan's relatively low level of development. In 1969/70, manufactured goods accounted for two-thirds of all exports. The structure of imports has also undergone substantial change, but in a different form.[46]

Trade between India and Pakistan declined sharply after the two countries gained independence in 1947. Pakistan's decision not to devalue the rupee with respect to sterling in 1949 was a key factor in the fall in bilateral trade. Because of the devaluation issue, the Commonwealth, including India, imposed a trade embargo on Pakistan. As a result, Pakistan's trade with India fell dramatically, from 70 per cent in 1947 to 18 per cent in 1949. From then on, trade between the two countries became almost negligible, mainly due to political differences and the wars of 1965 and 1971. In 1996, when India granted most favoured nation (MFN) status to Pakistan, trade between the two countries was a mere $180 million.

There are three main factors that have basically led to a change in Pakistan's position on trade with India. First, the current elected government of the Pakistan Peoples Party, as well as all the other mainstream political parties, is supportive of a friendly and peaceful relationship with India and favour stronger economic and commercial ties. Second, the business community in Pakistan has been a strong lobby group for normalising trade relations with India. Third, the Pakistani military's views on increased economic integration of the two neighbours are obviously keys to developing and improving trade ties.[47]

The process of trade normalisation was set in motion in 2004 during the Commerce Secretary level talks on Commercial and Economic

Co-operation between India and Pakistan. In this comprehensive dialogue, trade negotiations were to be discussed along with a dialogue on several other issues. This was the first step towards delinking trade negotiations from political issues. The bilateral trade dialogue that had started in 2004 continued for four more rounds of talks until 2007 and resulted in three major outcomes expansion of the positive list, opening of the road route in 2005, and amendment of the restrictive maritime protocol. As part of the Confidence Building Measures, in October 2008 the two governments permitted trade and travel across the Line of Control along Jammu and Kashmir.[48]

Although Pakistan trade with a large number of countries its exports are highly concentrated in few countries including USA, Germany, Japan, UK, Hong Kong, Dubai and Saudi Arabia which account for one-half of its exports. The United States is largest export market for Pakistan, accounting for 28.4 per cent of its exports followed by UK and Germany. Japan is fast vanishing as export market for Pakistan as its share in total exports has been on decline for one decade, reaching less than one per cent from 5.7 per cent a decade ago.[49]

Pakistan earns a lot in exporting raw cotton and cotton yarn but not stitched garments. Then it exports footballs from Sialkot and surgical instruments and cutlery from Wazirabad. Main products are Rice, Fruits and Textile. Pakistan is a fast growth country given that it is in a tough neighbourhood. For the last five years it has averaged 6-7 per cent growth. Pakistan has been burdened with a costly arms race with the eight times larger India. This has placed severe strain on her resources ever since her independence.[50] Two-way trade between Pakistan and the United States was more than $5 billion in 2012. Pakistan exports more products to the United States than to any other country in the world. In fact, American consumers purchased almost 20 per cent of Pakistan's exports last year. The United States also consistently ranks among the top sources of foreign direct investment in Pakistan.[51]

## Foreign Remittances

In 2013, Pakistan received a total of $14.9 billion from its nationals working abroad, says a report prepared by a US think-tank, Pew Research Centre.[52] Economists said the remittances are rising at the modest pace of 10 per cent that is quite encouraging for the capital and financial accounts of the country. The inflows of remittances from

Saudi Arabia and the UAE in the country stood at $2596.86 million and $1785.84 million, respectively, while the US, the UK, GCC countries, including Bahrain, Kuwait, Qatar and Oman, and the EU countries, sent $1441.42 million, $1309.31 million, $1048 million and $251.13 million, respectively.

Remittances received from Norway, Switzerland, Australia, Canada, Japan and other countries during the first seven months of the current fiscal year amounted to $600.85 million. In January, 2014, the inflows of remittances from Saudi Arabia, the UAE, US, the UK, GCC countries, including Bahrain, Kuwait, Qatar and Oman, and the EU countries amounted to $393.12 million, $213.50 million, $193.01 million, $169.46 million, $150.31 million and $34.56 million, respectively. In FY13 also, workers' remittances continued their increasing trend and reached $13.9 billion, almost meeting the annual plan target of $14 billion. The increase in FY13 was most pronounced from Bahrain, the UK, Australia and Sweden. The Middle East showed a mixed picture: robust economic activity in Saudi Arabia, Kuwait and Abu Dhabi helped increase Pakistan's remittances, inflows from Oman and Qatar were stagnant, while inflows from Dubai and Sharjah fell.[53]

## Conclusion

Pakistan is blessed with a variety of climatic and geographic regimes which are suitable to grow almost all kinds of food, fiber and cash crops including fruits and vegetables. Wheat and rice are the main staple food crops while cotton and sugarcane are the main cash/ industrial crops and the economy of the country is purely dependant on them. The Automotive industry has been an active and growing field for a long time. The Textile industry is the largest manufacturing industry. After independence, Muhammad Ali Jinnah took actions to establish a central bank in Pakistan which resulted in the new founding of the State Bank of Pakistan. Islamic Banking and finance growth has generated considerable interest in the financial world in recent years. The main destinations of choice for these tourists are the Khyber Pass, Peshawar, Karachi, Lahore, Swat and Rawalpindi.

The country's attraction range are from the ruin of the Indus Valley Civilisation such as Mohenjo-Daro, Harappa and Taxila, to the Himalayan hill stations, which attract those interested in winter sports. It is home to several mountain peaks over 7000 m. Road transport is the backbone of Pakistan's transport system. The 9,574 km long National Highway and Motorway network-which is 3.65 per cent of the total road network-carries 80 per cent of Pakistan's total traffic. The country possesses extensive reserves of mineral deposits such as coal, copper, gold, limestone etc. Exploration by government agencies as well as by multinational mining companies and various regional geological surveys, conducted in the recent past have confirmed the great potential in the metallic minerals like copper, gold, silver, platinum, chromites, iron, lead and zinc.

Pakistan produces about 81 per cent of its electricity through oil and gas which costs about 9.4 billion dollars. The origins of Pakistan's energy crisis can be traced back to the 1990s. A major energy crisis was actually averted in the 1970s, when the government launched the massive Mangla and Tarbela dams, leading to a short-lived period of robust hydro-driven energy generation that ably responded to demand. Pakistan trade with a large number of countries its exports are highly concentrated in few countries including USA, Germany, Japan, UK, Hong Kong, Dubai and Saudi Arabia which account for one-half of its exports. The United States is largest export market for Pakistan, accounting for 28.4 per cent of its exports followed by UK and Germany.

## References


1. *History of Pakistan (2014),* Retrieved from http://en.wikipedia.org/wiki/History_of_Pakistan.
2. *Economy of Pakistan-Challenges and prospects*, Retrieved from http://iba.edu.pk/News/speechesarticles_drishrat/Pakistan_Economy_Challenges_Prospects.pdf
3. *Highlights of Pakistan Economic survey 2012-13,* Retrieved from http://finance.gov.pk/survey/chapters_13/HGHLIGHTS%202013.pdf
4. *Overview of the economy,* Retrieved from http://finance.gov.pk/survey/chapters_13/executive%20summary.pdf
5. *Pakistan: Priorities for Agriculture and Rural Development*, Retrieved from http://web.worldbank.org/WBSITE/EXTERNAL/COUNTRIES/SOUTHASIAEXT/EXTSAREGTOPAGRI/0,,contentMDK:20273773~menuPK:548216~pagePK:34004173~piPK:34003707~theSitePK:452766,00.html
6. *Agriculture in Pakistan*, Retrieved from http://www.phclondon.org/commsection/london/invest_opportunities/Agriculture_in_Pakistan.pdf
7. *Agriculture in Pakistan*, Retrieved from http://simple.wikipedia.org/wiki/Agriculture_in_Pakistan

8. *Agriculture,* Retrieved from http://countrystudies.us/pakistan/49.htm
9. *Agriculture-Pakistan*, Retrieved from http://www.nationsencyclopedia.com/economies/Asia-and-the-Pacific/Pakistan-AGRICULTURE.html
10. See http://www.pkhope.com/role-of-agriculture-in-economic-development-of-pakistan/
11. Syed Ali Raza and Yasir Ali and Farhan Mehboob (2012), *Role of agriculture in economic growth of Pakistan*, Retrieved from http://mpra.ub.uni-muenchen.de/32273/1/MPRA_paper_32273.pdf
12. *Industry in Pakistan (2014),* Retrieved from http://en.wikipedia.org/wiki/Industry_of_Pakistan.
13. *Automotive industry in Pakistan,* Retrieved from http://en.wikipedia.org/wiki/Automotive_industry_in_Pakistan.
14. See http://www.dgtrdt.gov.pk/research/38th_syndicate_reports/6.pdf
15. *The Textile industry in Pakistan*, Retrieved from http://en.wikipedia.org/wiki/Textile_industry_in_Pakistan.
16. Yasin Ahmed, *Report on Textile Industry of Pakistan,* Retrieved from http://horizonpak.com/db/Reports/research.pdf
17. *Textile industry in Pakistan (2012),* Retrieved from http://sistemas.mre.gov.br/kitweb/datafiles/Islamabade/en-us/file/Report%20on%20Textile%20Industry-Final%20(2)%20(1).pdf
18. *Growth trends of Pakistan Textile Industry*, Retrieved from http://www.rcci.org.pk/wp-content/uploads/2012/12/gtopti.pdf
19. *Banking in Pakistan*, Retrieved from http://en.wikipedia.org/wiki/Banking_in_Pakistan.
20. *Islamic Banking Industry – Growing amid challenges*, Retrieved from http://www.meezanbank.com/docs/IBIG.pdf
21. *Strategic Plan Islamic Banking Industry of Pakistan 2014 – 2018*, Retrieved from http://www.sbp.org.pk/departments/pdf/StrategicPlanPDF/Strategy%20Paper-Final.pdf
22. See http://www.islamicfinancereview.co/wp-content/uploads/2013/05/02_Driving_Islamic_Banking_Forward.pdf
23. *Tourism in Pakistan (2014),* Retrieved from http://en.wikipedia.org/wiki/Tourism_in_Pakistan.
24. Saman Zulfqar, *Gloomy prospects of Tourism in Pakistan*, Retrieved from http://ipripak.org/articles/latest/gptp.pdf
25. *Pakistan: prospects of tourism*, Retrieved from http://www.dawn.com/news/1019749
26. *Transportation in Pakistan (2014),* Retrieved from http://simple.wikipedia.org/wiki/Transportation_in_Pakistan.
27. *Pakistan Transport Sector*, Retrieved from http://web.worldbank.org/WBSITE/EXTERNAL/COUNTRIES/SOUTHASIAEXT/

EXTSARREGTOPTRANSPORT/0,,contentMDK:20699058~menuPK:869060~pagePK:34004173~piPK:34003707~theSitePK:579598,00.html

28. *Transportation in Pakistan*, Retrieved from https://www.princeton.edu/~achaney/tmve/wiki100k/docs/Transport_in_Pakistan.html
29. Asad Ali, *Treasures of the deep: Mineral deposits in Pakistan*, Retrieved from http://www.utrade.co/magazine/utrade-magazine.aspx?key=250&title=treasures+of+the+deep+-+mineral+deposits+of+pakistan-title=Kumhar
30. *Minerals in Pakistan,* Retrieved from http://pakistan360degrees.com/minerals-of-pakistan/
31. *Hafsa Khawaja (2010),* Retrieved from http://lubpak.com/archives/19548
32. *Poverty in Pakistan,* Retrieved from http://en.wikipedia.org/wiki/Poverty_in_Pakistan.
33. *Poverty in Pakistan–40 per cent people living below poverty line!(2014),* Retrieved from http://www.geotauaisay.com/poverty-in-pakistan-40-people-living-below-poverty-line.html
34. *Rising poverty in Pakistan*, Retrieved from http://www.dailytimes.com.pk/opinion/14-Jun-2014/rising-poverty-in-pakistan.
35. *SDPI report: 58.7m Pakistanis living below poverty line (2014),* Retrieved from http://tribune.com.pk/story/675805/sdpi-report-58-7m-pakistanis-living-below-poverty-line/
36. N.A. Goheer, Poverty in Pakistan: Increasing Incidence, Chronic Gender Preponderance, and the Plausibility of Grameen-type Intermediation, *The Pakistan Development Review,* 38 : 4 Part II (Winter 1999) pp. 873–894, Retrieved from http://www.pide.org.pk/pdr/index.php/pdr/article/viewFile/1701/1674
37. *Unemployment in Pakistan set to increase in 2014: ILO report (2014),* Retrieved from http://tribune.com.pk/story/662013/ilo-report-pakistans-unemployment-rate-to-remain-same-till-2018/
38. Dr. Ghulam Muhammad Arif and Dr Shujaat Farooq, *Poverty, Inequality and Unemployment in Pakistan,* Retrieved from http://www.isdb.org/irj/go/km/docs/documents/IDBDevelopments/Internet/English/IDB/CM/Publications/Parnership_Strategies/Pakistan_MCPS_Background.pdf
39. See http://pakistanyouthmovement.com/articles/164-the-energy-crisis-in-pakistan-and-its-solutions?tmpl=component&print=1&page=
40. *5 steps to solving Pakistan's energy crisis (2012),* Retrieved from http://blogs.tribune.com.pk/story/10507/5-steps-to-solving-pakistans-energy-crisis/
41. *Solution for energy crisis in Pakistan*, Retrieved from http://ipripak.org/books/secp.pdf
42. *How to solve Pakistan's energy crisis?* Retrieved from http://www.stateofpakistan.org/how-to-solve-pakistans-energy-crisis

43. Michael Kugelman (2013), *From Conundrum to Catastrophe*, See http://www.nbr.org/research/activity.aspx?id=323

44. Dr M. Arshad Javaid et al. Electrical Energy Crisis in Pakistan and Their Possible Solutions, *International Journal of Basic and Applied Sciences* IJBAS-IJENS Vol: 11 No: 05, Retrieved from http://www.ijens.org/vol_11_i_05/110505-9393-ijbas-ijens.pdf

45. Nishat Fatima, *Analysing the Terms of Trade Effect for Pakistan*, Retrieved from http://www.pide.org.pk/pdf/Working%20Paper/WorkingPaper-59.pdf

46. Stephen Guisinger and Mohammad Irfan, *Trade Policies and Employment: The Case of Pakistan,* Retrieved from http://www.nber.org/chapters/c8736.pdf

47. Mohsin Khan, *India-Pakistan Trade Relations-A New Beginning*, Retrieved from http://newamerica.net/sites/newamerica.net/files/policydocs/Khan_India-PakistanTrade_NAF2.pdf

48. Nisha Taneja et al. (2013), *Normalizing India Pakistan Trade, Working Paper No. 267*, Retrieved from http://www.icrier.org/pdf/working_paper_267.pdf

49. *Major exports of Pakistan*, Retrieved from http://www.guesspapers.net/2921/major-exports-of-pakistan/

50. See http://wiki.answers.com/Q/What_are_the_major_imports_and_exports_of_Pakistan.

51. See http://www.dawn.com/news/791194/pakistani-businesses-can-export-over-3500-items-to-the-us-duty-free.

52. See http://www.dawn.com/news/1075799

53. See http://www.thenews.com.pk/Todays-News-3-231928-Foreign-remittances-rise-to-$9-billion-in-7-months.

# Chapter - 8

# Economy of Maldives

> *"I will not let anyone tell me we must spend more money. This crisis did not come about because we issued too little money but because we created economic growth with too much money and it was not sustainable growth."*
>
> ***—Angela Merkel***

## Introduction

Maldives is an island nation in the Indian Ocean–Arabian Sea area, consisting of a double chain of twenty-six atolls, oriented north-south, that lie between Minicoy Island and the Chagos Archipelago. The chains stand in the Laccadive Sea, about 700 kilometres (430 mi) south-west of Sri Lanka and 400 kilometres (250 mi) south-west of India. The Maldives is the smallest Asian country in both population and land area. With an average ground level elevation of 1.5 metres (4 ft 11 in) above sea level, it is the planet's lowest country. It is also the country with the lowest natural highest point in the world, at 2.4 metres (7 ft 10 in). Forecasts predicting future inundation of the Maldives due to rising sea levels are of great concern to its people.

On 26 December 2004, the 2004 Indian Ocean earthquake, the Maldives were devastated by a tsunami. Only nine islands were reported to have escaped any flooding, while fifty-seven islands faced serious damage to critical infrastructure, fourteen islands had to be totally evacuated, and six islands were destroyed. Maldives consists of 1,192 coral islands grouped in a double chain of 26 atolls, along the north-south direction, spread over roughly 90,000 square kilometres, making this one of the world's most dispersed countries. It lies between latitudes

1°S and 8°N, and longitudes 72° and 74°E. The Maldives has a tropical-monsoon climate, which is affected by the large landmass of South Asia to the north. Maldives is a presidential republic, with the President as head of government and head of state. The President heads the executive branch and appoints the cabinet which is approved by the People's Majlis (Parliament).[1]

From a 1980 level of 155,300, the population of the Maldives was estimated at 301,475 in July 2000. With the 2000 population growth rate at 3.06 per cent per annum (one of the highest population growth rates in the world), by 2010 the Maldives population is expected to have almost doubled. In 2000, the birth rate stood at 38.96 per 1,000, while the death rate was 8.32 deaths per 1,000. With the continuation of a similar population growth rate, the population of the Maldives will fail to stabilise for at least another 50 years.[2] The flag of Maldives is red with a large green rectangle in the centre bearing a vertical white crescent; the closed side of the crescent is on the hoist side of the flag. Today, Maldives is perhaps the only country with a hundred per cent Sunni Muslim population. Islam was introduced around AD 800, and the moderate form practiced in Maldives has remained virtually unchanged. The main tribes are Singhalese, Dravidian, Arab and African. No other religion, except Islam, is permitted.[3]

## Economy of Maldives

In ancient times the Maldives were renowned for cowry shells, coir rope, dried tuna fish, ambergris, and coco demer. Local and foreign trading ships used to load these products in Sri Lanka and transport them to other harbours in the Indian Ocean. The Maldivian government began an economic reform programme in 1989, initially by lifting import quotas and opening some exports to the private sector. The Maldivian economy is to a large degree based on tourism. Agriculture and manufacturing continue to play a lesser role in the economy, constrained by the limited availability of cultivable land and the shortage of domestic labour.[4]

At the same time the Maldives economy continues to be dominated by two sectors; tourism and fisheries. Largely as a result of the December 2004 tsunami, the Maldivian economy faced major economic, fiscal, and external financing difficulties in 2005 and 2006. Real GDP growth was -5 per cent in 2005, due mainly to a major decline in tourism following the tsunami. Although the tourism sector has recovered, other structural issues persist. For example, income inequality has not changed appreciably between 1997 to 2004; a high proportion of economic gains have been captured by the higher income groups in the population. An increasing regional disparity between northern and southern atolls is becoming an important political issue. In addition, the country is experiencing rising unemployment (14 per cent in 2004) especially among the youth (33 per cent).[5]

## Agriculture

The country's narrow economic base needs to be expanded, particularly agriculture, which presently accounts for less than three per cent of GDP. Most of the domestic agriculture demand is met through imports: the ratio of food imports to domestic food production is 10:1. While some islands contain sufficient soil and water conditions to support increased agricultural production for certain horticultural products, fishing is still seen as the traditional livelihood opportunity. The absence of a vibrant private land market limits the access to finance by prospective farmers. Transport and logistical issues also affect the supply of competitively priced inputs to agricultural islands, as well as the supply of high quality produce to the capital of Male and the major tourism islands; much as 25 per cent of perishable production can spoil before reaching Male.[6]

Agriculture, along with fisheries and forestry, accounted for five per cent of the Maldives' GDP in 2010. However, this was dominated by the significance of the fishing sector, compared to the relatively undeveloped agriculture industry. The sector is limited by the availability of good soil and arable land on the islands, with only around 10 per cent of the land suitable for cultivation, alongside the lack of a farming tradition. Growth largely consists of subsistence crops, with the main agricultural products including coconuts, corn, sweet potatoes, bananas, breadfruit, papayas, mangoes, taro, betel and onions. The small agriculture sector means the country is a net food importer and this meets most of its demands.[7]

The soothing rains of the monsoons provide a fertile land for Finger millet and Italian fox millets. Sweet potatoes are in some parts of the south, cassava. Southern islands offer a taro crops with maize, sorghum and bajara grown on many islands as well. The land can provide onions cucumbers, cabbages and green beans for a mixed salad or a local salad of green, chopped spinach, onions and lime juice for added flavour and is an island favourite. Although rice is not cultivated in the Maldives, it forms an important part of meals and is often imported from neighbouring countries. In Male, bakeries produce fresh bread, cakes and pastries, satisfying the plate of the most demanding gourmet.[8]

Traditional agricultural production in the Maldives is limited by poor soil, a low level of arable land, and a geographically split landmass which disallows large-scale commercial farming. In 1995, only 3,000 hectares of arable land was under permanent crops. There are a number of crops grown for domestic consumption. These include coconuts, bananas, breadfruit, other exotic fruits, betel, chiles, sweet potatoes, and onions.[9]

Like home gardens in other parts of Asia, those in the Maldives do not supply the main source of food or income for the household yet they continuously provide many of the varied household subsistence needs. Most of the species grown in the home garden, especially fruit and timber trees, are multipurpose in nature providing food, fuel wood, stimulants, dyes, medicines, wrapping, cordage, timber and so on. The major soil preparation methods used in home gardens are the preparation of beds and digging of planting holes. Planting holes are usually filled with old plant material, coconut husks, rusty cans and kitchen wastes.[10]

The coconut palm is one of the most abundant plants. While coconuts form an integral part of the Maldivian diet, current production is only used to a very marginal extent. Commercial use of coconuts for the production of copra has been phased out and value-added production from coconuts has not been realised. Currently, the productivity of coconut palms is low because of poor management, close planting, the almost non-existent use of fertilisers and damage from pests. Food and Agriculture Organisation was very active in supporting agriculture recovery in the post-tsunami period, including the establishment of an office in Malé staffed by a former Food and Agriculture Organisation Representative. After the initial severe salinisation of agricultural lands, most field crops and fruit trees suffered and many died. Food and Agriculture Organisation was quick to provide salinometers and practical advice to farmers on how to cope with salinity. Post-tsunami rainfall helped to remove the salt and the monsoon rains further cleansed the soil.[11]

## Fishing

The Maldivian economy was entirely dependent on fisheries and other marine products for centuries and fishing and related marine activities continue to employ a significant proportion of population. The government gives priority to the development of the fisheries sector, which at present contributes over 15 per cent of gross domestic product. About 30 per cent of the country's work force is engaged in the fisheries sector. It is the second most important sector after tourism.

The government established the Maldives Fishing Corporation in 1979 to exploit the country's vast fisheries resource. Maldives is a country without cows or buffalo. Manure is imported from India to be used as fertiliser. Goat and poultry production are two growing economic activities for out-lying island communities. Goats are in demand for cultural events while eggs are popular throughout the country and especially among the 100 plus high-end resort islands.[12]

## Industry

The Maldives' primary industry is the canning and processing of fish. In 1998, $19.06 million of canned fish, predominantly tuna, was exported. The development of the Felivaru Tuna Fish Cannery in the early 1990s was a key factor in the modernisation of this industry. The development of manufacturing is limited by the low level of domestic demand, limited skilled labour, and the lack of national resources. This means that many material and labour inputs into domestic goods rely heavily on imports.

The economy has diversified into the production of clothing, both for domestic consumption and for export. However, garment factories rely almost exclusively on the import of materials for the manufacture of their goods. The competitiveness of finished products is reduced due to the costs of passing through multiple tariff boundaries.[13]

## Tourism

Tourism is the largest economic industry, as it plays an important role in earning foreign exchange revenues and generating employment in the tertiary of the country. The archipelago is the main source of attraction to many tourists visiting the country worldwide. Tourism began in 1972. A United Nations mission on development which visited the Maldives Islands in the 1960s did not recommend tourism, claiming that the islands were not suitable. Ever since the launch of the first resort in 1972, tourism has flourished. Maldives is very famous for its natural beauty which includes the blue ocean and white beaches, accompanied by clean air and pleasant temperatures. The climate is ideal for visitors to get engaged in water sports. A tourist resort consists of an exclusive hotel on its own island, with its population entirely based on tourists and work force, with no local people or houses.[14]

Tourism and fishing together generate an estimated 31 per cent of GDP. This results in a very narrow economic base and puts Maldives at risk from economic downturn should one or both of these sectors decline, even temporarily, as evidenced by the drop in tourism following the tsunami. Tourism accounts for 23 per cent of GDP but the growth and development strategy needs to be reviewed. Maldives is a long haul destination, more than ten hours from originating markets in Western Europe with only one major airport, which is likely to be a severe constraint to market expansion. Newer investments seem to be targeted at non-traditional markets without adjustment in other parts of the supply chain to the new realities.[15]

## Mineral Industry

The mining industry in the Maldives consists of sand mining and coral mining. Sometimes coral pieces are removed for use as bricks or road-fill. Sand and limestone from coral reefs are made into cement for new buildings. But corals aren't only removed from their habitat for construction; they are also sold as souvenirs. Coral curios and jewellery are often sold to tourists and exporters in the markets of developing countries.[16]

## Energy

The Energy Authority of Maldives has announced the inception of $138 million renewable energy project which would generate 26 MW of electricity. Abdul Matheen, State Minister for Energy revealed that the project is expected to be completed within five years. Out of a total 26 MW of generated electricity, 16 MW will be supplied to the Male region, which constitutes 30 per cent of the total population of the country. This project is a part of a renewable energy investment plan of the government which has been developed under the Sustainable Renewable Energy Project of the Climate Investment Fund. The project would be funded by the World Bank, Asian Development Bank, and German and Japanese Banks. According to the Energy Authority of the Maldives, the project will be extended to 50 islands to promote the use of renewable energy.[17]

The Maldives declared a policy commitment in 2009 to become the world's first carbon neutral country by 2020. The most important action to achieve this objective is displacing its near total dependence on diesel-based power generation with renewable energy alternatives. The Government of Maldives has established a comprehensive policy framework for the development of renewable energy embedded in the Strategic Action Plan. The project will be launched in the second half of 2013 and will focus on RE mapping and geospatial planning, including ground-based data collection, data analysis, GIS mapping, strategic environmental assessment, and policy integration for the solar and wind resource.[18]

## Export-Import

The Maldives is increasingly relying upon imports. This is due to a lack of agricultural production and fossil fuel resources, a growing population and household incomes, and the high influx of tourists since the 1970s who demand certain foodstuffs and luxuries. In 1977, imports totalled \$11.1 million, whereas by 1998 they had boomed to \$354 million. The Maldives receives its imports from a wide range of countries. The European Union countries supplied \$65 million in 1998, of which the two largest partners, the UK and the Netherlands, provided \$18.5 million and \$12.5 million, respectively. Maldivian exports totalled \$76.2 million in 1998-a considerable growth from a 1977 level of \$4.8 million.

The main destination was the EU countries, which consumed \$20.1 million. The UK was the primary partner and purchased \$14.7 million in Maldivian exports, Germany imported \$5.1 million. Exports to the United States totalled \$15.7 million, nearby Sri Lanka \$13.1 million, Japan \$10.9 million, and Thailand \$9.8 million.[19] Maldives recorded a trade deficit of 118.90 USD Million in April of 2014. Balance of Trade in Maldives averaged -81.81 USD Million from 2005 until 2014, reaching an all time high of -43.30 USD Million in April of 2005 and a record low of -135.30 USD Million in February of 2013. Balance of Trade in Maldives is reported by the Maldives Monetary Authority.[20]

## Conclusion

Maldives is an island nation in the Indian Ocean–Arabian Sea area. In ancient times the Maldives were renowned for cowry shells, coir rope, dried tuna fish, ambergris, and coco demer. The country's narrow economic base needs to be expanded, particularly agriculture, which presently accounts for less than three per cent of GDP. Growth largely consists of subsistence crops, with the main agricultural products including coconuts, corn, sweet potatoes, bananas, breadfruit, papayas, mangoes, taro, betel and onions.

The Maldivian economy was entirely dependent on fisheries and other marine products for centuries and fishing and related marine activities continue to employ a significant proportion of population. The Maldives' primary industry is the canning and processing of fish. In 1998, $19.06 million of canned fish, predominantly tuna, was exported. Tourism is the largest economic industry, as it plays an important role in earning foreign exchange revenues and generating employment in the tertiary of the country. The archipelago is the main source of attraction to many tourists visiting the country worldwide. The mining industry in the Maldives consists of sand mining and coral mining. Sometimes coral pieces are removed for use as bricks or road-fill.

The Maldives is increasingly relying upon imports. This is due to a lack of agricultural production and fossil fuel resources, a growing population and household incomes, and the high influx of tourists since the 1970s who demand certain foodstuffs and luxuries.

## References

1. *Maldives (2014),* Retrieved from http://en.wikipedia.org/wiki/Maldives
2. *Maldives-country overview,* Retrieved from http://www.nations encyclopedia.com/economies/Asia-and-the-Pacific/Maldives.html
3. See http://www.mapsofworld.com/country-profile/maldives.html
4. *Maldives (2014),* Retrieved from http://en.wikipedia.org/wiki/Maldives
5. *Maldives: Priorities for Agriculture and Rural Development,* Retrieved from http://web.worldbank.org/WBSITE/EXTERNAL/COUNTRIES/SOUTHASIAEXT/EXTSAREGTOPAGRI/0,,contentMDK:21284029~menuPK:3636239~pagePK:34004173~piPK:34003707~theSitePK:452766,00.html

6. *Maldives: Priorities for Agriculture and Rural Development,* Retrieved from http://web.worldbank.org/WBSITE/EXTERNAL/COUNTRIES/SOUTHASIAEXT/EXTSAREGTOPAGRI/0,contentMDK:21284029~menuPK:3636239~pagePK:34004173~piPK:34003707~theSitePK:452766,00.html
7. See http://www.commonwealthofnations.org/sectors-maldives/business/agriculture/
8. *Agriculture in Maldives,* Retrieved from http://www.themaldives.net/maldives/maldives-agriculture.html
9. *Maldives-country overview,* Retrieved from http://www.nations encyclopedia.com/economies/Asia-and-the-Pacific/Maldives.html
10. *Maldivian Homegardens – A stable farming system in a fragile environment,* Retrieved from http://permaculturenews.org/2009/04/13/maldivian-homegardens-a-stable-farming-system-in-a-fragile-environment/
11. *Maldives and FAO Achievements and success stories,* Retrieved from http:/www.fao.org/fileadmin/templates/rap/files/epublications/MaldivesedocFINAL.pdf
12. *Maldives and FAO Achievements and success stories,* Retrieved from http://www.fao.org/fileadmin/templates/rap/files/epublications/MaldivesedocFINAL.pdf
13. *Maldives-country overview,* Retrieved from http://www.nations encyclopedia.com/economies/Asia-and-the-Pacific/Maldives.html
14. *Tourism in Maldives (2014),* Retrieved from http://en.wikipedia.org/wiki/Tourism_in_the_Maldives.
15. *Maldives: Priorities for Agriculture and Rural Development,* Retrieved from http://web.worldbank.org/WBSITE/EXTERNAL/COUNTRIES/SOUTHASIAEXT/EXTSAREGTOPAGRI/0,,contentMDK:21284029~menuPK:3636239~pagePK:34004173~piPK:34003707~theSitePK:452766,00.html
16. See http://www.commonwealthofnations.org/sectors-maldives/business/mining_and_minerals/
17. See http://cleantechnica.com/2012/10/20/138-million-maldives-renewable-energy-project-backed-by-world-bank-launched/
18. See http://www.esmap.org/RE_RESOURCE_MAPPING_MALDIVES
19. *Maldives-International trade,* Retrieved from http://www.nations encyclopedia.com/economies/Asia-and-the-Pacific/Maldives-INTERNATIONAL-TRADE.html
20. *Maldives Balance of Trade,* Retrieved from http://www.tradingeconomics.com/maldives/balance-of-trade.

# Chapter - 9

# Economy of Afghanistan

*"Economists who have studied the relationship between education and economic growth confirm what common sense suggests: The number of college degrees is not nearly as important as how well students develop cognitive skills, such as critical thinking and problem-solving ability."*

***—Derek Bok***

## Introduction

Afghanistan is a landlocked country located in Central Asia and South Asia. It has a population of around 31 million people making it the 42nd most populous country. It is bordered by Pakistan in the south and the east, Iran in the west, Turkmenistan, Uzbekistan, and Tajikistan in the north, and China in the far northeast and its territory covers 652,000 km$^2$ making it the 41st largest country in the world. From 1989 until 1992 Najibullah's government tried to solve the ongoing civil war without Soviet troops on the ground but with economic and military aid. Najibullah tried to build support for his government and tried to portray his government as Islamic, and in the 1990 constitution the country officially became an Islamic state and all references of communism were removed.

After the fall of Najibullah's government in 1992, the post-communist Islamic State of Afghanistan was established by the Peshawar Accord, a peace and power-sharing agreement under which all the Afghan parties were united in April 1992, except for the Pakistani supported Hezb-e Islami of Gulbuddin Hekmatyar. The Taliban's early victories in 1994 were followed by a series of defeats that resulted in heavy losses which led analysts to believe the Taliban movement had run its course. On 26 September 1996, as the Taliban with military support by Pakistan and financial support by Saudi Arabia prepared for another major offensive, Massoud ordered a full retreat from Kabul. Afghanistan is a multiethnic society, and its historical status as a crossroads has contributed significantly to its diverse ethnic makeup. The population of the country is divided into a wide variety of ethno-linguistic groups.[1]

Afghanistan occupies the northeastern area of the Plateau of Iran. The Hindu Kush Mountains stretching from Pakistan and their offsets shape a plateau in the centre of the country. Because of these geographical characteristics, much rainfall turn to snow which remain in high mountains, then flow into rivers in early spring as the temperature rises. Agriculture in Afghanistan has the form of a typical oasis agriculture seen in Central Asia drawing water from rivers.[2] Afghanistan is a mountainous country with the Hindu Kush system stretching about 966 kilometers and splitting the country from east to west. There are also several smaller mountain ranges. The lowest point of elevation is Amu Darya 258 masl and the highest one is Nowshak 7,485 masl. These mountainous areas are mostly barren or at most sparsely sprinkled with trees and stunted shrubs. In addition, the country has many rivers, lakes, and deserts. The four major river systems are the Amu Darya; the Helmand; the Harirud; and the Kabul.[3]

## Economy of Afghanistan

The economy of Afghanistan has improved significantly since 2002 due to the infusion of billions of dollars in international assistance and investments, as well as remittances from Afghan expats. The recent improvement is also due to dramatic improvements in agricultural production and the end of a four-year drought in most of the country. Agriculture production is constrained by an almost total dependence on erratic winter snows and spring rains for water. The Afghan economy has always been agricultural, despite the fact that only 12 per cent of its total land is arable and about 6 per cent is currently cultivated. As of 2007, the country's fruit and nut exports were at $113 million per year, but according to an estimate could grow to more than $800 million per year in 10 years given sufficient investment.

Wheat and cereal production is Afghanistan's traditional agricultural mainstay. The availability of land suitable for grazing has traditionally made animal husbandry an important part of the economy. The country has plenty of water reserves and suitable climate for fish farming. Fishing takes place in the lakes and rivers, particularly in the Kabul River around the Jalalabad area. Afghanistan's timber has been greatly depleted, and since the mid-1980s, only about three per cent of the land area has been forested, mainly in the east. Afghanistan is a member of SAARC, ECO, OIC, and has an observer status in the Shanghai Cooperation Organisation. It seeks to complete the so-called New Silk Road trade project, which is aimed to connecting South Asia with Central Asia and the Middle East.[4]

After more than a decade of western aid projects designed to make the Afghan economy self-sustaining, government revenue continues to fall short of projections, leaving the country in dire economic straits just as foreign funding begins to dry up. In spite of dozens of western-funded programmes aimed at increasing domestic revenue, the government is still almost entirely dependent on foreign donors to shore up its budget. Taxes and customs tariffs are the only significant sources of revenue, but those collection processes are still riddled with problems. Afghan soldiers and police are paid with foreign funds, so their salaries would not be affected for now. But the government is expected to take responsibility for a greater portion of its budget in future years and the current financial deficiencies are seen by many as a preview of future problems.[5]

## Agriculture

Agriculture has traditionally driven the Afghan economy, accounting for approximately 50 per cent of GDP before the Soviet invasion in 1979. Nevertheless, the agricultural sector has never produced at full capacity. Before the invasion, only 30 per cent of the total arable land of 15 million hectares was cultivated. At that time the main exports were sugarcane, sugar beets, fruit, nuts, vegetables, and wool. The continuing war reduced production significantly. In 2001, the principal food crops were corn, rice, barley, wheat, vegetables, fruits, and nuts. In Afghanistan, industry is also based on agriculture, along with raw materials.

The major industrial crops are cotton, tobacco, castor beans, and sugar beets. Sheep farming is also extremely valuable. The major sheep product exports are wool and sheep skins. The prices of staple foods have also increased in different parts of the country because demand is much higher than supply. The number of livestock was greatly reduced during the years of war.[6] Agriculture is the main source of income for the Afghan economy with up to 80 per cent of Afghan livelihoods consisting of farming, livestock or both. Decades of war, drought and social upheaval have devastated the country's agricultural sector.[7]

Wheat is the main staple cereal and accounts for about 70 per cent cropped area and cereal production each year and 70 per cent of total cereal consumption. Wheat cultivation was estimated to cover 2,575,000 hectare during 2008/09 crop season, which recorded one of the highest production levels in recent years. Cereals (barley, rice, maize) and pulses (chickpea and mung bean) are also important crops. Several summer and winter vegetables like potato, tomato, onion, okra, cauliflower, melon and watermelon are also produced both for domestic and export market. Cotton is also a widely cultivated crop. Fruits (apricots, cherries, figs, mulberries, pomegranates and grapes) and nuts (pistachios, walnuts) are among the most important export crops produced. There is a significant deficit in food production which results in food insecurity particularly for poor vulnerable households to meet the total national food and creating the need for emergency food aid.

Food security and distribution is also a major problem and both are sources of vulnerability for the Afghanistan given its 30 years history of violence and given the scale of Taliban and insurgent operations. Moreover, both agriculture and food distribution are caught up in the problems raised by Afghan dependence on opium cultivation, extortion and corruption in aid and transport operations at every level, and manipulation by national and local power brokers.[8]

Agriculture accounted for 47 per cent of estimated GDP in 2003, with agricultural and horticultural products accounting for roughly 50 per cent of exports. In the 1970s, Afghanistan was one of the world's largest exporters of raisins. Afghanistan uses less than one-third of its available water resources, yet poor water management combined with recent drought has led to water scarcity. Only an estimated 23 per cent of the population has access to safe drinking water. Between 1930 and 1979, Afghanistan had a small but thriving sugar industry based around a sugar factory located 250 kilometres northwest of Kabul in Baghlan, which supported thousands of small-scale sugar beet farmers.[9]

Agriculture and animal husbandry, mainly consisting of subsistence farming and pastoral nomadism, are, in more normal times, the most important elements of the gross domestic product, accounting for nearly half of its total value. Afghanistan is essentially a pastoral country. Only about one-eighth of the total land area is arable, and only about half of the arable acreage is cultivated annually. Much of the arable area consists of fallow cultivated land or steppes and mountains that serve as pasture land. Since much of the land is arid or semiarid, about half of the cultivated land is irrigated. Traditionally, as much as 85 per cent of the population drew its livelihood from a rural economy, mostly as farmers.[10]

The Ministry of Agriculture, Irrigation and Livestock is a national apex body responsible for overall policy formulation and implementation of all agriculture related activities in Afghanistan. There are two Deputy Ministries within in MAIL: Technical Affairs and Irrigation and Construction. The Deputy Ministry for Technical Affairs is responsible for agricultural research, extension, food quality control, animal husbandry and health, and natural resources. Afghanistan has the national seed policy, the seed law, and the seed rules, regulations and procedures with the National Seed Board serving as the focal point for coordinating all seed industry functions. The National Seed Board advises the Minister on all seed industry functions particularly matters relating to implementation of the Seed Law and National Seeds Policy.

The Ministry of Agriculture, Irrigation and Livestock adopted a National Seed Policy in September 2005, which is now in effect and implemented under the guidance of the National Seed Board. The Government enacted a Seed Law in 2009, which was published in Official Gazette 1005 of 16 December 2009. The Seed Law covers true agricultural seeds and vegetatively propagated planting materials. The Agricultural Research Institute of Afghanistan and Improved Seed Enterprise are key public sector implementing partners of the FAO/EU Seed Project.[11]

## Industry

Afghanistan is endowed with widespread natural resources, including extensive deposits of natural gas, petroleum, coal, copper, silver, gold, cobalt, chromite, talc, barites, sulphur, lead, zinc, iron ore, salt, rare earth elements, and precious and semiprecious stones.

Unfortunately, ongoing instability in certain areas of the country, remote and rugged terrain, and an inadequate infrastructure and transportation network have hampered improving and developing the mining sector, and there have been few serious attempts to further explore or exploit them.

The first significant investment in the mining sector is expected to commence soon, with the development of the Aynak copper deposit in east-central Afghanistan. Afghanistan has moderate to potentially abundant coal resources. The majority deposit of resources was observed in the Northeast and Northwest parts of Afghanistan. Coal has been used for a long time to powering the small industry. Nowadays we could count nine coal field and more than 42 coal occurrences in the country. The coal-bearing area occupies about 35 thousand square kilometers extending as a discontinuous belt for more than 700 kilometres from the North to west of the country.[12]

Public and private investment is not a new phenomenon in Afghanistan. Private sector cotton weaving and production of fabrics, scarves, local attire, cloths, traditional woollen hats, shawls and other relevant products have a long history in eastern Afghanistan. The production of these items is particularly widespread in the districts of Batikot, Kama Bihsud, and Rodat in Nangarhar province. Gulbahar textile plant is not completely a public textile manufacturing unit. The Kandahar cotton textile enterprise established in 1355/1976 is situated in Daman District of Kandahar province, covering an area of 24 hectares. Herat textile production facility established, in 1355/1976 is spread in an area of 25 hectares. Balkh cotton textile enterprise is a public company. It covers an area of 11 hectares.[13]

Thirty years of war not only destroyed the physical infrastructures in Afghanistan but also eradicated the regulatory, social, political and economic institutions which guarantee for an efficient environment for investment. Fortunately, since the fall of Taliban regime in 2001, the government has been engaged in establishing and developing the institutional requirements and arrangements which are necessary for investors to do business in Afghanistan. According to Mitchell (2008), Afghanistan has the potential to supply Middle Eastern and Asian markets with an almost unlimited amount of marble. According to some unverified reports, total estimated marble deposits in Afghanistan reach over 9 billion tons. Afghanistan annual marble production is around 124,000 to 155,000 tons. But over half of unprocessed marble goes to Pakistan and Iran. Total consumption of finished marble in Afghanistan is around 270,000 tons. Around 80 to 85 per cent of Afghan market is dominated by Pakistani marble. Currently the total value added of the Afghan marble industry is around $105 million which makes 0.6 per cent of GDP.[14]

Afghanistan's drug industry is a central issue for the country's state-building, security, governance, and development agenda. Recognising the critical importance and multifaceted nature of the drug problem in Afghanistan, the United Nations Office on Drugs and Crime and The World Bank embarked on a programme of cooperative research and policy-oriented analysis. The government's and the donor community's counter-narcotics efforts have had a limited impact so far on Afghanistan's opium production, which has remained at historically high levels in the last few years. Owing to the sustained growth of the licit economy, the size of the opium sector relative to the rest of the economy has declined significantly. Nevertheless, the opium sector remains Afghanistan's largest source of export earnings (although unrecorded) and a major source of incomes in the rural areas. Intensification of counter-narcotics efforts will therefore have a substantial economic and social impact.[15]

Since 2003, there have been huge private investments in Afghanistan–$1.8 billion foreign and $3.8 billion domestic investments. Most of these investments are allocated to the construction, telecommunications, banking, and transportation sectors. Other industries, such as the low-cost, labour intensive industries despite having huge potential for investors, have been overlooked. The plastics industry also plays an important role in enabling growth through innovation in a wide range of key European industries such as automotive, electrical and electronic, building and construction and food and beverage sectors. The success story for plastic is expected to continue as its unique properties lend itself to more and more innovation applications. Whilst global demand per capita is expected to grow by four per cent each year, consumption in Asia and new EU member states is significantly below that of mature industrial regions where growth rates are expected to remain slightly above GDP.[16]

The Afghan gem industry is operating in accordance with firmly entrenched ways of doing business that include smuggling of Afghan precious and semiprecious gems out of the country as raw material and family operated mine activities that rely on arms length deal making with the Ministry of Mines, if any government involvement at all. The Afghan gem industry is operating in a legal and regulatory vacuum. While the Minerals Law was adopted in 2005, capacity and understanding among government officials and mine operators remains considerably low and ineffective application of legal terms is the result. Strongly entrenched relationships and ways of doing business mean that government is not gaining national revenues that would ordinarily come in the form of taxes, custom collections, licensing and authorisation fees and royalties.[17]

## Banking

Afghanistan's banking sector remains fragile and in need of robust regulation by Da Afghanistan Bank. Forensic audits of major commercial banks in Afghanistan have identified systemic weaknesses in many areas of banking governance and operations, including personnel capacity, internal controls, accounting, credit analysis, and compliance with regulations. DAB's ongoing limitations and inability to conduct robust oversight allows such weaknesses in Afghan banks to remain unchecked, heightening the risk of another banking crisis.

In 2003, Afghanistan's central bank resumed regulatory functions necessary to ensure the stability of the country's banking sector. Since then, Afghanistan's banking sector has grown from two state-owned commercial banks and four state-owned special purpose development banks to nine privately-owned commercial banks, three state-owned commercial banks, and four foreign commercial banks, with more than 400 total branches across Afghanistan. Afghanistan's fragile banking sector requires robust financial supervision. According to the International Monetary Fund, a well-regulated financial system is essential for both domestic and international economic and financial stability. Further, assisting the Afghan government to develop the financial capabilities it needs to function independently is a key reconstruction objective of the U.S. and Afghan governments, as well as the international community.[18]

Seventeen banks with branches around the country are now operating, generating 5,000 jobs since 2003, when the Afghan Central Bank resumed licensing. Fueled by an infusion of international aid, the Afghan economy has been growing steadily in the past five years. The U.S. alone spent $31 billion on military and civilian aid to Afghanistan since 2002. According to the Central Bank, the 17 banks had deposits of $2 billion in January 2009, up 69 per cent from the previous year, and total outstanding loans of $1 billion, up 37 per cent year to year. The total assets of the banking system were $2.4 billion this year, up 66 per cent from 2008.

Most of the banks are owned by foreign regional investors or Afghan business people, with only one bank owned by a Western institution, Britain's Standard Chartered, which set up shop in Kabul in January 2004.[19] The Afghanistan Bank is the central bank of Afghanistan. It regulates all the banking and money handling operations in Afghanistan. The bank currently has 47 branches throughout the country, with five of these situated in Kabul, where the headquarters is also based. Da Afghanistan Bank is one of the leading and government recognised bank of Afghanistan which was established in 1939.[20]

## Mining

One of the important and basic pillars in the economy of every country is natural resources and its other subterraneous resources. By the growing demand of industry and technology, e.g. trees for paper and fuel production, iron ore for steel products, copper for wire, electrical equipment, and platinum are used for telecommunications equipment etc. Afghanistan is a country abundantly rich in natural resources. There are currently more than 1,400 mineral deposits that have been identified including energy minerals such as oil, gas and coal and other metallic and non-precious minerals such as lead, cement-grade limestone, gemstones, copper, iron, gold and salt.

The iron and copper deposits of Afghanistan can generate a bigger amount in the economy of the country if these mines are extracted in a proper and standard way with transparency. Since Afghanistan is a country rich in mining resources, it is facing a lot of problems in discovering and extracting its natural resources because the country does not have enough experts in the mining sector and technical facilities like machinery due to the three decades of war and conflict that left over development in Afghanistan.[21]

Afghanistan has considerable potential for the discovery of precious metal deposits such as porphyry and epithermal gold associated with younger Tertiary volcanic and high-level plutonic rocks. Currently, gold is produced almost solely by artisanal miners working the Samti Placer Deposit in Takhar Province. Gold deposits and prospects are known in rocks of Proterozoic to Neogene age. Many styles of gold mineralisation occur, in particular skarn, vein-hosted, porphyry and alluvial.

Afghanistan is relatively under-explored and has not yet been evaluated in the light of modern mineral deposit models and using up-to-date sophisticated analytical methods and exploration technique. Gold deposits, occurrences and showings discovered to date are the result of work conducted in the 1960s and 1970s, principally by Russian geologists who identified two main prospective regions: the northeast provinces of Badakhshan and Takhar, and the southern provinces of Ghanzi, Zabul and Kandahar. In 2002, the United States Geological Survey compiled a digital inventory of more than 1,079 mines and mineral occurrences in Afghanistan of which 112 are gold related.[22]

## Energy

Energy in Afghanistan describes energy and electricity production, consumption, import and export in Afghanistan. Energy is primarily provided by hydropower. The Afghan National Development Strategy has identified alternative energy, such as wind and solar energy, as a high value power source to develop. Alternative energy projects are already being tested across the country, from wind turbines in Panjshir Province to micro hydro dams in Badakhshan, to family-size biogas digesters throughout the country. The southern region of Afghanistan is lacking adequate electricity due to problems with the Kajaki power plant in Helmand, which has been destroyed and neglected for many years.

Natural gas was Afghanistan's only economically significant export in 1995, going mainly to Uzbekistan via pipeline de marde. Natural gas reserves were once estimated at 140 billion cubic metre. Discussions on electricity supplies began back in 2006; the Construction of a 442-kilometre (275 mi) high voltage transmission line from Uzbekistan to Afghanistan was completed by October 2008. It will run from Kabul through five Afghan provinces towards the country's border with Uzbekistan, and will then connect to the Uzbek electricity transmission system. Afghanistan is reported to have coal reserves totalling 100-400 million tons. These mines are located from Badakhshan and extend up to Herat Province.

In 1991, a new 72-collector solar installation was completed in Kabul at a cost of $364 million. An area of vast untapped potential lies in the heat energy locked inside the earth in the form of magma or dry, hot rocks. Geothermal energy for electricity generation has been used worldwide for nearly 100 years. Besides wind and sun, potential alternative energy sources for Afghanistan include biogas and geothermal energy. Biogas plants are fuelled by animal dung, and produce a clean, odourless and smokeless fuel. The digestion process also creates a high-quality fertiliser which can benefit the family farm. United States Agency for International Development has teamed up with the United States National Renewable Energy Laboratory to develop a wind map of Herat province. They have identified approximately 158,000 megawatts of untapped potential wind energy.[23]

Micro-hydropower plants supply cheap, renewable energy and offer new sources of income. In addition to building hydropower plants RESAP is also helping to build up a self-reliant industry around the plants. All the components for the plants are standardised, simplified and affordable, meaning that the plants can be built, installed and maintained by the Afghans themselves. In the future, the community itself will be responsible for operating and maintaining the plants. Afghan engineers, trained to use and maintain the hydropower plants, will be able to work on other hydropower projects, so that the small-scale use of hydropower can grow in Afghanistan, without foreign intervention. Hydropower plants will be installed in various parts of Afghanistan. Employees of local workshops and engineers will be given training. The components of the micro-hydropower plants will be continually developed and improved during the project.[24]

## Tourism

The tourism industry of Afghanistan, developed with government help in the early 1970s has been negligible since 1979 due to internal political instability. A passport and visa are required for entrance into Afghanistan. In 1999, the UN estimated the daily cost of staying in

Kabul at $70 USD. Approximately 61 per cent of these costs were estimated to be the price of a room in a guesthouse. Travel was highly restricted in the country due to the US-led campaign against the Taliban and al-Qaeda.[25]

The important historical places in Afghanistan offer glimpse of the past heritages and its various cultural aspects. One of the major aspects of the historical places lies in the fact that they stand tall, vividly representing the events that reshaped and modified the country. It is an important contributor to the country's economic growth. To enjoy the tourists' vacations in the country, they should spend time visiting the top 10 tourist spots in Afghanistan. Tourism in Afghanistan has reached five-year high, reports Wild Frontiers. The independent adventure travel company has revealed that in 2013 they have taken twice as many bookings for group tours to the region than they did in 2012. Once an ancient part of the Silk Road, the mountainous region is full of history and offers a unique destination for travellers who are in search of a road less travelled. However, with American troops set to withdraw in 2014, the future of the country is somewhat uncertain. Tour operators such as Hinterland Travel and Wild Frontiers have both travelled safely and successfully to the country since 2004 and 2005 respectively but visitors must still hold the utmost vigilance.[26]

## Export-Import

Afghanistan recorded a trade deficit of 8518 USD Million in 2013. Balance of Trade in Afghanistan averaged-3425.34 USD Million from 2003 until 2013, reaching an all time high of -1660.92 USD Million in 2005 and a record low of-8518 USD Million in 2013. Balance of Trade in Afghanistan is reported by the Central Statistics Organisation of Afghanistan.[27] Afghanistan's booming narcotics trade risks splintering the country into a "fragmented, criminal state" if the government and its western allies do not step up efforts to tackle opium production and the illicit economy it supports, a senior UN official warned. The cash is vital for all the officials and their supporters counting on the drugs for unorthodox campaign finance during presidential elections this year and parliamentary ones in 2015. When those are over, and there is more certainty about what Afghanistan might look like after foreign troops have left and Karzai has been replaced, prices may finally start to come down to levels justified by demand.[28]

Afghanistan has been at the junction of trade routes between central, south and west Asia for over 3000 years. Official trade during the 1990s was dominated by there-export of products, principally electronic goods and cosmetics, to Pakistan and other neighbouring countries. Major imports for domestic use include agricultural inputs, rice, wheat, fuel and cooking oil, while indigenous exports include fruit and nuts, primary materials and timber. Australia has limited trade with Afghanistan. The trade we do have is mainly in engines, machinery and telecommunications. In calendar year 2011, Australia was the 26th largest destination of exports from Afghanistan, and the 32nd largest origin of imports into Afghanistan.[29]

## Drug Trafficking

Opium is one of the world's oldest pain-relievers. Although the oldest opium poppy capsules have been found in Switzerland, the plant itself is thought to have originated somewhere between the eastern Mediterranean and Minor Asia. Opium poppy is the species of plant from which opium and poppy seeds are derived. Opium is the source of many narcotics, including morphine, thebaine, codeine, papaverine, and noscapine. The poppy is the only species of Papaveraceae that is an agricultural crop grown on a large scale. The opium poppy is the principal source of most naturally occurring ì-opioid receptor agonist opioids.[30]

The opium poppy is the root source of all opioids considered opiates. Opiates are extracted from opium and poppy straw. The total opium cultivation in 2008 in Afghanistan is estimated at 157,000 hectares (ha), a 19 per cent reduction compared to 2007. Of the 34 provinces in the country, 18 were poppy-free in 2008 compared to 13 in 2007. This includes the eastern province of Nangarhar, which was the number two cultivator in 2007 and now is free from opium cultivation. Afghanistan is already the world's largest producer of opium, and last year accounted for 75 per cent of the world's heroin supply.[31]

Afghanistan supplies about 90 per cent of the world's opium, from which heroin is made and its poppy-driven economy is helping to fuel the 12-year-long war. Uncertainty over the future after most foreign forces withdraw from Afghanistan by the end of 2014 could help cause a surge in opium growth as a means of generating cash.

Twelve provinces were forecast to show a rise in opium cultivation this year. Opium production has become particularly high in Helmand Province in the south, the country's major opium-producing area, and in Kandahar Province. In both places, the surge of American troops helped to beat back Taliban influence, but as those troops returned home last year, cultivation increased sharply. More than 70 per cent of opium production now takes place in three provinces where the surge occurred.[32]

Opium traders are often happy to provide seeds, fertilisers and even advance payments to encourage crops, leaving farmers who do not have western or government agricultural help very vulnerable to their inducements. Most of the worldwide production of illegal heroin, the drug refined from opium, comes from Afghanistan. The opium produced does not only go out along smugglers' trails through Pakistan and Iran, but also feeds a growing population of addicts in Afghanistan, now believed to be around one-million strong.[33]

In Afghanistan's poppy-rich south and southwest, a raging insurgency intersects a thriving opium trade. The 2001 invasion of Afghanistan caused the Taliban and al-Qaeda to scatter but failed to put down either group once and for all. Numerous mid-level Taliban lay low in Afghanistan's Pashto southwest, often in the fertile plains of western Kandahar and Helmand that also cultivated poppy. Taliban insurgents tax farmers in their control zones. In areas where the Taliban are dominant, the village-level Taliban sub-commander will hand out written receipts for the amount of opium collected. In the rural environment, where there is little use for hard cash, much economic dealing is done in opium and other commodities of value. The Taliban maintain opium warehouses across Afghanistan's southern poppy heartland, where insurgent commanders can deposit.[34]

Providing protection for the opium trade is another lucrative form of earning for the Taliban in the south. The Taliban raised about \$400 million in 2011 from sources that included donations, taxing local economies and extorting money from such targets as drug dealers, cell phone operators and aid projects. About \$275 million of that income reached Taliban leadership and the rest was collected, spent or misappropriated at the local level. Donations were another major source of funding, which also went directly to the Taliban leadership. Taliban's main source of income was Afghanistan's opium poppy economy. While it provides enough to finance much of the insurgency in the main poppy growing provinces of Helmand, Kandahar and Uruzgan, the money raised from the drug trade is insufficient to meet the cost of insurgent activity elsewhere.[35]

After the Cold War and the collapse of the Soviet Union, the illicit drug trade continued to fuel Asian conflicts, and Afghanistan and Burma became the world's two main opium-producing countries. Their national economies have now been affected for decades by an illicit agriculture that, to some extent and in some areas, grew detrimentally to food crops such as wheat and rice, even though most farmers grow the opium poppy as a cash crop to cope with extreme staple crops shortages. Illicit opium production thrives on war economies and poverty. Impacts and consequences of such economies vary according to time and location.[36]

Opium production threatens alimentary self-reliance and subjects growers to repression and even harsher life conditions. Despite significant eradication efforts, high opium prices led to an increase in poppy cultivation in Afghanistan. The increase in cultivation occurred in spite of a major push by the government to promote eradication efforts. The number of poppy-free provinces remains unchanged at 17, but Ghor province in the west lost that status in 2012 while Faryab province in the north regained it. Afghanistan has a small but effective counter-narcotics force, but as crop sales mostly fund local power brokers, criminal gangs and to a lesser degree the Taliban, it makes it difficult for the Afghan government to establish control in areas where the black market opium trade is driving the economy.[37]

Cultivating wheat will not even cover the cost of the fuel needed to pump out underground water. A number of farmers who have switched to traditional crops such as cotton complain the prices of these crops have fallen and that there is no market for them at home or abroad. The Afghan government estimates that in 2011, the livelihoods of some 191,500 rural households depended on the growing of illicit drug crops, primarily opium poppy.[38]

As part of its counter-narcotics strategy, the Afghan government has started a "Food Zone Programme" led by provincial governors, which includes schemes to help farmers with seeds and fertilisers.[39] But provincial governors usually complain that they don't get enough funds from the international community to help farmers properly and fulfill the promises they made to them. The U.S. military bombed about 300 tons of poppy seeds in a dusty field in southern Afghanistan in a dramatic show of force designed to break up the Taliban's connection to heroin. The military dropped a series of 1,000-pound bombs from planes on the mounds of poppy seeds and then followed with strikes from helicopters.[40]

## Conclusion

Afghanistan is a landlocked country located in Central Asia and South Asia. The economy of Afghanistan has improved significantly since 2002 due to the infusion of billions of dollars in international assistance and investments, as well as remittances from Afghan expats. Agriculture has traditionally driven the Afghan economy, accounting for approximately 50 per cent of GDP before the Soviet invasion in 1979.[41] Wheat is the main staple cereal and accounts for about 70 per cent cropped area and cereal production each year and 70 per cent of total cereal consumption. Food security and distribution is also a major problem and both are sources of vulnerability for the Afghanistan given its 30 year history of violence and given the scale of Taliban and insurgent operations.[42]

Afghanistan is endowed with widespread natural resources, including extensive deposits of natural gas, petroleum, coal, copper, silver, gold, cobalt, chromite, talc, barites, sulphur, lead, zinc, iron ore, salt, rare earth elements, and precious and semiprecious stones. Afghanistan's banking sector remains fragile and in need of robust regulation by Da Afghanistan Bank. One of the important and basic pillars in the economy of every country is natural resources and its other subterraneous resources. By the growing demand of industry and technology, e.g. trees for paper and fuel production, iron ore for steel products, copper for wire, electrical equipment, and platinum are used for telecommunications equipment etc.[43]

Energy in Afghanistan describes energy and electricity production, consumption, import and export in Afghanistan. Energy in Afghanistan is primarily provided by hydropower. The Afghan National Development Strategy has identified alternative energy, such as wind and solar energy, as a high value power source to develop. Nation supplies about 90 per cent of the world's opium, from which heroin is made and its poppy-driven economy is helping to fuel the 12-years-long war. Uncertainty over the future after most foreign forces withdraw from Afghanistan by the end of 2014 could help cause a surge in opium growth as a means of generating cash. Twelve provinces were forecast to show a rise in opium cultivation this year. Opium production has become particularly high in Helmand Province in the south, the country's major opium-producing area, and in Kandahar Province.[44]

## References


1. *Afghanistan (2014),* Retrieved from http://en.wikipedia.org/wiki/Afghanistan.
2. *Current Situation and Issues on Agriculture of Afghanistan,* Retrieved from http://nodaiweb.university.jp/desert/pdf/JALS-P78_345-348_color.pdf
3. Focus on Seed Programs, *The Afghanistan Seed Industry,* July 2011.
4. *Economy of Afghanistan,* Retrieved from http://en.wikipedia.org/wiki/Economy_of_Afghanistan.
5. *Afghan economy faces serious revenue shortfall as state undertakes transition*, Retrieved from http://www.theguardian.com/world/2014/apr/22/afghanistan-economy-revenue-budget-shortfall.
6. *Afghanistan-Agriculture,* Retrieved from http://www.nationsencyclopedia.com/economies/Asia-and-the-Pacific/Afghanistan-AGRICULTURE.html
7. See http://kabul.usembassy.gov/usda.html
8. *Agriculture, food and poverty in Afghanistan*, Retrieved from http://csis.org/publication/agriculture-food-and-poverty-afghanistan.
9. *Country profile: Afghanistan*, Retrieved from http://www.new-ag.info/en/country/profile.php?a=841
10. *Agriculture and forestry*, Retrieved from http://www.britannica.com/EBchecked/topic/7798/Afghanistan/21433/Agriculture-and-forestry.
11. Focus on Seed Programs, *The Afghanistan Seed Industry*, July 2011.
12. *Afghanistan's extractive industries transparency initistives*, Retrieved from http://mom.gov.af/Content/files/AEITI%20-%202nd%20Reconciliation%20Report%203_10_2012%20-%20English.pdf
13. *Textile & Clothing Industry of Afghanistan (2013),* Retrieved from http://www.aisa.org.af/study/Final%20Afghanistan%20Textile%20Industry%20Paper%20-%20MA.pdf
14. Abdul Ghafar Rassin (2012), *A comprehensive study of marble industry in Afghanistan*, Retrieved from http://www.aisa.org.af/study/Marble-industry-AFG-AISA-2012.pdf
15. *Afghanistan's Drug industry*, Retrieved from http://www.unodc.org/documents/data-and-analysis/Afgh_drugindustry_Nov06.pdf

16. *The Future of plastic industry in Afghanistan*, Retrieved from http://www.aisa.org.af/study/The%20Future%20of%20Plastic%20Industry%20in%20Afghanistan.pdf
17. See http://www.gems-afghan.com/ngo/USAID-SibleyFinalMayReport0607.pdf
18. *Afghanistan's Banking Sector: The Central Bank's Capacity to Regulate Commercial Banks Remains Weak,* Retrieved from http://www.sigar.mil/pdf/audits/SIGAR%2014-16-AR.pdf
19. *Banking on Afghanistan*, Retrieved from http://www.forbes.com/2009/04/17/afghanistan-banking-business-wall-street-afghanistan.html
20. See http://en.wikipedia.org/wiki/Da_Afghanistan_Bank
21. Saeeda Gouhari, *Mining in Afghanistan*, Retrieved from https://www.boell.de/sites/default/files/assets/boell.de/images/download_de/worldwide/Mining_in_Afghanistan_KorrekturenCL.pdf
22. *Mining in Afghanistan,* Retrieved from http://www.bgs.ac.uk/afghanminerals/docs/gold_a4.pdf
23. *Energy in Afghanistan*, Retrieved from http://en.wikipedia.org/wiki/Energy_in_Afghanistan.
24. *Renewable Energy Sources in Afghanistan Project*, Retrieved from http://english.rvo.nl/sites/default/files/2013/12/Hydropower%20-%20Afghanistan%20-%20International%20Assistance%20Mission.pdf
25. *Tourism in Afghanistan*, Retrieved from http://en.wikipedia.org/wiki/Tourism_in_Afghanistan.
26. *Tourism to Afghanistan increases by 100%,* Retrieved from http://www.wanderlust.co.uk/magazine/news/afghanistan-in-demand.
27. *Afghanistan Balance of Trade*, Retrieved from http://www.tradingeconomics.com/afghanistan/balance-of-trade.
28. *Drug trade could splinter Afghanistan into fragmented criminal state – UN,* Retrieved from http://www.theguardian.com/world/2014/jan/05/drug-trade-afghanistan-fragmented-criminal-state.
29. *Afghanistan country brief*, See https://www.dfat.gov.au/geo/afghanistan/afghanistan_country_brief.html
30. *Afghanistan (2013),* Retrieved from http://en.wikipedia.org/wiki/Afghanistan
31. *Illicit Drugs in Afghanistan,* Retrieved from http://www.unodc.org/afghanistan/en/illicit-drugs.html
32. *Agriculture in Afghanistan (2013),* Retrieved from http://www.fas.usda.gov/country/afghanistan/us-afghanistan.asp
33. *Production of Opium by Afghans Is Up Again (2013),* Retrieved from http://www.nytimes.com/2013/04/16/world/asia/afghanistan-opium-production-increases-for-3rd-year.html?_r=0

34. *Afghan farmers return to opium as other markets fail (2013),* Retrieved from http://www.bbc.co.uk/news/world-asia-22150482
35. *Afghanistan: high expectations of record opium crop (2013),* Retrieved from http://www.guardian.co.uk/world/2013/apr/15/afghanistan-expectations-record-opium-crop
36. Pierre-Arnaud Chouvy, Afghanistan's Opium Production in Perspective, *China and Eurasia Forum Quarterly,* Volume 4, No. 1 (2006), Retrieved from http://www.silkroadstudies.org/new/docs/CEF/Quarterly/February_2006/Pierre-Arnaud_Chouvy.pdf
37. Gretchen Peters (2009), *How opium profits the Taliban.*
38. *Taliban raked in $400 million from diverse sources-UN (2012),* Retrieved from http://www.reuters.com/article/2012/09/11/afghanistan-un-taliban-idUSL1E8KBAJH20120911
39. Papaver somniferum (2013), Retrieved from http://en.wikipedia.org/wiki/Papaver_somniferum
40. *Opium cultivation rises in Afghanistan despite major eradication push – UN report*, Retrieved from http://www.un.org/apps/news/story.asp?NewsID=43547#.UbrlT1KDH3Y
41. *Afghanistan expecting record opium crop,* Retrieved from http://rt.com/news/afghanistan-opium-record-crop-885/
42. Dawood Azami (2013), *Why Afghanistan may never eradicate opium*, Retrieved from http://www.bbc.co.uk/news/world-asia-21548230
43. *U.S. bombs poppy crop to cut Taliban drug ties (2009),* Retrieved from http://edition.cnn.com/2009/WORLD/asiapcf/07/21/afghanistan.poppy.strike/
44. Fredrik Dahl (2013), *Afghan opium cultivation to rise in 2013 - U.N. report*, Retrieved from http://www.reuters.com/article/2013/04/15/us-afhganistan-opium-idUSBRE93E0OR20130415.

# Chapter - 10

# Economy of India

*"I believe economic growth should translate into the happiness and progress of all. Along with it, there should be development of art and culture, literature and education, science and technology. We have to see how to harness the many resources of India for achieving common good and for inclusive growth."*

***—Pratibha Patil***

## Introduction

The Indus civilisation's economy appears to have depended significantly on trade, which was facilitated by advances in transport. Around 600 BC, the Mahajanapadas minted punch-marked silver coins. The period was marked by intensive trade activity and urban development. By 300 B.C., the Maurya Empire united most of the Indian subcontinent. Though ancient India had a significant urban population, much of India's population resided in villages, whose economy was largely isolated and self-sustaining. Agriculture was the predominant occupation of the populace and satisfied a village's food requirements besides providing raw materials for hand-based industries like textile, food processing and crafts. Religion, especially Hinduism and Jainism, played an influential role in shaping economic activities. In the joint family system, members of a family pooled their resources to maintain the family and invest in business ventures.[1]

The independence-era Indian economy (before and a little after 1947) was inspired by the economy of the Soviet Union with socialist practices, large public sectors, high import duties and lesser private participation characterising it, leading to massive inefficiencies and widespread corruption. However, later on India adopted free market principles and liberalised its economy to international trade under the guidance of Manmohan Singh, who then was the Finance Minister of India under the leadership of P.V. Narasimha Rao the then Prime Minister. Following these strong economic reforms, the country's economic growth progressed at a rapid pace with very high rates of growth and large increases in the incomes of people.

Social democratic policies governed India for sometime after India's Independence from the British. The economy was then characterised by extensive regulation, protectionism, public ownership, pervasive corruption and slow growth. Major industries include telecommunications, textiles, chemicals, food processing, steel, transportation equipment, cement, mining, petroleum, machinery, software and pharmaceuticals. Indian economic policy after independence was influenced by the colonial experience, which was seen by Indian leaders as exploitative, and by those leaders' exposure to democratic socialism as well as the progress achieved by the economy of the Soviet Union.[2]

## Economy of India

The Economy of India is the 10th largest in the world with a GDP (a year's goods and services) of $1.843 Trillion (U.S.). India's economy includes agriculture, handicrafts, industries, and a lot of services. Services are the main source of economic growth in India today, though two-thirds of Indian people earn their living directly or indirectly through agriculture. In recent times, due to its large number of well-educated people who can speak English, India became a pioneer in information technology.[3] The social problems India faces are the increasing population, poverty, lack of infrastructure (buildings, roads, etc.) and growing unemployment.

The India economy, the third largest economy in the world in terms of purchasing power, is going to touch new heights in coming years. As predicted by Goldman Sachs, the Global Investment Bank, by 2035 India would be the third largest economy of the world just after US and China. It will grow to 60 per cent of size of the US economy. This booming economy of today has to pass through many phases before it can achieve the current milestone of 9 per cent GDP. After India got independence from colonial rule in 1947, the process of rebuilding the economy started. For this various policies and schemes were formulated. First five year plan for the development of Indian economy came into implementation in 1952. These Five Year Plans, started by Indian government, focused on the needs of the Indian economy.[4]

## Agriculture

Agriculture, with its allied sectors, is unquestionably the largest livelihood provider in India, more so in the vast rural areas. It also contributes a significant figure to the Gross Domestic Product. Sustainable agriculture, in terms of food security, rural employment, and environmentally sustainable technologies such as soil conservation, sustainable natural resource management and biodiversity protection, are essential for holistic rural development. Indian agriculture and allied activities have witnessed a green revolution, a white revolution, a yellow revolution and a blue revolution.[5]

Agriculture in India has a long history dating back to ten thousand years. Today, India ranks second worldwide in farm output. India is the largest producer in the world of milk, cashew nuts, coconuts, tea, ginger, turmeric and black pepper, and has the world's largest cattle population (281 million). It is the second largest producer of wheat, rice, sugar, groundnut and inland fish. It is the third largest producer of tobacco. India accounts for 10 per cent of the world fruit production with first rank in the production of banana and sapota.[6]

Majority of farmers in India practices subsistence farming. This means farming for own consumption. In other words, the entire production is largely consumed by the farmers and their family and they do not have any surplus to sell in the market. In this type of farming, landholdings are small and fragmented. Cultivation techniques are primitive and simple. India grows almost each and every crop. Rice is the most important food crop of India. It is predominantly a Kharif or summer crop. It covers about one-third of total cultivated area of the country and provides food to more than half of the Indian population. Maximum population of India is of rice consumers.

Wheat is the second most important food crop of India next to rice. It is a Rabi or winter crop. It is sown in the beginning of winter and harvested in the beginning of summer. Normally (in north India) the sowing of wheat begins in the month of October-November and harvesting is done in the month of March-April. This is the staple food of millions of people particularly in the northern and north-western regions of India. Millets are short duration warm weather crops. These are coarse grain crops and are used for both food and fodder. These are kharif crop.[7]

Farming systems in India are range from subsistence farming to organic farming, to industrial or commercial farming. This variation is largely due to the fact that the climate varies significantly according to the different regions in India. India has a long agricultural history, which dates back approximately ten thousand years. Today, India has the second-highest crop output in the world and agriculture-related jobs employ nearly 60 per cent of the total workforce.[8]

In India, there are two main agricultural seasons in a year, i.e. The Kharif season or the summer season; and The Rabi season or the winter season. The Kharif season starts in June when the South-West monsoon starts. The Rabi Season starts in the middle of October when the south-west monsoon retreats and the north-east Monsoon begins.[9] Agriculture plays a crucial role in the life of an economy. It is the backbone of economic system. Agriculture not only provides food and raw material but also employment opportunities to a very large proportion of population. About 70 per cent of population is directly engaged in agriculture. Agriculture is the premier source of our national income.

According to National Income Committee and C.S.O., in 1960-61, 52 per cent of national income was contributed by agriculture and allied occupations. In 1976-77, this sector alone contributed 42.2 per cent while in 1981-82, its contribution was to the tune of 41.8 per cent. In 2001-02, it contributed around 32.4 per cent of national income. Agriculture sector also provides fodder for livestock (35.33 crores). It is the agricultural sector that feeds country's trade. The development of agricultural sector leads to marketable surplus. Agriculture has been the source of raw materials to the leading industries like cotton and jute textiles, sugar, tobacco, edible and non-edible oils etc. All these depend directly on agriculture.[10]

## Industry

Indian Chemical industry generates around 70,000 commercial goods are ranging from plastic to toiletries and pesticides to beauty products. It is regarded as the oldest domestic sector in India and in terms of volume it gives a sense of pride to India by featuring as the

12 largest producers of chemicals. India has 10 large cement plants governed by the different State governments. Besides this India have 115 cement plants and around 300 small cement plants. The big cement plans have installed competence of 148.28 million tons per annum whereas the mini cement plants have the total capacity of 11.10 million tons per annum. Indian Steel Industry is a 400 years old sector which has a past record of registering 4 per cent growth in 2005-06. The production during this period reached at 28.3 million tons. India steel industry is the tenth largest in the world. Petroleum industry started its operations in the year 1867 and is considered as the oldest Indian industry. India is one of the most flourishing oil markets in the world and in the last few decades has witnessed the expansion of top national companies like ONGC, HPCL, BPCL and IOC.[11]

The number of Industries in India have increased manifold in the last few years. The main business of Reliance is in the energy sector (oil and gas). It has also made its presence felt in the garments and telecommunication sectors.[12] Growth in the industrial sector is one of the vital figures that affect the Gross Domestic Product in India.[13] The automotive industry in India is one of the largest automotive markets in the world. India's passenger car and commercial vehicle manufacturing industry is the sixth largest in the world, with an annual production of more than 3.9 million units in 2011. The western hub near Mumbai and Pune contributes to 33 per cent of the market and the northern cluster around the National Capital Region contributes 32 per cent. In 2011, there were 3,695 factories producing automotive parts in all of India. The average firm made US$6 million in annual revenue with profits close to US$400 thousand.[14]

The Textile industry in India traditionally, after agriculture, is the only industry that has generated huge employment for both skilled and unskilled labour in textiles. The textile industry continues to be the second largest employment generating sector in India. It offers direct employment to over 35 million in the country. India is the second largest producer of fibre in the world and the major fibre produced is cotton. Other fibres produced in India include silk, jute, wool, and man-made fibers. Sixty per cent of the Indian textile Industry is cotton based. Government of India passed the National Textile Policy in 2000. The Indian Textile industries are mainly dominated by some government, semi-government and private institutions. The major Indian Industries include Bombay Dyeing, Fabindia, Grasim Industries, JCT Limited, Lakshmi Machine Works, Lakshmi Mills and Mysore Silk Factory.[15]

Iron and Steel industries are considered to the backbone of any nation. First Iron and Steel Company in India was established in Kulti (West Bengal) in the year 1874 AD Brakar Iron Company was the name of the establishment. Sugar industries are one of the oldest and important industries of India. The IT sector has been India's sunshine sector for quite some time now. The industry has contributed considerably to changing India's image from a slow developing economy to a global player in providing world class technology solutions. The Telecom Regulatory Authority of India too is targeting a 10-fold increase in broadband subscriber's to100 million by 2014.[16]

The Industrial Policy initiatives undertaken by the Government of India since July 1991 have been designed to build on the past industrial achievements and to accelerate the process of making Indian industry internationally competitive. It recognises the strength and maturity of the industry and attempts to provide the competitive stimulus for higher growth. Foreign investment had earlier played only a minor role as a source of finance. Several developing and less advanced countries have received foreign capital several times more than India. This is mainly because they had simplified their investment procedures. In conjunction with industrial deregulation, the government also liberalised substantially the process relating to foreign investment.[17]

Industrial Revolution in Gujarat dates back to Harappan Civilisation. As Gujarat has been writing and re-writing history, the early nineteenth century represented a significant watershed in Industrial Development. Gujarat's Industrial Policy 2009 is geared for catalysing Robust, Sustainable and Inclusive Growth. The only state to emerge as 'Investor friendly', Gujarat has achieved the distinction of being the top most industrially developed state in India in respect of investment in industrial sector and second among states in respect of value of production and value addition in industrial sector in India.[18]

The small-scale industries sector plays a vital role in the growth of the country. It contributes almost 40 per cent of the gross industrial value added in the Indian economy. The small-scale sector has grown rapidly over the years. The growth rates during the various plan periods have been very impressive. The number of small-scale units has increased from an estimated 0.87 million units in the year 1980-81 to over three million in the year 2000. SSI Sector in India creates largest employment opportunities for the Indian populace, next only to Agriculture. SSI Sector plays a major role in India's present export performance. 45-50 per cent of the Indian Exports is contributed by SSI Sector. Direct exports from the SSI Sector account for nearly 35 per cent of total exports. The product groups where the SSI sector dominates in exports are sports goods, readymade garments, woollen garments and knitwear, plastic products, processed food and leather products.[19]

The Ministry of Small Scale Industries is a defunct Indian government ministry. It was merged with the Ministry of Agro and Rural Industries to form the Ministry of Micro, Small and Medium Enterprises. The ministry was tasked with the promotion of micro and small enterprises. The Small Industries Development Organisation was under the control of the ministry, as was the public sector undertakings National Small Industries Corporation Limited. It was established in 1954 on the basis of the recommendations of the Ford Foundation. It has over 60 offices and 21 autonomous bodies under its management.[20]

The definition of small scale industries has undergone changes over the years in terms of investment limits is as follow as, in 1977, small scale industrial unit having investment of less than ₹ 10 lakh were defined as small scale industrial undertakings, while for ancillary units, the investment limit was ₹ 15 lakh. Units with investment of less than ₹ 1 lakh were defined as tiny enterprises. In 2000, the investment limit for small scale industries was ₹ 1 crore, for ancillary units ₹ 1 crore, and for tiny enterprise ₹ 25 lakh. The new definition for microenterprises, where the investment in plant and machinery does not exceed ₹ 25 lakh, small enterprises, where the investment limit was more than ₹ 25 lakh but does not exceed ₹ 5 crore and a medium enterprise, where the investment in plant and machinery is more than ₹ 5 crore but not exceed ₹ 10 crore.[21]

The small-scale sector occupies a position of prominence in the Indian economy, contributing to more than 50 per cent of the industrial production in value addition terms. The sector accounts for one-third of the export revenue and employs the largest manpower next to agriculture. In India's present liberalised economy, the survival and growth of small-scale industry largely depends on its ability to innovate, improve operational efficiency and increase productivity. In order to enable small scale enterprises adopt more efficient energy use patterns, it is essential to demonstrate positive impacts of reduced energy use to the entrepreneurs in terms of increased productivity and higher profitability.[22]

The liberalisation of the industrial policy and other government initiatives has given a definite impetus for entry, participation and growth of the private sector in the steel industry. Allowing foreign direct investment has been a positive step since India is heavily dependent on foreign technologies. These foreign technologies generally add life to the plant and production units, which ultimately lead to the country's economic growth. Iron ore export from India has showed a 253 per cent increase during the period October–December 2013, at 3.75 MT as against 1.06 MT in the corresponding period of the previous year, on the back of the opening of new mines in Chhattisgarh, Madhya Pradesh and Rajasthan, as per the Federation of Indian Mineral Industries.[23]

## Animal Husbandry

A large number of farmers in India depend on animal husbandry for their livelihood. In addition to supplying milk, meat, eggs, wool and hides, animals, mainly bullocks, are the major source of power for both farmers and drayers. Today, India has the world's largest dairy herd (composed of cows and buffaloes), at over 304 million strong, and stands first in milk production, with 112.5 million tonnes of milk produced in 2009-2010. The Department of Animal Husbandry, Dairying and Fisheries is responsible for issues related to livestock production, preservation, protection from disease and improvement of stocks and dairy development. Users can get detailed information on animal husbandry, dairy development and fisheries. Information is also provided on various schemes, trade, sanitary import permit, bird flu, swine flu, bull calves available for sale, etc.[24]

The Indian poultry industry has come along way from a backyard activity to an organised, scientific and vibrant industry. Despite the least attention from the planners, goat population in India has increased at the fastest rate among all major livestock species during last two decades. Pig husbandry is the most important activity in the animal husbandry sector in the northeastern region inhabited by tribal people.

The region also has a substantial pig population, which constitutes around 25 per cent of the country's pig population. Since the Second Plan, efforts have been made to control diseases namely, Rinderpest, Foot and Mouth Disease, Haemorrhagic Septicemia, Black Quarter and Anthrax. Oil cakes, maize and cereal by-products are important ingredients of animal feeds. Coarse grains and cottonseed are traditionally used as cattle feed.[25]

Animal husbandry includes domestication of animals to obtain animal products like milk, meat, wool, skin and Hyde etc. and to use them for draught and transportation. These animals are cow, buffalo, goat, sheep, pig, camel, horse, mule, donkey and yak etc. India has about 500 species of animals of which only few are domesticated for different uses. At state-level Bihar has the largest percentage (12.37) of cattle in the country followed by Uttar Pradesh (10.06), Madhya Pradesh (9.80), Maharashtra (9.09) and West Bengal (8.97). These five states together provide about 50 per cent of the country's cattle number. Sikkim (0.07 per cent), Arunachal Pradesh (0.23), Nagaland (0.19), Meghalaya (0.38), Manipur (0.26), and Tripura (0.62) have less than one per cent of the cattle in the country.[26]

Government of India is making efforts to increase the productivity of milch animals and thus increase the per capita availability of milk. Most of the milk is produced by small, marginal farmers and landless labourers who are grouped into cooperatives at the village level. To provide them a steady market and a remunerative price for the milk produced, about 12 million farmers have been brought under the ambit of more than one lakh village level cooperative societies in the country.[27]

## Plantation

Plantation crops constitute a large group of crops. The major plantation crops include coconut, areca nut, oil palm, cashew, tea, coffee and rubber; the minor plantation crops include cocoa. Their total coverage is comparatively less and they are mostly confined to small holdings. However, they play an important role in view of their export potential as well as domestic requirements and in employment generation and poverty alleviation programmes particularly in rural sector.[28]

Tea and coffee are the main and oldest industries in the country, which provide ample employment opportunities to the people at large and hold immense potential for export. India is one of the largest tea producers in the world. Coffee is the second largest traded commodity in the world and is an extremely important foreign exchange earner. The coffee industry of India is one of the largest producers of coffee in the world.[29]

Commercial production of tea in India began after the conquest of large areas by the British East India Company, at which point large tracts of land were converted for mass tea production. Today, India is one of the largest tea producers in the world, although over 70 per cent of its tea is consumed within India itself. A number of renowned teas, such as Assam and Darjeeling, also grow exclusively in India.[30] According to the ASSOCHAM report released in December, 2011, India, as the world's largest consumer of tea uses nearly 30 per cent of the global output. India is also the second largest producer of tea. Despite the production, India is also the largest exporter of tea after China. Tea is also mixed with these traditional herbs. The taste of chai (sweet and milky) helps disguise the stronger and bitterer flavours of some of the medicinal additives. The state of Assam is the world's largest tea-growing region, lying on either side of the Brahmaputra River, and bordering Bangladesh and Burma (Myanmar).

The cultivation and production of Assam tea in the first two decades (1840–1860) were monopolised by the Assam Company, which operated in districts of Upper Assam and through the labour of the local Kachari labour. The tea plant is grown in the lowlands of Assam, unlike Darjeeling's and Nilgiris, which are grown in the highlands. The Assam tea bush grows in a lowland region, in the valley of the Brahmaputra River, an area of clay soil rich in the nutrients of the floodplain. Assam tea is generally harvested twice, in a *"first flush"* and a *"second flush."* The first flush is picked during late March. The second flush, harvested later, is the more prized "tippy tea," named thus for the gold tips that appear on the leaves.[31]

Darjeeling, as well as being one of India's most popular hill stations, is surrounded by tea plantations that produce prized light coloured, floral smelling tea. Around 25 per cent of India's total tea output comes from Darjeeling. The mountainous Nilgiri district of Tamil Nadu, in south India, is known for its distinctive dark and intensely aromatic tea. Tea has been grown there for more than 100 years, and is the most important industry in the region. Wayanad, a lush mountainous agricultural area of Kerala, also produces a significant amount of tea (in addition to coffee and spices). Most of the tea plantations are located south of Kalpetta. The road to Chembra Peak will take you though a private estate, which is worth a look.[32]

Indian Coffee is shade grown and manually plucked. India produces Arabicas and Robustas, in both washed and unwashed forms and is the fifth largest producer and exporter of Coffee.[33] Central Coffee Research Institute and Extension wing of Coffee Board have brought out many publications covering the various technological aspects of coffee cultivation for use by coffee growers. In order to maintain the coffee estates in good condition and to increase the production and productivity, it is very important to follow and adopt the improved technologies like use of improved high yielding plant varieties, soil conservation and fertility maintenance, efficient use of agrochemicals and fertilisers, plant training, irrigation, shade management, post-harvest processing, integrated pest and disease management practices.[34]

South Indian states are the major producer of Coffees in India with Karnataka 53 per cent, Kerala 28 per cent, Tamil Nadu 11 per cent and remaining from the other states includes Andhra Pradesh, Orissa, Assam and Tripura. Hilly area and good monsoon in this region makes it best place for important varieties of coffee and tea plantation. Indian coffee is considers as one of the finest coffee in the world, they grown under the shade rather than direct sunlight. Chikmagalur is first place in India where coffee was introduced.[35]

Jute and Cotton are natural Fibres. India has a major share of cultivation of jute and cotton of the world. Jute is an important natural fibre. The share of Ganga delta contributes for about 85 per cent of the World-wide Jute cultivation. Jute is a cash crop of hot and moist climate. Bangladesh and India are the two chief jute producing countries. Hot and moist climate is ideal for jute. West Bengal is the largest producer of Jute in India followed by Assam, Bihar, Orissa, and Andhra Pradesh stagnant water nearly is needed for retting.[36]

India, China and Bangladesh are the three major producers in the cultivation or production of jute fiber. India has taken advantage of recent improvements in the cultivation of jute to become the largest producer or cultivator of jute in the world. Using advanced production techniques, India also has dominance over the worldwide products market. Bangladesh is currently the second largest producer of jute fiber, now overtaken by India. The Jat Area, popular for highest quality of jute fiber is located in Bangladesh. Therefore, Bangladesh is able to supply the highest quality of jute fiber in the world. China is the third largest in terms of jute cultivation.[37]

The Rubber Board has identified Assam as a "potential state" to "replicate the Tripura success story" and plans to bring two lakh hectares area under rubber plantation in the state in near future. It has set a target to bring at least 12,500 hectares area under rubber plantation in Assam and 35,000 hectares in North East in the twelfth five year plan. Sustained effort from the state government and the Rubber Board had made Tripura, a left ruled state in North East, the second largest producer of natural rubber in India within a short span. The Rubber Board, Assam has 28,102 hectares of land under rubber plantation currently, against its potential of two lakh hectares. Tripura on the other hand, has 55,415 hectares of land under plantation as against its potential of one lakh hectares. The land under rubber plantation in Kerala, which is the largest rubber producing state in India, is 5,25,408 hectares. Presently, India's rubber industry turnover is around ₹ 4,500 crore and the demand is expected to touch 1.78 lakh MT by 2025.[38]

## Transport

Transport is an important part of India's economy. Since the economic liberalisation of the 1990s, development of infrastructure within the country has progressed at a rapid pace, and today there is a wide variety of modes of transport by land, water and air. Public transport is the predominant mode of motorised local travel in cities. Traffic in Indian cities generally moves slowly, where traffic jams and accidents are very common. The oldest Indian state transport undertaking is North Bengal State Transport Corporation founded by the Raj Darbar of Koch Bihar Kingdom regime on 1 April 1945 with three buses and three trucks. Private vehicles account for 30 per cent of the total transport demand in urban areas of India. Rail services in India, first introduced in 1853, are provided by the state-run Indian Railways under the supervision of the Ministry of Railways.

Indian Railways provides an important mode of transport in India, transporting over 18 million passengers and more than two million tonnes of freight daily across one of the largest and busiest rail networks in the world. Rail links between India and neighbouring countries are not well-developed. Two trains operate to Pakistan-the Samjhauta Express between Delhi and Lahore, and the Thar Express between Jodhpur and Karachi. Bangladesh is connected by a bi-weekly train, the Maitree Express that runs from Kolkata to Dhaka.

India has a network of National Highways connecting all the major cities and state capitals, forming the economic backbone of the country. As of 2013, India has a total of 70,934 km (44,076 mi) of National Highways, of which 1,208 km (751 mi) are classified as expressways. As per the National Highways Authority of India, about 65 per cent of freight and 80 per cent passenger traffic is carried by the roads. The National Highways carry about 40 per cent of total road traffic, though only about two per cent of the road network is covered by these roads. Directorate General of Civil Aviation is the national regulatory body for the aviation industry. It is controlled by the Ministry of Civil Aviation. Air India is India's national flag carrier after merging with Indian Airlines in 2011 and plays a major role in connecting India with the rest of the world. IndiGo, Jet Airways, Air India, Spice jet and GoAir are the major carriers in order of their market share.

As of 2013, there are 346 civilian airports in India where 253 with paved runways and 93 with unpaved runways. As of 2013, there are 45 heliports in India. There are many major ports in India. Maritime transportation in India is managed by the Shipping Corporation of India, a government-owned company that also manages offshore and other marine transport infrastructure in the country. The ports are the main centres of trade. In India about 95 per cent of the foreign trade by quantity and 70 per cent by value takes place through the ports. India has an extensive network of inland waterways in the form of rivers, canals, backwaters and creeks. The total navigable length is 14,500 kilometers (9,000 mi), out of which about 5,200 km (3,231 mi) of river and 485 km (301 mi) of canals can be used by mechanised crafts.[39]

India's transport sector is large and diverse; it caters to the needs of 1.1 billion people. In 2007, the sector contributed about 5.5 per cent to the nation's GDP, with road transportation contributing the lion's share. Indian Railways is one of the largest railways under single management. Roads are the dominant mode of transportation in India. They carry almost 90 per cent of the country's passenger traffic and

65 per cent of its freight. India has 12 major and 187 minor and intermediate ports along its more than 7500 km long coastline. India has 125 airports, including 11 international airports.[40] India infrastructure is quite developed and the transportation network of the country contributes towards the economic development of the country.

The transportation network of India consists of roadways transport, railways, shoreline shipping, and airways transport etc. The transportation system of the nation is well-set and efficiently managed and is a key player in maintaining the financial development of the country. The quickest mode to travel to any corner of the world is air travel. Domestic flights are offered by the private carriers and Indian Airlines. At the same time, the international flights are offered by Air India. The four major airports in India are Kolkata, Chennai, Delhi, and Mumbai.[41] Despite ongoing improvements in the sector, several aspects of the transport sector are still riddled with problems due to outdated infrastructure, lack of investment, corruption and a burgeoning population.[42]

A dearth of adequate infrastructure and services has been recognised as one of the most important roadblocks in the sustainable development of Indian cities. National Urban Transport Policy was launched mid-2006 by the Ministry of Urban Development was created to motivate the building of people centric urban transport solutions instead of focusing on improving the conditions for private motor vehicles. Jawaharlal Nehru National Urban Renewal Mission was released by India's Prime Minister, Dr Manmohan Singh in December 2005 and administered by the Indian Ministry of Urban Development and Ministry of Poverty Alleviation to support state and local investment in urban development.

National Action Plan for Climate Change was launched in mid-2008 provided additional support and solidified India's commitment to sustainable transport solution. Auto Fuel Policy was issued in August 2002; the Auto Fuel Policy was developed by expert committee constituting experts from various ministries including environment, transport, industry, agriculture, petroleum and natural gas, non-conventional energy and consumer affairs to form a comprehensive and integrated national policy on the above. The National Environment Policy was released in early 2006 as a response to a national commitment to a clean environment, and as mandated in the Constitution of India - Articles 48A and 51 A (g). US-Environmental Protection Agency and Ministry of Environment and Forest have signed a MoU in January 2002, to improve Air Quality Management practices in India with additional support from the U.S. Agency for International Development and most recently the US Trade and Development Agency.[43]

## Mining

The Mining industry in India is a major economic activity which contributes significantly to the economy of India. The GDP contribution of the mining industry varies from 2.2 to 2.5 per cent only but going by the GDP of the total industrial sector it contributes around 10 to 11 per cent. India is the largest producer of sheet mica, the third largest producer of iron ore and the fifth largest producer of bauxite in the world. India's metal and mining industry was estimated to be $106.4 bn (£68.5bn) in 2010. The distribution of minerals in the country is uneven and mineral density varies from region to region. According to the 2008 Ministry of Mines estimates: 'India has stepped up its production to reach the second rank among the chromite producers of the world. Besides, India ranks third in production of coal and lignite, second in barites, fourth in iron ore, fifth in bauxite and crude steel, seventh in manganese ore and eighth in aluminum.'[44]

India has a long history of commercial coal mining covering nearly 220 years starting from 1774 by M/s Sumner and Heatly of East India Company in the Raniganj Coalfield along the western bank of river Damodar. Setting up of the National Coal Development Corporation, a Government of India Undertaking in 1956 with the collieries owned by the railways as its nucleus was the first major step towards planned development of Indian Coal Industry.[45]

India is well endowed in terms of most minerals. The National Mineral Policy, 2008 announced by the Union Government, was made to fulfill this aim. India produces as many as 87 minerals, which includes four fuel minerals, 10 metallic minerals, 47 non-metallic minerals, three atomic minerals and 23 minor minerals (including building and other materials). Minerals can broadly be divided into fuel and non-fuel minerals. Coal, lignite, petroleum and natural gas are the four fuel minerals. In a way, atomic minerals also can be clubbed under this category.[46]

In 2010-11; the number of reporting mines in India was 2,628. Most of the country's mining activities are concentrated in the states of Gujarat, Andhra Pradesh, Jharkhand, Madhya Pradesh, Rajasthan, Karnataka, Odisha, Tamil Nadu, Maharashtra, Chhattisgarh and West Bengal. Together, these 11 states account for 92 per cent of the mines in the country. India produced 842 minerals in 2010-11, valued at ₹ 2,00,609 crore. The Mines and Minerals (Development and Regulation) Act, 1948 was the first legal framework for regulation and development of mines in independent India. Enacted in 1957 by the Parliament, two set of rules were made under the Act–the Mineral Concession Rules and the Mineral Conservation and Development Rules (MCDR). The MMDR Act has been amended four times since 1957. The first amendment came in 1972 which enhanced government control over mining. The second amendment in 1986 further increased the Central government's control on mining and introduced the concept of an approved mining plan.[47]

Diamond mining isn't new to India and is said to have begun in the country in four AD along the Krishna River. Legend has it that the Kohinoor, once said to be the world's biggest diamond, was mined near a rivulet in present-day Guntur district in Andhra Pradesh. Other famous diamonds such as the Great Moghul, the Regent have also been mined in India. Diamonds are an allotrope of carbon formed at high pressure and temperature. The layers of the earth where conditions are most favourable for their formation are referred to as '*diamond* stability fields'.[48]

India has ranked sixth in the world with a Gold production of 19.5 tonns during the year 1905, whereas the production of gold from primary source during the year 2007 is only 2.490 tonnes. Kolar mine has produced more than 800 tonnes of gold before its closure in 2001. Presently gold is produced from three mines viz Hutti, Uti, Hirabuddni in Karnataka and as by product from base metal sulphide deposits of Khetri (Rajasthan), Mosabani, Singhbhum (Jharkhand), in public sector and Kundrekocha in private sector in the decreasing order.[49] India hardly produces any silver and is basically a silver importing country. It holds the 20th place in the list of silver producing countries and the total production of silver in India in 2004 was around 2.1 million ounces.

Rajasthan is the leading silver producing state in India with a production of around 32 thousand tons. Gujarat follows on the second place with a production of around 20 thousand tons. Over 50 per cent share of import of silver in India is held by Chinese silver. The major importing centre of silver in India was Mumbai but now it has been shifted to Ahmadabad and Jaipur due to high sales tax and octroi charges.[50] The three major silver producing states in India are Rajasthan, Gujarat and Jharkhand.

The Geological Survey of India estimates that platinum mining may be feasible in the mineral-rich belts of Baula-Nuasahi and Sukinda valley in the state. Baula-Nausahi, a 3-km-long belt, 170 km north-east of Bhubaneswar, is the only proven platinum group of elements (PGE) deposit in the country with an estimated 14.2 million tonns of deposits, confined to the active chromite mines. What is believed to be the oldest PGE mineralisation, the area has two types of PGE. The type-I is rich in platinum while the type-II is palladium-rich and is hydrothermal. PGE comprises six greyish to silver white metals including platinum, palladium, iridium, rhodium, osmium and ruthenium. These metals have attracted great interest from explorers and researchers across the world for their rarity and high commercial value, growing demand in jewellery, pharmaceutical industry, telecommunications and high-tech applications in fuel cell technology.

As per GSI assessment, Bangur in Keonjhar district, which lies within the chromite leasehold area of Orissa Mining Corporation in the southern extension of Baula-Nuasahi complex, is a potential PGE deposit area. Besides, a prominent PGE zone lies in the western part of the area.[51] The Geological Survey of India and Tamil Nadu Minerals Ltd will jointly explore the commercial viability of mining platinum group of minerals present in the Mettupalayalam and Namakkal areas of the state.[52]

Jaduguda in Singhbhum Thrust Belt (in the state of Jharkhand, formerly part of Bihar) is the first uranium deposit to be discovered in the country in 1951. The Singhbhum Thrust Belt is a zone of intense shearing and deep tectonisation with less than 1 km width and known for a number of copper deposits with associated nickel, molybdenum, bismuth, gold, silver etc. It extends in the shape of an arc for a length of about 160 km. Apart from discoveries in the Singhbhum Thrust Belt, several uranium occurrences have also been found in Cuddapah basin of Andhra Pradesh. These include Lambapur-Peddagattu, Chitrial,

Kuppunuru, Tumallapalle, and Rachakuntapalle which have significantly contributed towards the uranium reserve base of India.

In the Mahadek basin of Meghalaya in North-Eastern part of the country, sandsyone type uranium deposits like Domiasiat, Wahkhyn, and Mawsynram provide near-surface flat ore bodies amenable to commercial operations. Other areas in Rajasthan, Karnataka and Chhattisgarh hold promise for developing into some major deposits. The uranium mining in India made an exciting beginning with the formation of Uranium Corporation of India Ltd. in 1967 under the Department of Atomic Energy.

Since then, the uranium industry of the country has recorded phenomenal growth in production and upgradation of technology.[53] India may soon set up a new company to acquire uranium mines in foreign countries to ensure fuel supplies to its burgeoning nuclear power programme. The Atomic Energy Commission has recommended setting up of a joint venture company between Nuclear Power Corporation of India Limited and Uranium Corporation of India Limited to explore the possibility of acquiring uranium assets abroad.[54]

Decades of underinvestment have left the country with dire deficits in such critical areas as railways, roads, ports, airports, telecommunications and electricity generation. The airports and some ports have been privatised, and they're working pretty well. Power production is open to the private sector, but power distribution is still in the government's hands in most states. India has made extraordinary advances over the past 20 years, but it still lags behind China. The real problem is that the poor still do not think they're getting their share of economic growth. They need much greater compensation from employment to create economic uplift.[55]

## Export-Import

Foreign Trade in India includes all imports and exports to and from India. At the level of Central Government it is administered by the Ministry of Commerce and Industry. Prior to the 1991 economic liberalisation, India was a closed economy due to the average tariffs exceeding 200 per cent and the extensive quantitative restrictions on imports. Foreign investment was strictly restricted to only allow Indian ownership of businesses. Since the liberalisation, India's economy has improved mainly due to increased foreign trade.[56]

According to the Department of Commerce; the fifteen largest trading partners of India represent 62.1 per cent of Indian imports, and 58.1 per cent of Indian exports as of December 2010.[57] The EU and India are committed to further increase their trade in goods and services as well as bilateral investment through trade and investment liberalisation under the Free Trade Agreement negotiations that were launched in 2007.[58] The Ministry of Commerce and Industry is the most important organ concerned with the promotion and regulation of foreign trade in India. The Ministry has an elaborate organisational set up to look after the various aspects of trade. Its two important offices concerned with trade are the 'Directorate General of Foreign Trade, and the 'Directorate General of Commercial Intelligence and Statistics'. It is responsible for implementing the Foreign Trade Policy/Exim Policy with the main objective of promoting Indian exports. India is also engaged in trade negotiations and agreements at multilateral, regional and bilateral levels.[59]

The important items of export to are textiles and ready made garments, engineering goods such as bicycles and components thereof, mopeds, diesel engines, automotive components, hand tools etc., chemical and allied items like fine chemicals, dye and dye intermediates, tyres and tubes, rubber gloves. Besides, India also exports handicrafts items, sports goods, electronic items, jute, shellac, tea and spices to Latin America.[60]

India has become heavily import dependent on China when it comes to many essential and large volume drugs making it vulnerable to sudden disruption of supplies.[61] Imports in India increased to 39233.20 USD Million in May of 2014 from 35720 USD Million in April of 2014. Imports in India averaged 5824.86 USD Million from 1957 until 2014, reaching an all time high of 45281.90 USD Million in May of 2011 and a record low of 117.40 USD Million in August of 1958. Imports in India are reported by the Ministry of Commerce and Industry, India.[62]

## Banking

Banking in India is the modern sense originated in the last decades of the eighteenth century. The first banks were Bank of Hindustan (1770-1829) and The General Bank of India, established 1786 and since defunct. In 1969 the Indian government nationalised all the major banks that it did not already own and these have remained under government ownership. The government has developed initiatives to address this through the State Bank of India expanding its branch network and through the National Bank for Agriculture and Rural Development with things like microfinance. All banks which are included in the Second Schedule to the Reserve Bank of India Act, 1934 are Scheduled Banks.[63]

## Infrastructure Development

Infrastructure is a major sector that propels overall development of the Indian economy. The Secretariat for Infrastructure in the Planning Commission is involved in initiating policies that would ensure time-bound creation of world class infrastructure in the country.[64] Major infrastructure development requires a substantial influx of investment capital. The policies of the Indian Government seek to encourage investments in domestic infrastructure from both local and foreign private capital. The country is already a hot destination for foreign investors. Major infrastructure projects are governed by the concession agreements signed between public authorities and private entities.

India's roads are already congested, and getting more so. The Indian Government has also recognised existing infrastructure gaps and capacity constraints in the rail system, and as a consequence plans large scale investment over the five years from FY07-FY12. Increasing connectivity with inland transport networks is just one of many challenges currently facing India's ports, which have seen massive swells in the amount of goods transported. Traffic is estimated to reach 877 million tonnes by 2011-12, and containerised cargo is expected to grow at 15.5 per cent over the next seven years. Increased manufacturing activities and a growing population are also causing a surge in power usage.

Funding India's wide-ranging, US$500 billion programme of infrastructure expansion over a five-year period is likely to be beyond the means of total government funding, so policies have been designed to facilitate private investment to the maximum level possible. In order to make infrastructure projects more attractive for companies and investors, the Indian Government is re-examining the existing depreciation policy for such entities.[65]

The Twelfth Plan intends to continue its thrust on accelerating the pace of investment in infrastructure as this is critical for sustaining and accelerating growth. The Planning Commission in its Twelfth Five Year Plan Document (2012-17) expects investments in infrastructure projects to be worth of US$ one trillion over the five years of the plan. The total investment as a percentage of GDP is also expected to be in the range of 7-9 per cent. Since resource constraints will continue to limit public investment in infrastructure in other areas, PPP-based development needs to be encouraged wherever feasible. As per the Twelfth Plan Document, the Planning Commission targets to achieve 50 per cent private and PPP funding in total infrastructure investments, compared to a little more than 30 per cent in the Eleventh Plan.

The Indian power sector has attracted much private investment in the past years. With 56 projects for a total consideration of US$ 12.6 billion, the sector accounts for 18 per cent of the total value of PPP projects across sectors, though only seven per cent of the total number of PPP projects. According to the approach paper of the Twelfth Five Year Plan since more than two-third of the investment in the economy is by the private sector (households and corporate). Commercial banks stepped up lending to infrastructure companies largely by unwinding their excess investments in government securities maintained as statutory liquidity ratio. The Government of India has been encouraging private sector investment and participation in all infrastructure sectors. The National Development Council has made clear that 'Increased private participation has now become a necessity to mobilise the resources needed for infrastructure expansion and upgrading.'

In recent years, the PPP model in India has been fairly successful with several projects being implemented across sectors. One of the main problems confronting infrastructure and PPPs in India is the delay in implementing and executing large-scale projects resulting in time and cost overruns. Over the years, adoption of standardised documents, such as model concession agreements and bidding documents for award of PPP projects have been streamlined and there has also been accelerated decision-making by agencies in a manner that is fair, transparent, and competitive. Cochin International Airport also known as Nedumbassery Airport is the largest and busiest airport in Kerala.

The airport was the first to be developed under a PPP model. One of the single largest roadblocks for development of infrastructure would be the issue of land acquisition. Resistance from local communities has proven to be a potent force and has led to delays in infra projects.

Most of the infrastructure projects in India suffer from delays in completion. This is mainly due to an inadequate regulatory framework and inefficiency in the approval process.[66]

Two important steps are required for Indian Infrastructure sector. First, we need to setup an independent regulatory body like SEBI for infrastructure. The primary role of this body would be to attract private investments and protect the investor for various risks. Second, we need to have an authority which should take care of sovereign obstacles. The basic role of this body will be to remove the obstacles for public projects and monitor the development of the project. The new Public Private Partnership model has a lot of potential to carry out various infrastructure projects and provide a better infrastructure for each sector.[67]

## Foreign Direct Investment

Until the liberalisation of 1991, India was largely and intentionally isolated from the world markets, to protect its economy and to achieve self-reliance. Foreign trade was subject to import tariffs, export taxes and quantitative restrictions, while foreign direct investment was restricted by upper-limit equity participation, restrictions on technology transfer, export obligations and government approvals; these approvals were needed for nearly 60 per cent of new FDI in the industrial sector. The restrictions ensured that FDI averaged only around $200 million annually between 1985 and 1991; a large percentage of the capital flows consisted of foreign aid, commercial borrowing and deposits of non-resident Indians.[68]

## Foreign Remittance

Remittances to India are money transfers from Non-resident Indians, employed outside the country to family, friends or relatives in India. Money is sent to India either electronically or by demand draft. India and China are the two top destinations for flows, making up a third of the total amount. For India, $71 billion in remittances is nearly triple what it received from foreign direct investment in 2012. Remittances have grown steadily for the past three decades as migration increased, with only a slight dip during the financial crisis. Remittances can also help promote development, and are often the biggest source of foreign finance for developing economies.[69]

Top recipients of officially recorded remittances for 2013 are India (with an estimated $71 billion), China ($60 billion), the Philippines ($26 billion), Mexico ($22 billion), Nigeria ($21 billion), and Egypt ($20 billion). As a percentage of GDP, the top recipients of remittances, in 2012, were Tajikistan (48 per cent), Kyrgyz Republic (31 per cent), Lesotho and Nepal (25 per cent each) and Moldova (24 per cent). For a country like Tajikistan they constitute half the GDP. For Bangladesh, remittances provide vital protection against poverty. In terms of volume, India, with $71 billion of remittances, tops the global chart. Remittance volumes to developing countries, as a whole, are projected to continue growing strongly over the medium term, averaging an annual growth rate of nine per cent to reach $540 billion in 2016. Remittances are the most tangible and least controversial link between migration and development. Policymakers can do much more to maximise the positive impact of remittances by making them less costly and more productive for both the individual and the recipient country.[70]

## Conclusion

Agriculture, with its allied sectors, is unquestionably the largest livelihood provider in India, more so in the vast rural areas. It also contributes a significant figure to the Gross Domestic Product. Majority of farmers in India practices subsistence farming. This means farming for own consumption. In other words, the entire production is largely consumed by the farmers and their family and they do not have any surplus to sell in the market. The number of Industries in India have increased manifold in the last few years. The main business of Reliance is in the energy sector. A large number of farmers in India depend on animal husbandry for their livelihood.

The major plantation crops include coconut, areca nut, oil palm, cashew, tea, coffee and rubber; the minor plantation crops include cocoa. Their total coverage is comparatively less and they are mostly confined to small holdings. Transport in the Republic of India is an important part of India's economy. Since the economic liberalisation of the 1990s, development of infrastructure within the country has progressed at a rapid pace, and today there is a wide variety of modes of transport by land, water and air.

The Mining industry in India is a major economic activity which contributes significantly to the economy of India. The GDP contribution of the mining industry varies from 2.2 to 2.5 per cent only but going by the GDP of the total industrial sector it contributes around 10 to 11 per cent. Foreign trade in India includes all imports and exports to and from India. At the level of Central Government it is administered by the Ministry of Commerce and Industry. Prior to the 1991 economic liberalisation, India was a closed economy due to the average tariffs exceeding 200 per cent and the extensive quantitative restrictions on imports. The Twelfth Plan intends to continue its thrust on accelerating the pace of investment in infrastructure as this is critical for sustaining and accelerating growth.

## References


1. *Economic history of India*, Retrieved from http://en.wikipedia.org/wiki/Economic_history_of_India.
2. *Economy of The Republic of India*, Retrieved from http://www.capitalco.com.au/Portals/0/Docs/Economic_Data/Economy%20of%20India.pdf
3. *Economy of India*, Retrieved from http://simple.wikipedia.org/wiki/Economy_of_India
4. *Indian economy*, Retrieved from http://www.mapsofindia.com/india-economy.html
5. *Agriculture,* Retrieved from http://india.gov.in/topics/agriculture.
6. *Agriculture in India*, Retrieved from http://www.kish.in/agriculture-in-india/
7. *Agriculture in India,* Retrieved from http://www.nios.ac.in/media/documents/SecSocSciCour/English/Lesson-12.pdf
8. See http://aquaponicsinindia.com/tag/types-of-agriculture-in-india/
9. *Different Types of Farming in India*, Retrieved from http://dilipchandra12.hubpages.com/hub/Types-of-Farming-in-India
10. *What is the importance of Agriculture for our country?* See http://www.preservearticles.com/201107169225/what-is-the-importance-of-agriculture-for-our-country.html
11. *India Industry*, Retrieved from http://business.mapsofindia.com/india-industry/
12. *Industries in India*, Retrieved from http://business.mapsofindia.com/india-industry/industries.html
13. See http://india.gov.in/topics/industries
14. *Automotive industry in India*, Retrieved from http://en.wikipedia.org/wiki/Automotive_industry_in_India.
15. *Textile industry in India*, Retrieved from http://en.wikipedia.org/wiki/Textile_industry_in_India.

16. *5 Sectors on a Hiring Spree (2011)*, Retrieved from http://businesstoday.intoday.in/story/retail-infrastructure-healthcare-sectors-to-hire-more-in-india/1/19528.html
17. *Medium and Large Industries,* Retrieved from http://www.spc.tn.gov.in/tenthplan/CH_10_1.PDF
18. See http://www.gujaratindia.com/business/major-indus.htm
19. See http://www.dcmsme.gov.in/ssiindia/performance.htm
20. *Ministry of Small Scale Industries*, Retrieved from http://en.wikipedia.org/wiki/Ministry_of_Small_Scale_Industries.
21. *The role of small scale industry in reduction of poverty in India*, Retrieved from http://www.indiastat.com/article/49/mallika/full%20text.pdf
22. Girish Sethi and Prosanto Pal, *Energy Efficiency in Small Scale Industries-An Indian Perspective,* Retrieved from http://www.cosmile.org/papers/general_energyefficiencysmallscaleindustriesperspective.PDF
23. *Steel Industry in India*, Retrieved from http://www.ibef.org/industry/steel.aspx
24. *Animal husbandry*, Retrieved from http://india.gov.in/topics/agriculture/animal-husbandry.
25. *Animal husbandry and dairying, chapter 5.2,* Retrieved from http://planningcommission.nic.in/plans/planrel/fiveyr/10th/volume2/v2_ch5_2.pdf
26. *Complete information on Animal Husbandry in India*, Retrieved from http://www.preservearticles.com/2012020322595/complete-information-on-animal-husbandry-in-india.html
27. *Animal Husbandry and Dairying*, Retrieved from http://business.gov.in/agriculture/animal.php
28. *Plantation crops,* Retrieved from http://www.archive.india.gov.in/sectors/agriculture/index.php?id=24
29. *Plantation Crops*, Retrieved from http://business.gov.in/agriculture/plantation_crops.php
30. *History of tea in India*, Retrieved from http://en.wikipedia.org/wiki/History_of_tea_in_India
31. *Assam tea,* Retrieved from http://en.wikipedia.org/wiki/Assam_tea
32. *5 Places to Visit India Tea Plantations*, Retrieved from http://goindia.about.com/od/topdestinations/tp/5-Best-India-Tea-Gardens.htm
33. See http://www.nkgjayanti.com/productsandgradesfromindia
34. See http://www.indiacoffee.org/Pasupathi/Coffee%20Cultivation%20Guide%20-%20Coffee%20Kaipidi.pdf
35. See http://www.walkthroughindia.com/location/top-10-major-coffee-and-tea-plantation-regions-in-india/

36. *Cultivation of Cotton and Jute in India,* See http://www.importantindia.com/4405/cultivation-of-jute-and-cotton-in-india/

37. *Jute cultivation,* Retrieved from http://en.wikipedia.org/wiki Jute_cultivation

38. *Business Standard (July 6, 2014)*, Assam Rubber Board to bring 12,500 hectares under plantation, Retrieved from http://www.business-standard.com/article/markets/assam-rubber-board-to-bring-12-500-hectares-under-plantation-111082500070_1.html

39. *Transport in India*, Retrieved from http://en.wikipedia.org/wiki/Transport_in_India.

40. *India Transport Sector*, Retrieved from http://web.worldbank.org/WBSITE/EXTERNAL/COUNTRIES/SOUTHASIAEXT/EXTSARREGTOPTRANSPORT/0,,contentMDK:20703625~menuPK:868822~pagePK:34004173~piPK:34003707~theSitePK:579598,00.html

41. *India Infrastructure*, Retrieved from http://www.mapsofindia.com/infrastructure/

42. *Transport in India*, Retrieved from https://www.princeton.edu/~achaney/tmve/wiki100k/docs/Transport_in_India.html

43. *India: Policies and Initiatives,* Retrieved from http://embarqindia.org/node 99

44. *Mining in India*, Retrieved from http://en.wikipedia.org/wiki/Mining_in_India.

45. *Coal Mining in India: The Past*, Retrieved from http://www.coal.nic.in/abtcoal.htm

46. *Development of Indian Mining Industry–The Way Forward (2013)*, Retrieved from http://www.ficci.com/spdocument/20317/Mining-Industry.pdf

47. *Mining in India,* Retrieved from http://www.cseindia.org/userfiles/Mining_India.pdf

48. *The Economic Times (Sep 28, 2013),* Tamil Nadu, Andhra Pradesh sitting on bed of diamonds: Report, See http://articles.economictimes.indiatimes.com/2013-09-28/news/42481579_1_diamond-traders-diamond-mining-biggest-diamond

49. See http://www.portal.gsi.gov.in/portal/page?_pageid=127,721726&_dad=portal&_schema=PORTAL

50. See http://www.crnindia.com/commodity/silver.html

51. The Times of India (August 12, 2011), Rich platinum deposits found in state, says GSI, Retrieved from http://timesofindia.indiatimes.com/city/bhubaneswar/Rich-platinum-deposits-found-in-state-says-GSI/articleshow/9571424.cms

52. See http://www.commodityonline.com/news/platinum-deposits-found-in-tamil-nadu-29647-3-29648.html.

53. R. Gupta and A. K. Sarangi, Emerging trends in uranium mining: The Indian scenario, Presented in the IAEA symposium on *"Uranium production and raw materials for the nuclear fuel cycle-Supply and demand, economics, the environment and energy security"*, Vienna; Jun. 20-24, 2005
54. See http://www.wise-uranium.org/upin.html
55. See http://www.pwc.com/gx/en/capital-projects-infrastructure/assets/gridlines-india-article-2013.pdf
56. Foreign trade in India, Retrieved from http://en.wikipedia.org/wiki/Foreign_trade_of_India.
57. See http://en.wikipedia.org/wiki/List_of_the_largest_trading_partners_of_India.
58. See http://ec.europa.eu/trade/policy/countries-and-regions/countries/india/
59. See http://business.gov.in/trade/index.php
60. See http://commerce.nic.in/flac/maj_item.htm
61. *The Economic Times (Jul 4, 2014),* India heavily dependent on drug imports from China: Study, See http://articles.economictimes.indiatimes.com/2014-07-04/news/51076494_1_essential-drugs-drug-imports-clinical-trials
62. *India Imports*, See http://www.tradingeconomics.com/india/imports
63. *Banking in India*, Retrieved from http://en.wikipedia.org/wiki/Banking_in_India.
64. See http:// india.gov.in/topics/infrastructure
65. *Infrastructure in India: A vast land of construction opportunity*, Retrieved from https://www.pwc.in/en_IN/in/assets/pdfs/infrastructure-in-india.pdf
66. Geethanjali Nataraj, *Infrastructure Challenges in India: The Role of Public-Private Partnerships*, Retrieved from http://iegindia.org/wshop2526july/paper5.pdf
67. See http://theindianeconomist.com/infrastructure-in-india-problems-and-solutions/
68. *Economy of The Republic of India*, Retrieved from http://www.capitalco.com.au/Portals/0/Docs/Economic_Data/Economy%20of%20India.pdf
69. *The Hindu (Oct 4, 2013),* India, a top destination for global remittances, Retrieved from http://www.thehindu.com/todays-paper/tp-business/india-a-top-destination-for-global-remittances/article5198897.ece
70. *The Times of India (Oct 3, 2013)*, India tops global chart of remittances, Retrieved from http://timesofindia.indiatimes.com/india/India-tops-global-chart-of-remittances/articleshow/23457369.cmshttp://timesofindia.indiatimes.com/india/India-tops-global-chart-of-remittances/articleshow/23457369.cms

# Chapter - 11

# Foreign Direct Investment in South Asia

*"All those predictions about how much economic growth will be created by this, all of those new jobs, would be created by the things we wanted-the extension of unemployment insurance and middle class tax cuts. An estate tax for millionaires adds exactly zero jobs. A tax cut for billionaires-virtually none."*

***—Anthony Weiner***

## Introduction

Foreign direct investment is a measure of foreign ownership of productive assets, such as factories, mines and land. Increasing foreign investment can be used as one measure of growing economic globalisation. It was proven to be a significant source of investment for developing countries which helps to bridge saving-investment gap, creation of employment opportunities, transfer of technology, and ultimately increasing economic growth of the host countries. It is important to ensure an attractive investment climate. Consistent macroeconomic policies, good governance, economic stability, guarantee of property rights, rule of law and absence of corruption are among the conditions required to attract FDI.

Foreign investment comes in several forms. Portfolio investment, foreign loans and foreign direct investment are the three important types. Of these foreign direct investments in industry and services are the most useful. Foreign loans are generally used for investment in infrastructure. There are two types of FDI: inward foreign direct investment and outward foreign direct investment, resulting in a net FDI inflow (positive or negative) and "stock of foreign direct investment", which is the cumulative number for a given period. Direct investment excludes investment through purchase of shares. FDI is one example of international factor movements.

## Importance of Foreign Direct Investment

Economic growth leads to foreign direct investment due to the fact that higher levels of economic growth will be attained through efficiency of use of resources, which reduces cost per unit of output, and it creates market for the output produced. It leads to foreign direct investment due to the fact that as the market size of the host country increases with a high rate of economic growth, resulting from the expected higher level of profitability. Foreign Direct Investment helps in the growth of the economy of the country by developing the competitive markets with more advanced and modified international industries and also provides the chance to learn and experience the new technologies in an international environment which capable and recognise the employees internationally.

It provides jobs opportunities, management skills, and new technology besides bridging the gaps between saving and investment. FDI can be a source of valuable technology and know-how while fostering linkages with local firms, which can help jumpstart an economy. Based on these arguments, industrialised and developing countries have offered incentives to encourage foreign direct investments in their economies.

## Foreign Direct Investment in Bangladesh

Despite being a recent phenomenon, several underlying factors have contributed to increasing the FDI inflow in Bangladesh, such as trade and exchange liberalisation, current account convertibility, emphasis on private sector led development, liberalisation of the investment regime, opening up of infrastructure and services to the private sector-both domestic and foreign, and above all the interest of foreign investors in energy and telecommunication sector. Overall, FDI has a positive impact on economic growth but the magnitude of the effect depends on the availability of complementary resources, especially on the domestic stock of human capital.

The central bank's data showed that net FDI inflows were recorded at \$673 million during the five months starting from July, as against

$664 million in the same period last fiscal. Net FDI inflows in the country in 2012-13 FY (July 2012-June 2013) stood at $1.47 billion, as against $1.19 billion in 2011-12 fiscal year. FDI inflow to Bangladesh has traditionally been lower, even compared with other South Asian countries. The consecutive failures of attracting the FDI and even meeting the targets should not be taken casually. The dual targets of maintaining growth and controlling inflation may be affected in near future if the consumption growth and overall investment growth continue with these declining trends of FDI. These two important factors can make Bangladesh an alluring destination for foreign investors. Lowest wage rates among the Asian countries, tolerable inflation rate, reasonably stable (except previous year) exchange rate, investment friendly custom regulations and attractive incentive packages make Bangladesh a favourable investment destination.

## Foreign Direct Investment in Sri Lanka

The current total in FDI is a 41 per cent increase over the corresponding period of the past year. The port sector has received 19 per cent, telecom 17 per cent and property development has garnered 13 per cent out of the total FDI during the first three quarters of 2013. China ranks as the single biggest investor bringing in 24 per cent of the total investments. Hong Kong follows with 12 per cent, Singapore with 10 per cent, Netherlands eight per cent, Malaysia and UK bringing in seven per cent, each, and India with five per cent.

Gateway Industries, a firm that has been given approval to develop a heavy industrial zone in Trincomalee in Eastern Sri Lanka has also invested 20 million US dollars and has started building a jetty. The government is looking forward to build several new investment zones in the island. Sri Lanka will sign $2 billion worth foreign direct investment deals, including the $1.3 billion investment from China Communications Construction Co. Ltd to build a port city. The country missed many opportunities to attract foreign investments in industry owing to the ethnic conflict.

## Foreign Direct Investment in Maldives

More than 950,000 tourists visit annually, forming the backbone of the economy. The Government of the Maldives has aggressively promoted building new island resorts, and an additional 14 islands are expected to be leased out in 2013. Foreign investments have primarily involved resort management, but also include telecommunications, accounting, banking, insurance, air transport, courier services, and some manufacturing. The Ministry of Economic Development is tasked with promoting and regulating foreign investments in all sectors, except for the tourism sector.

Foreign investment in Maldives is governed by Law No. 25/79, governing agreements between the government and investors. Foreign direct investment, net inflows in Maldives was 13.73 as of 2011. Its highest value over the past 31 years was 13.73 in 2011, while its lowest value was -6.01 in 1982. United Nations Conference on Trade and Development has stated that Maldives had a total of $284 million in Foreign Direct Investment in 2012, an increase of 11 per cent compared to 2011.

## Foreign Direct Investment in Pakistan

FDI has been on the decline since 2008 in the wake of security concerns, weak law and order situation and energy and power outages in the country. The oil and gas exploration sector emerged as the biggest recipient of FDI with $296.2 million, followed by the financial sector with $102.8 million in the July-February period in FY14. Foreign investment in food, chemical and tobacco and cigarette sectors was recorded at $75.1 million, $71.6 million and $55.5 million, respectively. The level of FDI is still too low to have much of an impact on the country's financial account. Foreign portfolio investment at the Karachi Stock Exchange is encouraging despite no listing of new companies at the local equity market.

Foreign direct investment, net outflows in Pakistan was 0.03 as of 2011. Its highest value over the past six years was 0.09 in 2006, while its lowest value was 0.03 in 2010. Foreign direct investment, net inflows in Pakistan was 0.62 as of 2011. Its highest value over the past 41 years was 3.90 in 2007, while its lowest value was -0.06 in 1973. Pakistan received $416 million in foreign direct investment in the first half of the current 2013/14 fiscal year compared with $568.8 million received during the same period a year earlier. In December 2013, foreign direct investment fell to $85.4 million year-on-year from $253 million in the same month of 2012. Foreign Private Investment (Promotion and Protection) Act, 1976 and the Furtherance and

Protection of Economic Reforms Act, 1992 provide legal cover for protection of foreign investors/investment in Pakistan.

## Foreign Direct Investment in Afghanistan

Afghanistan is strategically located between the energy rich republics of Central Asia and the major seaports in South Asia providing a key transit route for central Asian oil and gas to markets in South Asia as well as overseas. The Government of the Islamic Republic of Afghanistan recognises that the development of a vibrant private sector is crucial to the reconstruction of an economy ravaged by decades of conflict and mismanagement.

The newly established High Economic Council, chaired by the president and including ministers as well as representatives from academia and the private sector may play an increasing role in investment policy development. In general, investments may be 100 per cent foreign-owned and there is no requirement for foreigners to secure an Afghan partner. However, the Afghan Constitution and the PIL prohibit foreign ownership of land, which compels most foreign firms to work with an Afghan partner. Afghanistan's legal and regulatory frameworks and enforcement mechanisms are nascent.

## Foreign Direct Investment in Nepal

For a least developed-country like Nepal with huge saving-investment gap; limited, albeit growing, revenue to gross domestic product ratio; and limited amount of foreign aid flow, foreign direct investment is considered an indispensible mode of development financing. Nepal's Ministry of Industry that is holding talks in regards to raising the FDI threshold with the stakeholders said that the move was planned to control low-level foreign investors whose interest is not to establish industries genuinely but to prolong their stay in Nepal for whatsoever interests.

The move is aimed at encouraging quality investment and attracts genuine investors. Nepal has been accentuating foreign investment by dislodging the control on foreign investment and furnishing a number of facilities. The Foreign Investment and Technology Transfer Act 1992, which was amended in 2000, enacted in line with open and liberal economic strategies. The intent of the Act was to invite and bring in foreign investment in the form of equity participation, direct investment in domestic production, reinvestment of the earnings gleaned from such investment and transfer of technology, inter alia. Additionally, the Act stipulated that industries established with foreign investment were also qualified to enjoy all the services and inducements plus income tax facilities provided to domestic investors under the Industrial Enterprises Act 1992.

The new Industrial Policy 2010 was created to replace the Industrial Policy of 1992 with the primary objective of attracting domestic and foreign investments by improving the industrial environment, increasing industrial production and productivity, creating more employment opportunities, substituting imports through the promotion of export-based industries, and improving Nepal's balance of payment by minimising the trade deficit. The Industrial Infrastructure Development Programme was brought into effect in 2008-09 in order to develop Nepal's physical infrastructure, establish and operate feasible industries, and promote an investment-friendly environment for industrialists and entrepreneurs. The Industrial Policy, 2010 was created to bring about positive changes in the overall economic and social sectors of the country through speedy industrial development.

## Foreign Direct Investment in Bhutan

Bhutan is keen to attract Indian investors in areas like generation of hydel power, information and communication technology, hospitality, agriculture and infrastructure. Primarily, Bhutanese industries have been affected by low levels of productivity and this is clearly related to the lack of technological development and low levels of human capital. FDI and joint ventures are some of the mechanisms that must be actively promoted to help jump start the process.

Foreign Direct Investment over the Ninth Plan showed a positive growth trend but has largely been directed exclusive into the hospitality sector and has stagnated of late. The share of FDI in the GDP of Bhutan remains relatively low compared to other developing countries. Geographical factors hold back the region; the country is hemmed in and very mountainous, which makes infrastructure construction very difficult and costly. In the present scenario, Bhutan has about 40 FDI applications out of that around 14 are from India, many of them are already in operation. Bhutan and India traditionally have enjoyed a very special relationship which is based on trust, India truly recognises Bhutan as very special partner in development and growth with equity.

## Foreign Direct Investment in India

Mauritius has been one of the biggest sources of FDI into India, which attracted inflows of $78.15 billion FDI from that country between April 2000 and February 2014. Mauritius accounts for 37 per cent of the country's total foreign direct investment. Foreign investments are crucial for India, which needs about $1 trillion by March 2017 to overhaul infrastructure such as ports, airports and highways and boost growth. Foreign direct investment into India grew for the second consecutive month in February in 2014 to $2.01 billion, up 12.29 per cent. In February 2013, the FDI was at $1.79 billion according to the data by the Department of Industrial Policy and Promotion. Foreign direct investment to India declined marginally by 0.6 per cent to $20.76 billion in the first 11 months of the 2013-14 financial years ended March 31.

Investments in the services sector, which includes banking, insurance, research and development and outsourcing among others, dipped by 54 per cent to $2.18 billion during April-February period of the last fiscal. In order to strengthen bilateral economic relations, India has allowed foreign direct investment from Pakistan. Without engaging with Pakistan, South Asia Free Trade Agreement cannot move forward. To allow investments from Pakistan, the Department of Industrial Policy and Promotion had sent a proposal to Finance Ministry for changes in Foreign Exchange Management Act. In a move that will strengthen commercial ties between India and Pakistan, Reserve Bank of India has permitted foreign direct investment from Pakistan into India which had been banned hitherto. The central bank added that this notification overrides the earlier regulation under the foreign exchange management act which bars citizens of Pakistan or any entity incorporated outside India in Pakistan from purchasing shares or bonds of an Indian company under the foreign direct investment scheme.

### *Multi-Brand Retail Sector*

The 51 per cent foreign direct investment in multi-brand retail is likely to include foreign portfolio investment as well, as the government is keen to ensure that the restriction on foreign ownership is not breached. The government is wary that any breach in the limit will give more fodder to those opposed to opening of the sector to foreign investors, a hard fought reform for the UPA government that lost some key allies on the issue. There will be a composite 51 per cent cap for both FDI and FII investment in multi-brand retail.

Under the current rules, investment by foreign institutional investors can go up to 24 per cent in a listed company and can be further raised with a shareholder resolution to up to the sectoral limit cap. Amazon may be fighting tooth and nail with its brick-and-mortar counterparts such as Wal-Mart and Tesco in the West, but in India it has laid the green carpet for Indian retail chains for its just-launched online marketplace. The world's largest online retailer plans to enter into selling partnership with many leading retail chains, including Future Group, Shoppers Stop, Crossword, Viveks, UniverCell, Spencer's Retail and Woodland, to sell their wares through the Amazon India marketplace.

Walmart Stores Inc, the world's largest supermarket, looks set to become the first foreign company to invest in multi-brand retail by buying a 49 per cent stake in Cedar Support Service, the holding company for Bharti Retail, for ₹ 455.8 crore. Wal-mart will convert compulsory convertible debentures, purchased in March 2010, into 42.6 crore equity shares, according to internal documents detailing the venture's future plans that were reviewed by ET. India's decision to allow foreign direct investment in multi-brand retail towards the end of 2012 and its FDI policy modified in April 2013 put the country back on the retailing map of the world. In 1997, the government approved 100 per cent FDI in *"cash and carry"* wholesale stores under the automatic route and, in 2006, 51 per cent FDI was allowed in single-brand retailing, although with prior approval from the government.

### *Pharmaceutical Sector*

The Reserve Bank said the non-compete clause will not be applicable in acquisition of existing pharma companies by foreign entities or investors except in certain special cases. India allows 100 per cent FDI in pharma sector. While FDI is permitted through automatic route in case of Greenfield investment or new venture, government approval is required in case of Brownfield or existing companies.

### *Indian Railway*

The department of industrial policy and promotion will push for a decision on foreign direct investment in railways before the general elections are announced after putting in a mechanism to address concerns raised by the home ministry. The Ministry of Commerce and Industry has sought approval of the Election Commission of India to move ahead with its proposal to liberalise the overseas investment policy in railways. The Cabinet can take a decision on the matter only after the Election Commission's approval. The Department of Industrial Policy and Promotion under the ministry has proposed to relax the foreign direct investment policy in certain railway sectors.

The DIPP proposes to allow 100 per cent FDI in high-speed train systems, suburban corridors, high-speed tracks and freight lines connecting ports and mines. For 2012- 13, railways posted a loss of about 26,000 crore. Main earnings of the railways come from its freight operations which cross subsidies the losses on running passenger trains. Goods trains are made to wait to let passenger trains pass as there are not enough tracks to accommodate such a large number of trains. India has the world's fifth largest rail network, after US, Russia, Canada and China. However, it is lagging behind the others and has deteriorated over the years due to heavy congestion of the tracks and the failure to modernise.

### *Shipping Industry*

Thirteen years after India allowed 100 per cent foreign direct investment in shipping. The Indian flag suffers from certain barriers in terms of tax and duty structures which have impeded the flow of FDI into the shipping sector. Global fleet-owners say that India is not a commercially viable place to register ships. India adopted a globally followed taxation system for the shipping industry in 2004 by introducing a tax based on the cargo carrying capacity of ships. Besides, Indian-registered ships lack government policy support or preference to carry Indian cargo. The government does not offer any kind of premium to Indian-registered ships for carrying Indian cargo.

### *Telecom Industry*

The Telecom Commission has approved the enhancement of the foreign direct investment limit in the telecom sector from 74 per cent to 100 per cent. The cumulative FDI between 2000 and 2012 was ₹ 57079 crore or nearly $10 billion. By improving connectivity through the highest quality of connectivity and competition, it will further empower the aam aadmi of the country in a meaningful manner. The National Telecom Policy 1994 allowed up to 49 per cent FDI in telecom services. India's mobile sector not just flourished, but also became one of the largest sources for attracting global FDI between 1994 and 2013. The FDI peaked during 2007-2010, and then declined sharply from ₹ 12,270 crore in 2009-10 to ₹ 7,542 crore in 2011.

### *Food Processing Sector*

The potentials of food processing industry are looking very promising to investors. Many large foreign players have already entered into the Indian food processing scenario by merging with prominent domestic players. It is anticipated that this trend will rise more strongly in the next couple of years. It provides an excellent opportunity to the local players in extending their product portfolios. FDI complements and adds to domestic investments. Besides capital, it brings in the latest knowledge, skills, and professionalism, thus allowing for the growth of technologies.

Government has taken steps to encourage FDI and one of the significant measures was declaring the Food Processing Sector under 100 per cent FDI through automatic route. The extant policy permits FDI under the automatic route, inter alia, Food Processing Industries. Foreign Direct Investment also brings new products, new technology and improved quality in the Food Processing Sector resulting in reduction in wastage of agri products, safe and hygienic foods, higher employment and also enhancing export potential of processed foods.

### *Steel Industry*

According to the Ministry of Steel, Steel producers have signed 222 MOU's with various states for a planned capacity of about 275.7 million tonnes in 2009-10. Indian investment policy stipulates 100 per cent foreign direct investment through the automatic route in the Indian steel sector. Some of the initiatives taken by the government to promote the steel sector include National Steel Policy 2005, which seeks to facilitate the removal of procedural and policy bottlenecks that affect the availability of production inputs, increased investment in research and development, and the creation of road, railway and port infrastructure. Moreover, in order to encourage R&D activities in iron and steel sector, Ministry of Steel is providing financial assistance from Steel Development Fund and Plan Fund.

### *Cement Industry*

In 1989, industry was considered to be prepared for free market competition and all price and distribution controls were withdrawn. The cement sector was liberalised and today 100 per cent FDI is permitted in the cement industry.[68] In the past decade, there was a wave of consolidation in the Indian cement industry. A number of large mergers and acquisitions were witnessed. In most cases, global companies have acquired regional players. Grasim as a part of Aditya Birla Group acquired a controlling stake in Ultratech Cement from L&T in 2004. In the same year, Holcim acquired 40-45 per cent stake in Gujarat Ambuja Cements and ACC. Recently, Grasim merged into Ultratech to create a single entity.

### *Defence Sector*

The government's decision to let the Cabinet Committee on Security clear FDI proposals beyond 26 per cent in the defence sector technically leaves it open for CCS to even allow 100 per cent foreign investment. Indian companies keen on foreign tie-ups include L&T, Mahindra & Mahindra and the Tatas. US firm Lockheed Martin is understood to be interested in collaboration with the Tatas. India Inc cheered the changes. Large number of sectors has either seen an increase in FDI cap or has moved under the automatic route from the Foreign Investment Promotion Board approval. The government deferred a decision on increasing the cap in civil aviation from 49 per cent to 74 per cent as said FDI could wait as there were no interested parties waiting in the wings.

### *Civil Aviation Sector*

Foreign Direct Investment of 49 per cent in aviation is the single most important policy decision that would transform the country's civil aviation sector. Various policy measures taken by the government had begun to yield results and hoped that the general aviation business would emerge as an important player of regional connectivity and economic development. The government liberalised grant of traffic rights to Indian carriers to boost international air travel. Indian government expects investment of USD 12.1 billion during the Twelfth Plan Period, of which USD 9.3 billion is expected to come from the private sector.

### *Insurance Sector*

The government has clarified that the 26 per cent cap on foreign investments in the insurance sector applies to intermediaries such as brokers, third party administrators and surveyors. In the case of insurance companies, the 26 per cent cap will include foreign direct investment, foreign institutional investments (FIIs) and investments from non-resident Indians (NRIs).

The earlier policy only talked about allowing 26 per cent FDI in the insurance sector without elaborating on what activities were covered under the cap and how FII and NRI investments were to be treated. India's insurance regulator has set up a committee to study the option of allowing 100 per cent FDI in insurance intermediaries, third-party administrators, surveyors and loss assessors.

### *Banking Sector*

The aggregate foreign investment (FDI, FII and NRI) cannot exceed 74 per cent in private sector banks while the ceiling is at 20 per cent for nationalised banks, State Bank of India and its associate banks. As regards the FDI limit in insurance sector, the government introduced the Insurance Laws Amendment Bill, 2008 in Parliament to increase it from 26 per cent to 49 per cent. The penetration of life insurance in India has increased from 2.15 per cent in 2001 to 3.17 per cent in 2017 which is above Brazil, Russia, Malaysia, Pakistan, China, Sri Lanka, Australia and Germany.

Reforms were introduced in the banking sector to strength Indian banks and make them internationally competitive and banks to play a vital role in the economic development of the country. The banking sector was opened up for private participation and the entry of new private banks increased competition. The efficiency of the banking sector improved as suggested by indicators such as gradual in cost of intermediation and decline in nonperforming loans.

### *Automobile Industry*

FDI in automotive industry was permitted. In 1993, it was also allowed in the passenger car segment. It inflows to Automobile Industry have been at an increasing rate as India has witnessed a major economic liberalisation over the years in terms of various industries. The Indian auto industry has been recording tremendous growth over the years and has emerged as a major contributor to India's gross domestic product. The cumulative foreign direct investment inflows into the Indian automobile industry during the period April 2000 to January 2014 was recorded at US$ 9,344 million, an increase of four per cent to the total FDI inflows in terms of US$, according to data published by Department of Industrial Policy and Promotion, Government of India.

### *Indian Airport*

Government allowed 100 per cent foreign investment in power trading, development of Greenfield airports and infrastructure creation for petroleum marketing. In addition, the Cabinet also decided to permit 100 per cent FDI in captive mining of coal and lignite, laying of natural gas and LNG pipelines, besides exploration of diamonds and other precious stones. These investments will now be permitted through the automatic route and investors will not be required to approach FIPB for prior permission to set up Indian ventures. At present, 74 per cent FDI is permitted in the development of new airports, while no foreign investment was allowed in electricity trading.

### *Agriculture Sector*

India government has permitted FDI up to 100 per cent, under the automatic route, subject to certain conditions mentioned in Consolidated FDI Policy, in the agricultural activities like as floriculture, horticulture, apiculture and cultivation of vegetables and mushrooms under controlled conditions; development and production of seeds and planting material; animal husbandry (including breeding of dogs), pisciculture, aquaculture, under controlled conditions; and services related to agro and allied sectors. Hundred per cent FDI is also permitted in tea sector.

## Conclusion

Foreign direct investment is a measure of foreign ownership of productive assets, such as factories, mines and land. It helps in the growth of the economy of the country by developing the competitive markets with more advanced and modified international industries and also provides the chance to learn and experience the new technologies in an international environment which capable and recognise the employees internationally. It provides jobs opportunities, management skills, and new technology besides bridging the gaps between saving and investment. Mauritius has been one of the biggest sources of FDI into India, which attracted inflows of $78.15 billion FDI from that country between April 2000 and February 2014. Mauritius accounts for 37 per cent of the country's total foreign direct investment.

The 51 per cent foreign direct investment in multi-brand retail is likely to include foreign portfolio investment as well, as the government is keen to ensure that the restriction on foreign ownership is not breached. India allows 100 per cent FDI in pharma sector. India allowed 100 per cent foreign direct investment in shipping. The Telecom Commission has approved the enhancement of the foreign direct investment limit in the telecom sector from 74 per cent to 100 per cent. Government has taken steps to encourage FDI and one of the significant measures was declaring the Food Processing Sector under 100 per cent FDI through automatic route.

Indian investment policy stipulates 100 per cent foreign direct investment through the automatic route in the Indian steel sector. The cement sector was liberalised and today 100 per cent FDI is permitted in the cement industry. The government's decision to let the Cabinet Committee on Security clear FDI proposals beyond 26 per cent in the defence sector technically leaves it open for CCS to even allow 100 per cent foreign investment. Indian companies keen on foreign tie-ups include L and T, Mahindra and Mahindra and the Tatas. Indian government has permitted FDI up to 100 per cent, under the automatic route, subject to certain conditions mentioned in Consolidated FDI Policy, in the agricultural activities.

## References

1. *100 per cent FDI, but nine shipping companies leave India,* Retrieved from http://www.sunday-guardian.com/news/100-fdi-but-nine-shipping-companies-leave-india.
2. *2013 Investment Climate Statement–Maldives*, Retrieved from http://www.state.gov/e/eb/rls/othr/ics/2013/204687.htm

3. *2013 Investment Climate Statement*, Retrieved from http://www.state.gov/e/eb/rls/othr/ics/2013/205289.htm
4. *49 per cent FDI can transform Indian aviation sector: Civil Aviation Minister*, Retrieved from http://www.travelbizmonitor.com/49-fdi-can-transform-indian-aviation-sector-civil-aviation-minister-19737
5. Atri Mukherjee, *Regional Inequality in Foreign Direct Investment Flows to India: The Problem and the Prospects,* Retrieved from http://www.rbi.org.in/scripts/bs_viewcontent.aspx?Id=2597
6. *Automobile Industry in India (2014).* Retrieved from http://www.ibef.org/industry/india-automobiles.aspx
7. *Bangladesh Economic Update Foreign Direct Investment (FDI)* February 2012, Retrieved from http://www.unnayan.org/documents/Governance%20Capability/MEU_Feb_2012_FDI.pdf
8. *Bhutan and India Talk FDI*, Retrieved from http://www.thebhutanese.bt/bhutan-and-india-talk-fdi-2/
9. *Bhutan: Foreign Investment*, Retrieved from https://en.santandertrade.com/establish-overseas/bhutan/investing-3?&actualiser_id_banque=oui&id_banque=0&memoriser_choix=memoriser
10. *Business Line (Feb 5, 2014).* Govt clarifies policy on FDI in insurance, Retrieved from http://www.thehindubusinessline.com/economy/macro-economy/govt-clarifies-policy-on-fdi-in-insurance/article5657432.ece
11. *Business Standard (March 13, 2013).* Govt has set norms for attracting FDI for development of airports: Ajit Singh to LS, Retrieved from http://www.business-standard.com/article/economy-policy/govt-has-set-norms-for-attracting-fdi-for-development-of-airports-ajit-singh-to-ls-113031300200_1.html
12. *Business Standard (March 13, 2014).* FDI in railways: Comm Min seeks EC approval, Retrieved from http://www.business-standard.com/article/elections-2014/fdi-in-railways-comm-min-seeks-ec-approval-114031300925_1.html
13. *Business Standard (May 11, 2014).* Foreign investments to India will surge if Modi becomes PM, Retrieved from http://www.business-standard.com/article/news-ians/foreign-investments-to-india-will-surge-if-modi-becomes-pm-114051100329_1.html
14. *Business Today (Jan 29, 2014).* India received $28 bn FDI in 2013: UNCTAD, Retrieved from http://businesstoday.intoday.in/story/india-received-fdi-flow-in-2013-unctad/1/202804.html
15. *Consolidating the Cement Industry – Brick by Brick*, Retrieved from http://iimaconsulting.wordpress.com/tag/fdi/
16. *Diplomatic missions promoting Nepal for FDIs*, Retrieved from http://www.thehimalayantimes.com/fullNews.php?headline=Diplomatic+missions+promoting+Nepal+for+FDIs&NewsID=414278&a=3

17. Dr S Rameshkumar and Dr C U Tripura Sundari, *Causal nexus between foreign direct investment and economic growth in SAARC countries*, Retrieved from http://aisc-india.in/AISC2013_web/papers/papers_final/paper_136.pdf

18. Dr N. K. Sathya Pal Sharma and Professor Krishna B. S. (2013). Role of FDI in Banking, in generating wealth to Indian Economy, *International Journal of Advancements in Research & Technology*, Volume 2, Issue 5, Retrieved from http://www.ijoart.org/docs/Role-of-FDI-in-Banking-in-generating-wealth-to-Indian-Economy.pdf

19. Erum Zaidi (March 15, 2014). *FDI rises by 17 per cent in eight months,* Retrieved from http://www.thenews.com.pk/Todays-News-3-238245-FDI-rises-by-17-percent-in-eight-months.

20. *FDI Opportunities in the Indian Renewable Energy Sector*, Retrieved from http://nexusnovus.com/fdi-opportunities-renewable-energy-sector-india

21. *Food Processing*, Retrieved from http://www.investindia.gov.in/?q=food-processing-sector.

22. *Foreign Direct Investment (FDI) in Pakistan*, Retrieved from http://masoodandmasood.com/foreign-direct-investment-fdi-pakistan-law-lawyer-consultant-help/

23. *Foreign Direct Investment in Nepal: Current status, prospects and challenges*, Working Paper No. 01/13, South Asia Watch on Trade, Economics and Environment, Retrieved from http://www.sawtee.org/Research_Reports/R2013-01.pdf

24. *Foreign direct investment: Constraints and challenges*, Retrieved from http://www.thehimalayantimes.com/fullNews.php?headline=Foreign+direct+investment%3A+Constraints+and+challenges+&NewsID=401954

25. *Foreign investors inject $284m into Pakistan's economy*, Retrieved from http://tribune.com.pk/story/633552/foreign-investors-inject-284m-into-pakistans-economy/

26. *Government Control & FDI in Cement in India (2011),* Retrieved from http://www.gktoday.in/government-control-fdi-in-cement-in-india/

27. *Government Encouraging FDI in Food Processing Sector*, Retrieved from http://www.pib.nic.in/newsite/erelease.aspx?relid=83658

28. *Government likely to seek 100 per cent FDI in Railways*, Retrieved from http://indiatoday.intoday.in/story/government-mulling-to-bring-100-per-cent-fdi-in-railways/1/335347.html

29. http://www.academia.edu/4177603/Determinants_of_Inflow_of_Foreign_Direct_Investment_FDI_into_Pakistan.

30. *India eyes $100 bn FDI in nuclear energy*, Retrieved from http://www.livemint.com/Politics/rwmAbGZJVUej4IoVjMrVfI/India-eyes-100-bn-FDI-in-nuclear-energy.html

31. *India opens gate to 100% FDI in select agricultural sectors,* Retrieved from http://www.commodityonline.com/news/india-opens-gate-to-100-fdi-in-select-agricultural-sectors-55895-3-55896.html
32. *India's FDI policy may lead to boom in textile sector,* Retrieved from http://www.fibre2fashion.com/news/textile-news/india/newsdetails.aspx?news_id=122623
33. *Indian states that attracted highest FDI*, Retrieved from http://www.rediff.com/business/slide-show/slide-show-1-indian-states-that-attracted-highest-fdi/20120829.htm
34. *Inflows of Foreign Direct Investment,* Retrieved from http://www.boi.gov.bd/index.php/investment-climate-info/fdi-in-bangladesh
35. *Investment Climate in Nepal,* Retrieved from http://www.investnepal.gov.np/portal/index.php?p1=content&p2=8#.U2-KpztQHFw
36. *Investment Opportunities in the Indian Food Processing Sector,* Retrieved from http://nexusnovus.com/opportunities-foreign-investments-indian-food-processing-sector.
37. *Investment opportunities, Embassy of the Maldives-Japan,* Retrieved from http://www.maldivesembassy.jp/investment-opportunities.
38. *Maldives-Foreign direct investment,* Retrieved from http://www.indexmundi.com/facts/maldives/foreign-direct-investment
39. Md. Arif Billah, *Foreign Direct Investment Scenario: Bangladesh Perspective*, Thoughts on Economics, Vol. 22, No. 01, Retrieved from http://www.ierb-bd.org/wp-content/uploads/2012/10/FDI-Arif-billah-Revised-08-03-2012.pdf
40. Md. Sajedur Rahman; and Md. Ali Ahsan (2012). Foreign Direct Investment as an Instrument for promoting Economic Development in Bangladesh, *Asian Business Review*, Volume 3, Number 4, Retrieved from http://oaji.net/articles/800-1398826336.pdf
41. Muhammad Amir Hossain, *Impact of Foreign Direct Investment on Bangladesh's Balance of Payments: Some Policy Implications,* Retrieved from http://notunprojonmo.com/wp-content/uploads/2011/07/E18-pn0805.pdf
42. *Nepali gov't plans to raise FDI threshold to 200,000 USD,* Retrieved from http://www.shanghaidaily.com/article/article_xinhua.aspx?id=217608
43. Nimal Sanderatne, *The importance of Foreign Direct Investment*, Retrieved from http://www.sundaytimes.lk/110529/Columns/eco.html
44. Nimal Sanderatne, *The importance of Foreign Direct Investment*, Retrieved from http://www.sundaytimes.lk/110529/Columns/eco.html
45. *Opportunities and Challenges-Bhutan,* Retrieved from http://www.asiatradehub.com/bhutan/industry.asp

46. *Pakistan net FDI falls 26 per cent,* Retrieved from http://www.brecorder.com/top-news/108-pakistan-top-news/154231-pakistan-net-fdi-falls-26-per cent.html

47. See http://archive.indianexpress.com/news/india-permits-fdi-from-pakistan/982460/

48. See http://www.banglanews24.com/English/detailsnews.php?nssl=b7ea447e02f21e56b1593ac87a4f7fff&nttl=1102201486444

49. See http://www.cjasr.com/volumesandissues/issued-articles/2013/100-cjasr/164-march-2013-2-3-11

50. See http://www.dnb.co.in/SMEMumbai/Textile%20overview.asp

51. See http://www.eai.in/ref/services/ime_consulting.html

52. See http://www.idsa.in/TWIR/7_1_2013_Maldives

53. See http://www.indexmundi.com/facts/pakistan/foreign-direct-investment

54. See http://www.moneycontrol.com/news/real-estate/fdimulti-brand-retail-hopeabeyance_1020882.html

55. *Sourangsu Banerji (2013). Effects of Foreign Direct Investment (FDI) in the Indian Economy,* Retrieved from http://hal.inria.fr/docs/00/84/68/25/PDF/Effects_of_Foreign_Direct_Investment_FDI_in_the_Indian_Economy.pdf

56. *Sri Lanka earns $870m in Foreign Direct Investment in 2013 (Dec 10, 2013).* Retrieved from http://www.therepublicsquare.com/business/2013/12/09/sri-lanka-receives-870-m-in-foreign-direct-investment/

57. *Sri Lanka targets US$2.5bn in FDI in 2014 (Jan 10, 2014).* Retrieved from http://www.lankabusinessonline.com/news/sri-lanka-targets-us$2.5bn-in-fdi-in-2014/41566371

58. *Sri Lanka to sign $2 bln FDI deals including port city – minister (Nov 13, 2013).* Retrieved from http://www.reuters.com/article/2013/11/13/srilanka-investments-idUSL4N0IY2L720131113

59. *Steel:* Sector Overview, *Retrieved from* http://www.investindia.gov.in/?q=steel-sector

60. *T. Rajesh and A.S. Dileep (2013).* Foreign Direct Investment in Automobile Industry, Retrieved from http://www.ijcrar.com/vol-3/T.%20Rajesh%20and%20A.S.%20Dileep.pdf

61. *The Economic Times (Apr 7, 2014).* India Inc wants BJP to reconsider stand on FDI in retail, Retrieved from http://economictimes.indiatimes.com/news/politics-and-nation/india-inc-wants-bjp-to-reconsider-stand-on-fdi-in-retail/articleshow/33398550.cms

62. *The Economic Times (April 21, 2014).* Non-compete clause for FDI in pharmaceutical companies will not be applicable: Reserve Bank of India, Retrieved from http://economictimes.indiatimes.com/industry/healthcare/biotech/pharmaceuticals/non-compete-clause-for-fdi-in-pharmaceutical-

companies-will-not-be-applicable-reserve-bank-of-india/articleshow/34057120.cms

63. *The Economic Times (June 07, 2013).* Amazon seeks tie-up with local retailers like Future Group, Shoppers Stop to boost sales, Retrieved from http://economictimes.indiatimes.com/tech/internet/amazon-seeks-tie-up-with-local-retailers-like-future-group-shoppers-stop-to-boost-sales/articleshow/20469392.cms
64. *The Economic Times (June 07, 2013).* FDI in retail: Walmart, Tesco will not be able to acquire existing retailers, Retrieved from http://economictimes.indiatimes.com/industry/services/retail/fdi-in-retail-walmart-tesco-will-not-be-able-to-acquire-existing-retailers/articleshow/20469522.cms
65. *The Economic Times (June 29, 2009).* Bhutan liberalizes FDI laws to attract Indian investors, Retrieved from http://articles.economictimes.indiatimes.com/2009-06-29/news/28456126_1_india-and-bhutan-bhutanese-hydel-power
66. *The Economic Times (March 03, 2014).* Cabinet likely to consider FDI in Railways next week, Retrieved from http://articles.economictimes.indiatimes.com/2014-03-03/news/47859621_1_fdi-proposals-dipp-foreign-investment-promotion-board
67. *The Economic Times (May 11, 2014).* FDI from Mauritius to India dips 50 per cent in April-February period , Retrieved from http://economictimes.indiatimes.com/news/economy/finance/fdi-from-mauritius-to-india-dips-50-per-cent-in-april-february-period/articleshow/34963090.cms
68. *The Economic Times (May 29, 2013).* Walmart to buy 49 per cent in holding company of Bharti Retail, Cedar Support for ₹ 455.8 cr., Retrieved from http://economictimes.indiatimes.com/industry/services/retail/walmart-to-buy-49-in-holding-company-of-bharti-retail-cedar-support-for-rs-455-8-cr/articleshow/20319850.cms
69. *The Economic Times (May 30, 2013).* 51% FDI in multi-brand retail likely to include FIIs, Retrieved from http://economictimes.indiatimes.com/news/economy/policy/51-fdi-in-multi-brand-retail-likely-to-include-fiis/articleshow/20341521.cms
70. *The Economic Times (May 7, 2014).* India has huge potential to attract FDI from Europe: Report, Retrieved from http://economictimes.indiatimes.com/news/economy/indicators/india-has-huge-potential-to-attract-fdi-from-europe-report/articleshow/34786951.cms
71. *The Economic Times (May 7, 2014).* India needs to modify Intellectual Property Rights regime to attract FDI: Report, Retrieved from http://economictimes.indiatimes.com/news/international/business/india-needs-to-modify-intellectual-property-rights-regime-to-attract-fdi-report/articleshow/34792094.cms

72. *The Hindu (April 14, 2012).* India to open FDI gate to Pakistan http://www.thehindu.com/business/Economy/india-to-open-fdi-gate-to-pakistan/article3310677.ece
73. *The Hindu (July 3, 2013).* Telecom Commission approves hike in FDI to 100 per cent.
74. *The Hindu (June 08, 2012).* India to allow FDI from Pakistan: Sharma, Retrieved from http://www.thehindu.com/business/india-to-allow-fdi-from-pakistan-sharma/article3505040.ece
75. *The Hindu (May 14, 2013).* India's defence needs FDI, Retrieved from http://www.thehindu.com/opinion/lead/indias-defence-needs-fdi/article4712277.ece
76. *The Hindustan Times (August 23, 2013).* No proposal to hike FDI limit in banks: Govt, Retrieved from http://www.hindustantimes.com/business-news/businessbankinginsurance/no-proposal-to-hike-fdi-limit-in-banks-govt/article1-1111903.aspx
77. *The Hindustan Times (July 18, 2013).* The irony of steel : FDI limits raised but Posco, Arcelor pull out, Retrieved from http://www.hindustantimes.com/india-news/the-irony-of-steel-fdi-limits-raised-but-posco-arcelor-pull-out/article1-1094345.aspx
78. *The Impact of Foreign Direct investment on Pakistan Economic Growth*, Retrieved from http://journal-archieves30.webs.com/287-296.pdf
79. *The Times of India (Aug 22, 2012).* India allows FDI from Pakistan.
80. *The Times of India (Dec 24, 2013).* India called for relaxing FDI cap in defence sector, Retrieved from http://timesofindia.indiatimes.com/business/india-business/India-called-for-relaxing-FDI-cap-in-defence-sector/articleshow/27834560.cms
81. *The Times of India (Dec 8, 2012).* FDI in retail strongly supported by Punjab farmers: PM Manmohan Singh, Retrieved from http://timesofindia.indiatimes.com/india/FDI-in-retail-strongly-supported-by-Punjab-farmers-PM-Manmohan-Singh/articleshow/17532818.cms
82. *The Times of India (Jan 26, 2006).* 100% FDI okayed for new airports, Retrieved from http://timesofindia.indiatimes.com/business/india-business/100-FDI-okayed-for-new-airports/articleshow/1386153.cms
83. *The Times of India (July 16, 2013*). Govt allows 100% FDI in telecom, hikes insurance cap to 49%, Retrieved from http://timesofindia.indiatimes.com/business/india-business/Govt-allows-100-FDI-in-telecom-hikes-insurance-cap-to-49/articleshow/21106372.cms
84. *The Times of India (Sep29, 2012).* India's FDI retail saga: From Wal-Mart to Agarwal-Mart?, Retrieved from http://timesofindia.indiatimes.com/business/international-business/Indias-FDI-retail-saga-From-Wal-Mart-to-Agarwal-Mart/articleshow/16604326.cms

85. *Times of India (Jul 17, 2013).* Call on aviation FDI cap of 74 % deferred, Retrieved from http://timesofindia.indiatimes.com/business/india-business/Call-on-aviation-FDI-cap-of-74-deferred/articleshow/21113214.cms

86. *Why India has failed to attract foreign investment in shipping,* Retrieved from http://www.livemint.com/Opinion/tNSdqc7faVU6A3BCYHaX7I/Why-India-has-failed-to-attract-foreign-investment-in-shippi.html

87. *Why investment in Afghanistan,* Retrieved from http://www.dsafghan.in/pdf/why-invest-in-afghanistan.pdf

# Chapter - 12

# Balance of Payment Situations of South Asian Countries

*"Without in any way minimising the economic and psychological blow that people experience when they lose their jobs, the unemployed in affluent countries still have a safety net, in the form of social security payments, and usually free healthcare and free education for their children. They also have sanitation and safe drinking water."*

***—Peter Singer***

## Introduction

An economic transaction occurs when something of economic value is provided by one party to another. Transactions that are considered to have economic value comprise those in goods, services, income and financial assets and liabilities. The transactions recorded in a balance of payments statement stem from dealings between two parties, one usually being a resident and the other a non-resident. The types of transactions included in the balance of payments are exchanges, one-sided transactions and imputed transactions.

One-sided transactions refer to gifts, grants, taxes etc. where one transactor provides something of economic value to another, but does not receive a quid pro quo to which an economic value can be assigned. To maintain the double entry system of accounting, the value provided is matched in the accounts by an offsetting entry which is referred to as transfer.[1] International financial transactions such as foreign exchange interventions have considerable effect on monetary policy. The balance of payments is a bookkeeping system for recording all payments that have a direct bearing on the movement of funds between a nation (private sector and government) and foreign countries.[2]

There is no bookkeeping requirement that the sums of the two sides of a selected number of balance-of-payments accounts should be the same, and it happens that the balances shown by certain combinations of accounts are of considerable interest to analysts and government officials. It is these balances that are often referred to as surpluses or decits in the balance of payments.[3] The term "balance of payments" did not gain immediate acceptance because it was only Ricardo among the classical economists who made use of it. With the publication of Sir James Steuart's book "An Inquiry into the Principles of Political Economy" in 1767, greater recognition started being given to the term balance of payments. In addition, he pointed out that it was wrong that a deficit on the balance of payments had to be financed by means of specie, because it could also be achieved by incurring debt or by changes in foreign investment. With the realisation of these interrelationships, a new era dawned in international trade and financial statistics.[4]

The world economic slowdown and reduction in oil prices brought down the trade deficit but still it remained unreasonably high as compared to the potential of the economy. The decreased deficit of the services account is mainly attributable to the lower payments on account of transportation because of lower imports, and the other major cause being the lower payments for other business services.[5]

## What is Balance of Payment?

Balance of Payment of a country is defined as the record of all economic transactions between the residents of a country and the rest of the world in a particular period (over a quarter of a year or more commonly over a year). These transactions are made by individuals, firms and government bodies. Balance of payments includes all visible and non-visible transactions of a country during a given period, usually a year.

Balance of payments accounts are an accounting record of all monetary transactions between a country and the rest of the world.[6] Balance of Payments, International Investment Position and External Debt statistics are important macroeconomic aggregates that summarise the external transactions and positions of an economy with the rest of the world. They are important for monetary and financial monitoring and policy deliberations in both the domestic and international contexts.[7]

## Components of Balance of Payments

BOP is an accounting of a country's international transactions by individuals, firms and government agencies) for a specific time period (quarter or year). It is comprised of two major accounts: (a) *Current account*–includes merchandise trade, services, interest and dividend income, and one-way transfers. (b) *Financial account*–includes financial assets (stocks, bonds) and direct foreign investment (businesses, real estate). As an accounting principle the current account balance and financial account balance must equal zero. When they do not the central bank must buy or sell currency to resolve the imbalance.[8]

The basic convention applied in constructing the balance of payments is the double-entry accounting system. Every transaction is represented by two entries with equal values but opposite signs, a debit (–) and a credit (+). With double-entry bookkeeping, the sum of all credits should in principle be identical to the sum of all debits, and the overall balance must equal zero. In this sense, the balance of payments is always in balance. The time period for recording balance of payments flows may be of any length.[9]

Most items entered in the current account of the standard components should show gross debits and credits. Most entries in the capital and financial account should be made on a net basis; that is, each component should be shown only as a credit or a debit.[10] The current account measures all transactions (other than those in financial assets and liabilities) that involve economic values and occur between resident and non-resident entities. It also includes offsets to current economic values provided or acquired without something of economic value in exchange. The financial account covers all transactions, including the creation and liquidation of financial claims, associated with change of ownership in international financial assets and liabilities.[11]

Three types of investment (direct investment (FDI), portfolio and other investment) make-up the financial account, along with financial derivatives and reserve assets. A positive value for the financial account indicates that inward investment flows (inward FDI, portfolio and other investment liabilities) exceed reserve assets and outward investment flows (outward FDI, portfolio and other investment assets).[12]

Under current account of the BoP, transactions are classified into merchandise (exports and imports) and invisibles. Invisible transactions are further classified into three categories, namely (a) Services-travel, transportation, insurance, government not included elsewhere and miscellaneous (such as, communication, construction, financial, software, news agency, royalties, management and business services); (b) Income; and (c) Transfers (grants, gifts, remittances, etc.) which do not have any quid pro quo. Under the Capital Account, capital inflows can be classified by instrument (debt or equity) and maturity (short or long-term). The main components of the capital account include foreign investment, loans and banking capital.[13]

The current account records all receipts and payments from goods and services transactions with foreigners. These transactions are divided into three distinct categories: goods and services, investment income and current transfers. In addition to various goods, "goods and services" includes travel, transportation, commercial services and government services. Investment income includes interest as well as profits and dividends on direct investments, portfolio investments and other investments. Current transfers include payments to individuals and institutions, including pensions, withholding taxes and official contributions, such as Canadian aid to other countries.[14]

## Type of Balance of Payment

Balance of trade is the difference between a country's expenditures on imports and its income from exports of goods and services. The balance of trade in goods is known as *"the visible balance"*. The balance of trade in services is known as "the invisible balance". Balance on the current account is found by adding all transactions (expenditures on imports plus income from exports) in the current account. If a country spends more on imports than it earns from exports, it is said to have a "current account deficit" or a "trade deficit". If a country earns more from its exports than it spends on imports, it is said to have a current account surplus or a trade surplus.[15]

Current account deficit is usually accompanied by depletion in foreign-exchange assets because those reserves would be used for investment abroad. The deficit could also signify increased foreign investment in the local market, in which case the local economy is liable to pay the foreign economy investment income in the future. A surplus is indicative of an economy that is a net creditor to the rest of the world. It shows how much a country is saving as opposed to investing.[16] If credits are more, i.e. exports are more, than it is a positive sign for the economy and it is known as a favourable balance of payment. If debits are more, i.e. imports are more, then it is a negative sign for the economy and it is known as an unfavourable balance of payment.[17]

## Approaches to the Balance of Payment

There are three analytical approaches to the BOP: (i) the elasticity's approach (ii) the absorption approach and (iii) the monetary approach.

1. *The Elasticities Approach*: Robinson developed this approach originally in 1930's. It concentrates on the elasticity condition necessary for a devaluation to improve the current account component of BOP. It is a partial equilibrium model, which focus on the response of exports and imports to charges in relative prices and ignores income effects, capital flow, and the money market.
2. *The Absorption Approach:* This approach emphasises the fact that payments imbalances are characterised by ex ante divergences between aggregate income receipts and aggregate domestic expenditures. This approach focuses specific attention upon the product market, rather less on the exchange rate market and appears to ignore completely the money market.
3. *The Monetary Approach*: According to this approach it would appear that what is happening to a country's BOP will depend, given the demand for money in that country and in the rest of the world, upon the rate of the growth of the money supply in the country vis-à-vis the rate of growth of the money supply in the rest of the world. The key feature of the monetary approach is the automatic balance of payments adjustment mechanism i.e., a BOP surplus or deficit is removed by adjustment of money supply to money demand.[18]

## Significance of Balance of Payments

The balance of payment has been an important indicator of the growing economic activities in all countries. The balance of payment has been an important indicator of the growing activities in all countries of the world. It shows the extent to which a country is developed technically and also competitive in the world market. Since the balance of payment deals with transactions and thus deals with flows rather than stocks.[19] Running a deficit on the current account means that an economy is not paying its way in the global economy. There is a net outflow of demand and income from the circular flow of income and spending. Spending on imported goods and services exceeds the income from exports. Many countries operate with a trade and current account surplus–good examples are China, Germany, Japan, Norway and emerging market countries with strong export sectors.[20]

The balance-of-payments resides at the crux of development. It illustrates the intersection of trade and finance and reveals the relationship of a given economy to the international marketplace. The reasons for balance-of-payments crises among developing countries stem from the basic obstacles that they face in trying to become industrialised, and also illuminate why those difficulties are so entrenched. A nation's balance-of-payments is where its trade and finance flows converge.[21] Balance of payments and international investment position data are critical in formulating national and international economic policy. Certain aspects of the balance of payments data, such as payment imbalances and foreign direct investment, are key issues that a nation's economic policies seek to address. Economic policies are often targeted at specific objectives that, in turn, impact the balance of payments. The greatest importance of balance of payments lies in its serving as an indicator of changing international economic position of a country.[22]

The balance of payments is the economic barometer which can be used to appraise a nation's short-term international economic prospects, to evaluate the degree of its international solvency, and to determine the appropriateness of the exchange rate of country's currency.[23] In some countries, considerable progress has already been made towards the elimination of discriminatory restrictions; in others, much remains to be done. Recent international financial developments have established an environment favourable to the elimination of discrimination for balance of payments reasons. There has been a substantial improvement in the reserve positions of the industrial countries in particular and widespread moves to external convertibility have taken place.[24]

## Reasons for Current Account Deficit in Balance of Payments

A current account deficit occurs when the value of imports (of goods, services and investment incomes) is greater than the value of exports. A deficit occurs when more money is leaving the country than coming in. This is when imports of goods and services as well as income and transfer payments abroad exceed exports and income and transfer payments coming in to the country. A deficit can arise out of two reasons; one is that the country's residents are buying more abroad than overseas residents have spent on the country's products. This may be due to a changing exchange rate.

Another cause for a deficit on the trade of goods and services is changes in income. Structural problems can also lead to a deficit in trades in goods and services. This is where domestic firms are producing poor quality goods and are inefficient. If this is the case, demand is likely to fall and a deficit will persist. If there has been a large transfer of income abroad, this will lead to a current account deficit.[25]

BOP problem in developing countries is not caused by a single reason rather there are multi-reasons due to which this problem take place. Many developing countries can face the problem of dis-equilibrium in the balance of payment because of persistent deficits in their trade with developed countries. Developing countries has to make huge imports from advanced countries for the sake of implementation their economic development. The inflow of grants from developed countries and foreign capital to these countries is far short of their needs. As a result those countries are loosing their reserves of foreign currencies and facing very serious difficulties in this regards.

The developing countries basically based on agriculture. The production of agriculture is highly uncertain. In case of any decrease, draught etc. the output of agriculture can come down and the agricultural export decline sharply. The developing countries are highly populated with higher population growth rate. These situations increase the use of domestic goods and increase the demand of imported goods. Developing countries are often in a state of uncertainty; the political situation in most of the time is disturbing the environment.[26] There are various factors which could cause a current account deficit:

1. *Fixed Exchange Rate:* If the currency is overvalued, imports will be cheaper and therefore there will be a higher Q of imports. Exports will become uncompetitive and therefore there will be a fall in the quantity of exports.
2. *Decline in Competitiveness:* Sometimes there has been decline in the exporting manufacturing sector, because it has struggled to compete with developing countries in the Far East. This has led to a persistent deficit in the balance of trade.
3. *Economic Growth:* If there is an increase in national income, people will tend to have more disposable income to consume goods. If domestic producers can not meet the domestic demand, consumers will have to import goods from abroad.[27]
4. *Import of Oil:* Petroleum oil and lubricants (POL) has been the single most important item in India's import bill. During seventies and eighties constituted nearly one-third of total imports of the country.
5. *Deficits on Capital Transactions:* In recent years, there has been the growing deficit on capital account due to country's rising obligations to meet amortisation payments. The situation is worsened due to a fall in the availability on concessional aid to finance the deficits and flattering out private remittances.
6. *Import Liberalisation*: Due to import liberalisation during the eighties there has been a quantum jump in imports of capital goods and modern technology. The new economic and trade policies of 1991 have favoured a further liberalisation of imports.[28]

## Balance of Payments in Pakistan

Pakistan has been facing BOP problem since the independence. It has been under deficit since then. Pakistan is an agro-based economy and its exports mainly depend on rice and raw cotton. Whenever there is an international price shock or internal draught situation the export situation of these agricultural products is affected badly increasing the deficit gap. The overall BOP deficit is being financed largely by foreign credits, which increase our future debt, services liabilities and which would cause strains on the future balance of payments. The net private transfer in Pakistan consists of the home remittances of Pakistani nationals abroad and this is a temporary phenomenon. High population growth has been a hurdle and main problem in BOP as this has been increasing the import bill.

There is a lack of continuity in the government policies that is also discouraging the foreign as well as local investors. Political instability is one of the major hurdles to improve the BOP situation of the country. Implementation of Fiscal and Monetary policies and Pakistani Tariffs on exports and imports are not being implemented properly and with proper knowledge, which is not improving the BOP situation. Pakistan is suffering from acute external and internal debt problems, which is also one cause of deteriorating the BOP situation.[29]

Pakistan has suffered in the past due to perception of poor governance and reneging of contracts. This government has taken actions to introduce transparency, predictability, rule of law and accountability in the system. Even the worst critics of this government do recognise that the overall governance has improved although a lot of reforms are either underway or planned to strengthen judiciary, police, civil service and other institutions.[30]

Pakistan has reached a critical balance of payments situation and will need another package from the International Monetary Fund. The government is facing a stubborn Taliban insurgency and a worsening sectarian conflict in which thousands have been killed. In 2008, Pakistan averted a balance of payments problem by securing an $11 billion IMF loan package, but the IMF suspended the programme in 2011 after economic and reform targets including widening the country's miniscule tax base were missed. The ADB, along with the IMF, has been encouraging Pakistan's unpopular government to carry out politically-sensitive reforms to strengthen the economy and widen the country's revenue base.[31]

Pakistan has one of the smallest tax bases in the world. About 0.5 per cent of the population of 180 million pays income tax in a country which receives billions of dollars in financial support from the United States and other Western allies. There are many payments that need to be made to international organisations, most importantly the IMF. There is a big chunk in payments to be done over the next two years that is not matched by inflows.[32] Pakistan's merchandise trade deficit has been improved by 13.9 per cent in July-April 2008-09 from $ 14,218 million to $ 12,238 million during July-April 2009-10. Unlike last year when the decline in trade deficit was mainly contributed by massive fall in import expenditures due to decline in international prices, this year's improvement in trade deficit remained broad based, with both exports and imports contributing to the decline.

Exports recorded growth of 8.0 per cent during July-April 2009-10 on the back of recovery in export markets of the country, exchange rate depreciation, and improved production of crops. Moreover, during July-April 2009-10, export receipts of the country surpassed the full year official target of 6.0 per cent exports growth for 2009-10. Textiles are a major driver of the exports. Low value added products like raw cotton and cotton yarn fetches the major share of contribution in the textile group on the back of factors like early and better production of these crops along with restoration of external demand specifically from China.[33]

## Balance of Payment in Nepal

Despite large recorded trade deficits, Nepal often maintains a surplus in its current account thanks to surpluses in services (including tourism), official aid transfers, and increasingly large remittances from Nepalese living abroad, and in spite of unrecorded trade and smuggling across the Indian border. The IMF reported small surpluses on Nepal's current account of $24 million and $28 million respectively, for the fiscal years 1998/99 and 1999/2000, even exclusive of official aid transfers.[34]

The country's trade deficit has increased by 25.5 per cent whereas remittance growth rate has declined by 19.6 per cent in 2014. Nepali migrant workers sent home ₹ 266.08 billion during the review period. The remittance growth rate had increased by 34.7 per cent during the same period in 2013. According to Nepal Rastra Bank (NRB), the imports of merchandise and services have increased significantly compared to last year. The country's trade deficit has increased by 25 per cent to ₹ 309.5 billion.[35] The central bank said a substantial rise in imports, slow remittance growth and decreased foreign assistance resulted in poor BoP situation. NRB Research Department Chief Min Bahadur Shrestha said the BoP situation deteriorated as a huge amount went outside the country at the end of the seventh month for the payment of import bills.[36]

Nepal has managed to dramatically bring down the balance of payment deficit to ₹ 2.62 billion, but a huge current account deficit continued to trouble the country on the back of a massive trade deficit that widened by more than ₹ 100 billion in Fiscal Year 2009/10 alone. The country's exports declined by 9.7 per cent to ₹ 61.13 billion during the year as instability, insecurity and lack of initiative by the government to address labour and power outage problems took a toll on industrial output and drove away investment. Mainly commodities like woollen carpet, readymade garments, pashmina, pulses and herbs failed to retain their markets during the year. The central bank said import of petroleum products, vehicles and spare parts, MS billet, gold, telecommunication equipment and steel rod and sheet, among others played a huge role to drive up the imports.[37]

## Balance of Payments in Bhutan

Bhutan's current account deficit was at a low of 11.1 per cent of GDP in 1998, the year construction began on the Tala hydroelectric project. This ratio more than doubled the next year, to 24.1 per cent of GDP in 1999, reflecting increased capital goods imports and rising factor service payments for the project dependent on foreign labour and expertise. The proportional deficit on the current account ranged even higher in 2000 and 2001, to 28.4 per cent of GDP and 26.8 per cent of GDP, respectively, and was expected to be yet higher for 2002.[38] Economic growth continued to moderate from 6.5 per cent to an estimated 5.2 per cent in Fiscal Year 2013 (ended 30 June 2013), rates well below the average growth of 8.4 per cent over the past decade. The slowdown largely reflects policy measures adopted in 2012 to alleviate growing shortages of Indian rupee reserves. The measures entailed credit and import restrictions, particularly in import-heavy activities such as construction and transport that required large rupee payments.[39]

The robust growth in the industrial sector in FY2010/11 kept pace with the average rate recorded in the past decade, but contribution of individual subsectors varied across the years. The services sector in FY2010/11 also grew at the healthy average growth rate of around eight per cent in the past decade, with all subsectors growing strongly.

The Bhutanese ngultrum is pegged to the Indian rupee, and India is Bhutan's key trading partner. Food prices rose through 2009 in both countries. As food prices in India declined in 2010, they also moderated in Bhutan. Meanwhile, the recent fuel price hike in India has contributed to rising non-food prices because of possible feed-through effects. Since the poor have a high ratio of food spending in total expenditure, it is possible that this affects poor households disproportionately. The government has limited mechanisms to influence food prices. A bilateral free-trade agreement with India allows duty-free imports of all food and agricultural commodities. India supplies approximately 50 per cent of Bhutan's requirements for rice. The government has undertaken several reforms to modernise the financial sector and strengthen the institutional framework for financial management.[40]

## Balance of Payment in Bangladesh

Bangladesh has had an unfavourable balance of payment for many years due to its dependency on imports. In Bangladesh, import, export, and exchange rate, are the most important economic variables in recent times as they help in balancing the balance of payment. Remittances from Bangladeshis working overseas, mainly in the Middle East are the major source of foreign exchange earnings; exports of garments and textiles are the main sources of foreign exchange earnings. Though liberalisation has taken place, still the condition of balance of payment in Bangladesh is not satisfactory. There are many reasons for this problem such as: the ICT sector is not strong enough, our export items are limited, lack of skillfulness etc. There are many components that affect the trade balance of an economy and Balance of payment also has many indices. The effects of trade balance can be checked in different ways.[41]

Bangladesh's current account on foreign trade has recorded huge balance of payments surplus as investment has dried up in the country due to political turmoil. The surplus in foreign transactions was registered at $1.38 billion in the first five months (July-Nov) of the 2013-14 fiscal, which is three times higher than the corresponding period of the last fiscal. The surplus was $433 million in the July-Nov period of 2012-13 fiscal. The surplus in the current account means Bangladesh need not to take loans for daily transactions. The total surplus stood at $2.52 billion in 2012-13 fiscal while in 2011-12 there was a deficit of $447 million.[42] Bangladesh's overall balance of payments surplus reached over five billion U.S. dollars in the last fiscal year 2012-13 concluded in June due mainly to healthy current account balance on the back of an increase in exports and inflow of remittances.[43]

Due to crop failures caused by devastating floods that occurred most frequently as well as drought, and devastating cyclonic storm, Bangladesh occasionally had to import large amount of food grain on cash payment, which resulted in a massive deterioration in the country's balance of payments situation in the post-liberation period of end of the past century. In addition, the terms of trade consistently deteriorated due to rising import prices and instability in export earnings, causing continuous deficits in trade accounts of balance of payments.[44]

## Balance of Payment in Sri Lanka

Trade deficits have been a characteristic feature of Sri Lanka's export-import economy. Despite persistent trade deficits, it has been possible to achieve much smaller balance of payments deficits, and in some years, to even realise balance of payments surpluses. Workers' remittances have been mostly responsible for offsetting the large trade deficits. In 2013, in spite of a trade deficit of US$ 7.6 billion, the balance of payments recorded an overall surplus of nearly US$ 1 billion. The prospect of the trade deficit declining to about US$ 6 billion in 2014 provides the possibility of achieving a significant overall balance of payments surplus this year. Trade deficits have been massive in recent years; there have been balance of payments surpluses in some years.

In 2011, the trade deficit was a massive US$ 9.7 billion, yet the deficit in the overall balance of payments was only US$ 1.1 billion. In 2012, despite the trade deficit of 9.4 billion, the country achieved a small overall balance of payments surplus of US$ 151 million. With the trade deficit declining to US$ 7.6 billion in 2013, an overall balance of payments surplus of US$ 991 million was achieved. International transfers, better known as workers' remittances, have been the main source of funds that have enabled an improvement in the balance of payments. Remittances have continued to increase over the years and especially after 2009. In 2012, remittances amounted to US$ 6 billion and offset 64 per cent of the trade deficit of 9.4 billion.

In 2013, remittances grew by a further 13 per cent from that of the previous year to US$ 6.8 billion to offset as much as 90 per cent of the trade deficit of US$ 7.6 billion. These remittances were mainly responsible for the overall balance of payments surplus of nearly US$ 1 billion in 2014. The second important means of offsetting the trade deficit has been earnings from services that have also been increasing after 2010. Foreign inflows of funds as foreign direct investments and net inflows into the stock market too contributed to the balance of payments.[45]

Sri Lanka's balance-of-payments position is highly sensitive to price changes in the world market because it depends in large part upon a few export crops to pay for its imports. Since 1983, sharply rising defence expenditures, a decline in tourism caused by continuing civil violence, and slumping world tea and coconut prices combined to exert pressure on the balance of payments.[46] Sri Lanka's foreign reserves rose 4.6 per cent to 7,200 million in December 2013 from a year earlier, despite payments to the International Monetary Fund and losses on gold holdings. In 2013, Sri Lanka recorded an estimated 991 million US dollar 'balance of payments surplus', according to Central Bank estimates, which is a broad measure of the difference between external payments (outflows) and receipts (inflows) of a country within a period. The gap between the two was largely caused by a repayment of over 500 million US dollars to the IMF.[47]

## Balance of Payment of Maldives

Balance of payments deficits during the first half of the 1980s were caused largely by the international shipping recession, the collapse of world tuna prices, and a brief downturn in tourism caused by the violence in nearby Sri Lanka. The government began an economic reform programme in 1989, by lifting import quotas and opening some exports to the private sector. In recent years, it has encouraged more foreign investment by liberalising regulations.[48]

Tourism is Maldives' largest economic activity, accounts for 28 per cent of GDP and more than 60 per cent of foreign exchange receipts. Fishing is the second leading sector, but the fish catch has dropped sharply in recent years. Agriculture and manufacturing continue to play a lesser role in the economy, constrained by the limited availability of cultivable land and the shortage of domestic labour.[49]

## Balance of Payment in India

The Reserve Bank of India is responsible for compiling the balance of payments for India. It obtains data on the balance of payments primarily as a by-product of the administration of the exchange control. In accordance with the Foreign Exchange Management Act of 1999, all foreign exchange transactions must be channelled through the banking system, and the banks that undertake foreign exchange transactions must submit various periodical returns and supporting documents prescribed under the FEMA.

In respect of the transactions that are not routed through banking channels, information is obtained directly from the relevant government agencies, other concerned agencies, and other departments within the RBI. Under the exchange control rules, authorised dealers (i.e., banks authorised to deal in foreign exchange) are required to report details in respect of transactions.[50] India's balance of payments swung back into surplus during the October-December quarter, helped by government curbs in gold imports, after two quarters in deficit. India returned to a surplus of $19.1 billion for October-December, much higher than a nearly $800 million surplus a year ago.[51]

The Indian economy is exhibiting early signs of recovery, as indicated by improvements in purchasing managers index, moderation in inflation, return of investor confidence through surge in portfolio investment flows and buoyant equity markets. India's BoP was under stress during 2011-12, as the trade and current account deficit widened. Though capital inflows increased, it fell short of fully financing current account deficit, resulting in drawdown of foreign exchange reserves. India's foreign exchange reserves comprise foreign currency assets, gold, special drawing rights and reserve tranche position in the International Monetary Fund. The level of foreign exchange reserves is largely the outcome of the Reserve Bank of India intervention in the foreign exchange market to smoothen exchange rate volatility and valuation changes due to movement of the US dollar against other major currencies of the world.[52]

## Conclusion

BOP is an accounting of a country's international transactions by individuals, firms and government agencies) for a specific time period (quarter or year). BOP is comprised of two major accounts: (a) Current account and (b) Financial account. The balance of payments is always in balance. The time period for recording balance of payments flows may be of any length. The balance of payment has been an important indicator of the growing economic activities in all countries.

The balance of payment has been an important indicator of the growing activities in all countries of the world. It shows the extent to which a country is developed technically and also competitive in the world market. The balance-of-payments resides at the crux of development. It illustrates the intersection of trade and finance and reveals the relationship of a given economy to the international marketplace.

## References

1. *Balance of Payments and International Investment Position, Australia, Concepts, Sources and Methods, 1998* , See http://www.abs.gov.au/Ausstats/abs@.nsf/0/8B440ED82BF8F72BCA25697E0018FDF5?opendocument
2. *Balance of Payments,* Retrieved from http://wps.aw.com/wps/media/objects/5294/5421792/appendices/appendixch14.pdf
3. Norman S. Fieleke, What is the Balance of Payments? See
4. The Use of Balance of Payments Statistics in the Determination of http://en.wikipedia.org/wiki Monetary and Fiscal Policy, Retrieved from https://www.imf.org/external/pubs/ft/bop/2002/02-51.pdf
5. M. Ashraf Janjua, *Pakistan's balance of payment prospects and policy proposals,* Retrieved from http://www.iobm.edu.pk/PBR/1007/PBR_1007_Complete.pdf
6. Balance of payments (2014), Retrieved from http://en.wikipedia.org/wiki/Balance_of_payments.
7. *Balance of payments*, Retrieved from http://www.censtatd.gov.hk/hkstat/sub/sc260.jsp
8. *Balance of Payments*, Retrieved from http://apcentral.collegeboard.com/apc/public/repository/balance-of-payments.pdf
9. *Balance of Payments Accounts, Analysis and Forecasting,* Retrieved from http://rbidocs.rbi.org.in/rdocs/content/pdfs/L-9.pdf
10. Balance of payment manuals, Retrieved from https://www.imf.org/external/pubs/ft/bopman/bopman.pdf
11. *Balance of Payments: Categories and Definitions,* Retrieved from http://faculty.washington.edu/danby/bls324/macro/categories.html
12. *Balance of payments statistics*, Retrieved from http://epp.eurostat.ec.europa.eu/statistics_explained/index.php/Balance_of_payment_statistics

13. *Balance of payments,* chapter 4, Retrieved from http://mospi.nic.in/Mospi_New/upload/SYB2013/CH-4-BALANCE%20OF%20PAYMENT/Chapter%20No.4.pdf
14. See http://publications.gc.ca/Collection-R/LoPBdP/CIR/8610-e.htm
15. See http://blogs.yis.ac.jp/macaulayp/files/2013/08/Balance-of-Payments-PDF-1a9lgil.pdf
16. See http://www.investopedia.com/articles/03/061803.asp
17. *Bangladesh's Balance of Payments: an Econometric Analysis,* Retrieved from http://www.euacademic.org/UploadArticle/25.pdf
18. Hafeez ur Rehman and Hafiz Abdur Rashid, *The balance of payment problem in developing countries, especially in Pakistan,* Retrieved from http://joc.hcc.edu.pk/articlepdf/JOC_Rehman__Rashid_31_52.pdf
19. *Causes of Balance of Payment Problems in Emerging and Developing Economies,* See http://www.studymode.com/essays/Causes-Of-Balance-Of-Payment-Problems-918967.html
20. *Balance of Payments - Deficits and Surpluses (2012),* See http://tutor2u.net/economics/revision-notes/a2-macro-balance-of-payments-deficits.html
21. Chantal Thomas (2000), Balance-of-Payments Crises in the Developing World: Balancing Trade, Finance and Development in the New Economic Order, *American University International Law Review,* Volume 15 | Issue 6, Article 3, pp.1251-53.
22. *Balance of payments,* Retrieved from http://www.investopedia.com/terms/b/bop.asp
23. See http://www.shareyouressays.com/112127/importance-of-balance-of-payments-for-a-country-explained
24. *Discrimination for balance of payments reasons*, Retrieved from https://www.imf.org/external/pubs/ft/sd/index.asp?decision=955-(59/45)
25. See http://thepeaktimes.wordpress.com/2013/04/23/the-causes-and-consequences-of-a-deficit-and-a-surplus-on-the-current-account-of-the-balance-of-payments/
26. Hafeez ur Rehman and Hafiz Abdur Rashid, *The balance of payment problem in developing countries, especially in Pakistan,* Retrieved from http://joc.hcc.edu.pk/articlepdf/JOC_Rehman__Rashid_31_52.pdf
27. *Factors which cause a current account deficit in the balance of payments,* Retrieved from http://www.economicshelp.org/macroeconomics/bop/cause-of-deficit/
28. *What are the Causes of India's Balance of Payment?* See http://www.preservearticles.com/2012020122309/what-are-the-causes-of-indias-balance-of-payment.html
29. Hafeez ur Rehman and Hafiz Abdur Rashid, The balance of payment problem in developing countries, especially in Pakistan, Retrieved from http://joc.hcc.edu.pk/articlepdf/JOC_Rehman__Rashid_31_52.pdf

30. Pakistan's balance of payments: Historical Perspective, *Current Situation and Future Evolution,* Retrieved from http://ishrathusain.iba.edu.pk/speeches/economicManagementPolicies/2001/pakistans_balance_of_payments.pdf
31. *Pakistan in critical balance of payments situation, may need $9 billion – ADB,* See http://in.reuters.com/article/2013/03/06/pakistan-economy-idINDEE92507F20130306
32. *Pakistan in critical balance of payments situation, may need $9b,* See http://www.nation.com.pk/business/07-Mar-2013/pakistan-in-critical-balance-of-payments-situation-may-need-9b
33. *Balance of Payments,* Retrieved from http://www.finance.gov.pk/survey/chapter_10/07_balance_of_payments.pdf
34. See http://www.nationsencyclopedia.com/Asia-and-Oceania/Nepal-BALANCE-OF-PAYMENTS.html
35. See http://www.nepaldispatch.com/2013/04/balance-of-payment-surplus-stands-at-rs-11-78-billion/
36. See http://www.ekantipur.com/the-kathmandu-post/2013/03/15/money/nepal-rastra-bank-macro-economic-report/246456.html
37. See http://archives.myrepublica.com/portal/index.php?action=news_details&news_id=23080
38. *Bhutan - Balance of payments*, See http://www.nationsencyclopedia.com/Asia-and-Oceania/Bhutan-BALANCE-OF-PAYMENTS.html
39. See http://www.adb.org/countries/bhutan/economy
40. *Bhutan Economic Update, September 2011*, Retrieved from http://siteresources.worldbank.org/BHUTANEXTN/Resources/BhutanEconomicUpdate.pdf
41. M.S. Rahman, *Bangladesh's Balance of Payments: an Econometric Analysis,* See http://www.euacademic.org/UploadArticle/25.pdf
42. See http://bdnews24.com/economy/2014/01/14/huge-balance-of-payments-surplus
43. See http://news.xinhuanet.com/english/world/2013-08/26/c_132664553.htm
44. See http://www.banglapedia.org/HT/B_0079.htm
45. *Achieving balance of payments surpluses despite trade deficits,* See http://www.sundaytimes.lk/140316/columns/achieving-balance-of-payments-surpluses-despite-trade-deficits-89269.html
46. See http://www.nationsencyclopedia.com/Asia-and-Oceania/Sri-Lanka-BALANCE-OF-PAYMENTS.html
47. *Sri Lanka ends 2013 with US$7.2bn in foreign reserves*, Retrieved from http://www.lankabusinessonline.com/news/sri-lanka-ends-2013-with-us$7.2bn-in-foreign-reserves/456167261

48. See Read more: http://www.nationsencyclopedia.com/Asia-and-Oceania/Maldives-BALANCE-OF-PAYMENTS.html#ixzz3ApuhhFyR
49. See http://www.theodora.com/wfbcurrent/maldives/maldives_economy.html
50. See http://stats.oecd.org/mei/default.asp?lang=e&subject=13&country=ind
51. See http://in.reuters.com/article/2014/03/05/india-current-account-rbi-idINDEEA240C220140305
52. *Balance of Payments,* Retrieved from http://indiabudget.nic.in/es2012-13/echap-06.pdf

# Chapter - 13

# Terrorism in South Asian Countries

*"There is no life to be found in violence. Every act of violence brings us closer to death. Whether it's the mundane violence we do to our bodies by overeating toxic food or drink or the extreme violence of child abuse, domestic warfare, life-threatening poverty, addiction, or state terrorism."*

—***Bell Hooks***

## Introduction

The word terrorism, in and of itself, was coined during the French Revolution's Reign of Terror (1793–1794). In the Reign of Terror, a group of rebels, the Jacobins, used the term when self-reflexively portraying their own actions in the French Revolution. The Reign of Terror was a campaign of large-scale violence by the French state; between 16,000 and 40,000 people were killed in a little over a year. It is not surprising, then, that the French National Convention proclaimed in September 1793 that "terror is the order of the day."[1]

Terrorism has been practiced by a broad array of political organisations to further their objectives. In November 2004, a United Nations Secretary General report described terrorism as any act "intended to cause death or serious bodily harm to civilians or non-combatants with the purpose of intimidating a population or compelling a government or an international organisation to do or abstain from doing any act."[2] Terrorism is a criminal act that influences an audience beyond the immediate victim. The strategy of terrorists is to commit acts of violence that draws the attention of the local populace, the government, and the world to their cause. The terrorists plan their attack to obtain the greatest publicity, choosing targets that symbolise what they oppose. The effectiveness of the terrorist act lies not in the act itself, but in the public's or government's reaction to the act.[3]

## Meaning of the Concept

The difficulty in defining "terrorism" is in agreeing on a basis for determining when the use of violence is legitimate; therefore, the modern definition of terrorism is inherently controversial. The Arab Convention for the Suppression of Terrorism was adopted by the Council of Arab Ministers of the Interior and the Council of Arab Ministers of Justice in Cairo, Egypt in 1998. Terrorism was defined in the convention as: *"Any act or threat of violence, whatever its motives or purposes, that occurs in the advancement of an individual or collective criminal agenda and seeking to sow panic among people, causing fear by harming them, or placing their lives, liberty or security in danger, or seeking to cause damage to the environment or to public or private installations or property or to occupying or seizing them, or seeking to jeopardize national resources."*

UN Security Council Resolution 1566 (2004) gives a definition: *"criminal acts, including against civilians, committed with the intent to cause death or serious bodily injury, or taking of hostages, with the purpose to provoke a state of terror in the general public or in a group of persons or particular persons, intimidate a population or compel a government or an international organisation to do or to abstain from doing any act."* The United Kingdom's Terrorism Act 2000 defines *"terrorism to include an act "designed seriously to interfere with or seriously to disrupt an electronic system". An act of violence is not even necessary under this definition."* FBI definition of terrorism: *"The unlawful use of force or violence against persons or property to intimidate or coerce a government, the civilian population, or any segment thereof, in furtherance of political or social objectives."*[4]

## Types of Terrorism[5]

Different types of terrorism have been defined by lawmakers, security professionals and scholars:

- *State Terrorism*: It can also be argued that states can, and have been terrorists. States can use force or the threat of force, without declaring war, to terrorise citizens and achieve a political goal. Germany under Nazi rule has been described in this way. It has also been argued that states participate in international terrorism, often by proxy.

- *Bioterrorism:* Bioterrorism refers to the intentional release of toxic biological agents to harm and terrorise civilians, in the name of a political or other cause. The US Center for Disease Control has classified the viruses, bacteria and toxins that could be used in an attack.
- *Cyber terrorism:* Cyber terrorists use information technology to attack civilians and draw attention to their cause. This may mean that they use information technology, such as computer systems or telecommunications, as a tool to orchestrate a traditional attack. More often, cyber terrorism refers to an attack on information technology itself in a way that would radically disrupt networked services.
- *Ecoterrorism:* Ecoterrorism is a recently coined term describing violence in the interests of environmentalism. In general, environmental extremists sabotage property to inflict economic damage on industries or actors they see as harming animals or the natural environment.
- *Nuclear terrorism:* Nuclear terrorism refers to a number of different ways nuclear materials might be exploited as a terrorist tactic. These include attacking nuclear facilities, purchasing nuclear weapons, or building nuclear weapons or otherwise finding ways to disperse radioactive materials.
- *Narcoterrorism:* Narcoterrorism has had several meanings since its coining in 1983. It once denoted violence used by drug traffickers to influence governments or prevent government efforts to stop the drug trade.

## Causes of Terrorism

People choose terrorism when they are trying to right what they perceive to be a social or political or historical wrong, when they have been stripped of their land or rights, or denied these.[6] Terrorism is the threat or use of violence against civilians to draw attention to an issue. Terrorism was originally theorised in the context of insurgency and guerrilla warfare, a form of organised political violence by a non-state army or group. Terrorism isn't a random or crazy choice, but is chosen as a tactic in service of a larger goal. Socio-economic explanations of terrorism suggest that various forms of deprivation drive people to terrorism, or that they are more susceptible to recruitment by organisations using terrorist tactics.

Poverty, lack of education or lack of political freedom are a few examples. In the 1990s a new form of terrorism fueled by religious fervour was on the rise. They pointed to organisations such as Al Qaeda, Aum Shinrikyo (a Japanese cult) and Christian identity groups. Religious ideas, such as martyrdom, and Armageddon, were seen as particularly dangerous.[7] Some of the factors that lead to terrorism are: (a) Frustration and desperation to achieve a goal; (b) Confused emotion; (c) Shortsightedness and Impulsive action; (d) Belief in a non-verifiable concept of heaven and merit; a childish concept of God favouring some and angry at others, thereby undermining the omniscience and omnipotence of the Divine; (e) Terrorism induces fear psychosis in all, increases poverty, suffering and loss of life with no apparent gains.[8] One of the most popular explanations is that poverty breeds terrorism and hence is a cause of terrorism. Some argue that nondemocratic governments breed conditions that terrorists can exploit to further their own agenda. Some argue that ethnicity and injustices (perceived or real) is one of the root causes of terrorism.[9]

## Global Terrorism

Terrorism is defined as premeditated political violence against civilians with the objective of maximising media exposure to the act and, ultimately, to the terror group and/or to its cause. Because it targets non-military personnel (that is, because the focus of terrorist activities are civilians or non-combatants), terrorist acts fundamentally differ from civil wars, guerrilla warfare and riots. Because the aim is to raise the profile of the cause, one main objective of terrorism is to maximise media exposure so as to further the atmosphere of fear.[10]

Terrorists manipulate fear through the use of violence to achieve their objectives. While the root causes must be tackled to decrease the number of terrorists, an understanding of the enabling factors for terrorists is also needed in order to reduce their capacity to act. It is all the more necessary because reducing the motivation behind terrorism is a task for a generation or more, and reducing their capacity will demand constant attention in the meantime.[11] Terrorism has come to be defined in the background of the terrorist attacks on the United States (US) on September 11, 2001. "9/11" thus has become the basis for defining the global response to terrorism since that time.[12]

Al-Qaeda is a global militant Islamist and Wahhabist organisation founded by Osama bin Laden, Al-Qaeda has attacked civilian and military targets in various countries, including the September 11 attacks, 1998 US embassy bombings and the 2002 Bali bombings. The US government responded to the September 11 attacks by launching the War on Terror. Characteristic techniques employed by al-Qaeda include suicide attacks and simultaneous bombings of different targets. Al-Qaeda's management philosophy has been described as *"centralisation of decision and decentralisation of execution."*

The radical Islamist movement in general and al-Qaeda in particular developed during the Islamic revival and Islamist movement of the last three decades of the twentieth century, along with less extreme movements. The origins of al-Qaeda as a network inspiring terrorism around the world and training operatives can be traced to the Soviet War in Afghanistan (December 1979–February 1989). Toward the end of the Soviet military mission in Afghanistan, some *mujahedeen* wanted to expand their operations to include Islamist struggles in other parts of the world, such as Israel and Kashmir. A number of overlapping and interrelated organisations were formed, to further those aspirations.[13]

The September 11 attacks were a series of four coordinated terrorist attacks launched by the Islamic terrorist group al-Qaeda upon the United States in New York City and the Washington, D.C., metropolitan area on Tuesday, September 11, 2001. The attacks killed almost 3,000 people and caused at least $10 billion in property and infrastructure damage. Four passenger airliners were hijacked by 19 al-Qaeda terrorists so they could be flown into buildings in suicide attacks. Two of those planes, American and United Airlines Flight 175, were crashed into the North and South towers, respectively, of the World Trade Center complex in New York City. Suspicion quickly fell on al-Qaeda. Al-Qaeda and bin Laden cited U.S. support of Israel, the presence of U.S. troops in Saudi Arabia, and sanctions against Iraq as motives for the attacks. The United States responded to the attacks by launching the War on Terror and invading Afghanistan to depose the Taliban, which had harbored al-Qaeda.[14]

Since 2001, global terrorism has become one of the biggest domestic and international challenges for Germany. Internationally, Germany has been keen to emphasise a more multilateralist approach, opposing the Iraq war and stressing the need to address the root causes of terrorism rather than merely its violent manifestations.[15] The world community is waging an unprecedented campaign to disrupt the ow of money to terrorist networks and cripple their ability to operate on a global scale. The United States is working closely with other governments and international institutions to block terrorist assets overseas, take preventive measures to keep assets out of terrorist hands, and offer training and assistance to governments that seek to improve their institutional ability to carry out anti-money laundering strategies.[16]

Increasingly, international terrorism is recognised as a threat to US foreign, as well as domestic, security. Both timing and target selection by terrorists can affect US interests in areas ranging from preservation of commerce to nuclear nonproliferation to the Middle East peace process. Terrorists have been able to develop their own sources of financing, which range from NGOs and charities to illegal enterprises such as narcotics, extortion, and kidnapping. Colombia's FARC is said to make hundreds of millions of dollars annually from criminal activities, mostly from "taxing" of, or participating in the narcotics trade.[17]

### *Global Terrorism* Index

The Global Terrorism Index (GTI) is an attempt to systematically rank the nations of the world according to terrorist activity. The index combines a number of factors associated with terrorist attacks to build a thorough picture of the impact of terrorism over a 10-year period, illustrating trends, and providing a data series for analysis by researchers and policymakers. It is the product of Institute for Economics and Peace and is based on data from the Global Terrorism Database (GTD) which is collected and collated by the National Consortium for the Study of Terrorism and Responses to Terrorism at the University of Maryland. The GTD has codified over 104,000 cases of terrorism.[18]

### Terrorism in Pakistan

Terrorism in Pakistan has become a major and highly destructive phenomenon in recent years. The state and its Inter-Services

Intelligence, in alliance with the CIA, encouraged the *"mujahedeen"* to fight a proxy war against Soviet forces present in Afghanistan. At the end of the Soviet war in Afghanistan, between 1990 and 1996, the Pakistani establishment continued to organise, support and nurture mujahedeen groups on the premise that they could be used for proxy warfare in the Indian state of Jammu and Kashmir and in support of the doctrine of *"strategic depth"* in Afghanistan through the use of the Taliban. The post-9/11 War on Terrorism in Pakistan has had two principal elements: the government's battle with jihad groups banned after the attacks in New York, and the U.S. pursuit of Al-Qaeda, usually (but not always) in co-operation with Pakistani forces.[19]

Ninety-seven per cent of Pakistan's population is Muslim, but it is not a monolithic whole. The two major sects of Islam in Pakistan are Sunni and Shia. Sunnis can be considered as adherents of the conservative Muslim school of thought, who perceive themselves as following the Sunna or tradition of the Prophet Mohammed. Religion is used for the instigation of terrorism by two sets of actors in Pakistan. First, there are sectarian groups belonging to the Sunni and Shia sects of Islam that are active in terrorist activities which are mostly directed against the people from the opposite sect. The Sunni militant organisations call for Pakistan to be declared a Sunni state while Shias fight for specific political rights to safeguard their distinct status. The second set of actors are jihadi groups that were considered by the Government of Pakistan up to 2001 as strategic tools to be used in Afghanistan and Kashmir, some of whom have now turned against the government and become involved in terrorist activities inside the country.[20]

South Asia is viewed as a key arena in the fight against militant religious extremism, most especially in Pakistan and as related to Afghan stability. The United States also remains concerned with indigenous extremist groups in Pakistan, and with the ongoing *"cross-border infiltration"* of Islamist militants who traverse the Kashmiri Line of Control and other borders to engage in terrorist acts in India and Indian Kashmir.[21] With varying motives, using the newest weapons, engulfing wider area, and claiming more lives, terrorism in Pakistan has attracted considerable local and global attention.[22] Throughout history, terrorists have tended to live to see their acts rewarded. In such cases and as far as religious suicide bombings are concerned, the cost/

benefit calculations do not take place on earth for the reward promised is a heavenly one. Islamic militancy has always been prolific in Pakistan.[23]

## Terrorism in Jammu and Kashmir

Jammu and Kashmir is a state in Northern India, granted autonomy under Article 370 of Indian constitution. Jammu and Kashmir consists of three regions: Jammu, the valley and Ladakh. Srinagar is the summer capital, and Jammu is the winter capital. Formerly a part of the erstwhile Princely State of Kashmir and Jammu, which governed the larger historic region of Kashmir, the region is the subject of a territorial conflict among China, India and Pakistan. On 25 October 1947 Maharaja Hari Singh signed the Instrument of Accession on 26 October 1947 and it was accepted on 27 October 1947 by the Governor General of India. Jammu and Kashmir has a Muslim majority population, though Islam is practised by about 67 per cent of the population of the state and by 97 per cent of the population of the Kashmir valley.

In Jammu, Hindus constitute 65 per cent of the population, Muslims 31 per cent and Sikhs, 4 per cent. Jammu and Kashmir is the only state in India which enjoys special autonomy under Article 370 of the Constitution of India, according to which no law enacted by the Parliament of India, except for those in the field of defence, communication and foreign policy, will be extendable in Jammu and Kashmir unless it is ratified by the state legislature of Jammu and Kashmir. Subsequently, jurisdiction of the Supreme Court of India over Jammu and Kashmir has been extended.[24]

The erstwhile princely state of Jammu and Kashmir acceded to India on 26 October 1947 through an Instrument of Accession executed by Hari Singh, the then ruler. Pakistan alleged that Hari Singh had no right to execute the accession when the Standstill Agreement was in force with it, while India maintained that it was legal. Through Shimla agreement (1972), both India and Pakistan agreed to settle their differences over Jammu and Kashmir through peaceful bilateral negotiations. Pending the final settlement of any of the problems, neither side would unilaterally alter the situation.[25]

Terrorist attacks by Pakistan-backed groups since 9/11 in places as far as Hyderabad, Kolkata, Varanasi, Rampur, Lucknow, Delhi,

Mumbai, Ajmer, Gandhinagar, Faizabad, Ayodhya, Panipat, Malegaon and Bangalore, as well as the detection and disruption of terrorist modules virtually across the country. In combination, afflicting as many as 15 states outside J&K and the Northeast are evidence of a complex and long-term war of attrition by Pakistani state agencies and their jihadi surrogates. The blasts in Bangalore and Ahmadabad mark a further step in the ISI-sponsored pan-Indian spread of the jihad. When the Mumbai blasts of March 1993 occurred, analysts saw them as the beginning of an attempt by the ISI to target India's economic sinews, when the Indian Institute of Science was attacked in Bangalore in December 2005, India's technological and scientific capacities were thought to be the *'new target'*, when the temple at Varanasi, and much later, a mosque in Malegaon, were hit, it was seen as an attempt to disrupt India's 'communal harmony'.[26]

The first and foremost problem that troubled India-US ties during the first Clinton's first term was the Kashmir dispute, as both human rights and nuclear proliferation issues have had been related to this dispute. The US attitude towards this problem was of course, not positive to India. Since US policy makers and strategic thinkers viewed Kashmir issue as a potential nuclear flashpoint, the Clinton administration took efforts to bring both India and Pakistan towards better understanding and resolving their differences through persistent dialogue and also initiating a series of confidence building measure.[27]

The dynamics of Kashmir conflict have undergone a drastic change since 9/11 due to dramatic changes wrought by US War on Terrorism in the region. The US focus on fighting terrorism, extremism and Islamic fundamentalism, most of the times all linked together has put tremendous pressure on Pakistan's Kashmir policy. President Musharraf, in his speech at the SAARC Summit in 2002 stated: *"We regard terrorism as a grave threat to civil society. We abhor violence. We are determined to eliminate terrorism and therefore, fully implement the SAARC Convention for Combating Terrorism."* However, he emphasised on the need for the elimination of the root causes of terrorism. At the 57th session of UN General Assembly, in 2002 reflecting on roots of terrorism he stated: "it was not religion which impels a terrorist act, it is often a sense of frustration and powerlessness to redress persistent injustice."[28]

Isolated incidents of terrorism related to Jammu and Kashmir (J&K) used to take place even before 1989. Large groups of Kashmiri youth, which were critical of the Government of India, started clandestinely going to Pakistan for being trained in camps in Pakistani-occupied Kashmir set up by Pakistan's Inter-Services Intelligence. Initially, the Jammu and Kashmir Liberation Front, which demands independence for the entire J&K, including those parts which are under Pakistani and Chinese occupation, was in the forefront of the insurgency. Alarmed by this, Pakistan, which claims that the entire state should have come to it at the time of the partition of India by the British in 1947, encouraged the Jamaat-e-Islami of J&K to form its own militant organisation called the Hizbul Mujahideen (HM) to advocate the merger of the State with Pakistan.[29] Militant violence led by Jammu Kashmir Liberation front has caused ethnic cleansing of several hundred thousand Kashmiri Hindu Pandits, who comprises an estimated three per cent of the Kashmir valley's population.[30]

## Jammu Kashmir Liberation Front (JKLF)

The Jammu Kashmir Liberation Front, founded by Amanullah Khan and Maqbool Bhat, is a Kashmiri nationalist organisation founded in Birmingham, England on May 29, 1977. From then until 1994 it was an active terrorist organisation. The JKLF claims that they are not Islamist, but are nationalist, and opposes the emergence of the territories into either Pakistan or India but rather wants the region of Kashmir to separate from the two countries and become independent. The JKLF split into two factions after the group based in Indian-administered Kashmir led by Yasin Malik publicly renounced violence in 1995.[31]

## Jaish-e-Mohammed

The group's primary motive is to separate Kashmir from India and it has carried out several attacks primarily in Indian state of Jammu & Kashmir. In March 2000, Maulana Masood Azhar formed Jaish-e-Mohammed, a terrorist organisation from a split within Harkat-ul-Mujahideen (HUM) (another terrorist organisation) shortly after his December 1999 release from prison in exchange of Passengers of Indian Airlines flight IC 814 which was hijacked and was taken to Kandahar. In January 2002, the government of President Pervez Musharraf banned the group. In response JeM changed its name to Khaddam ul-Islam.[32]

## Lashkar-e-Taiba

It is one of the largest and most active terrorist organisations in South Asia, operating mainly from Pakistan. It was founded in 1990 by Hafez Saeed, Abdullah Azzam and Zafar Iqbal in Afghanistan. Lashkar-e-Taiba has been accused by India of attacking military and civilian targets in India, most notably the 2001 Indian Parliament attack and the 2008 Mumbai attacks. Its stated objective is to introduce an Islamic state in South Asia and to liberate Muslims residing in Indian Kashmir. Its training camps are presently located at a number of locations in Pakistan. These camps, which include its base camp, Markaz-e-Taiba in Muridke near Lahore and the one near Manshera, are used to impart training to militants. In 1987, LeT established two training camps in Afghanistan. The first one was the Muaskar-e-Taiba at Jaji in Paktia Province and the second one was the Muaskar-e-Aqsa in Kunar Province.[33]

## Insurgency in Northeast India

Northeastern India consists of Assam, Meghalaya, Tripura, Arunachal Pradesh, Mizoram, Manipur, and Nagaland. Tensions exist between these states and the central government as well as amongst the tribal people, who are natives of these states, and migrant peoples from other parts of India. Assam has been a refuge for militants, for a number of years, due to its porous borders with Bangladesh and Bhutan. The main causes of the friction include anti-foreigner agitation in the 1980s, and the simmering Assam-Bodo tensions.

The United Liberation Front of Assam was formed in April 1979 to establish a sovereign state of Assam through an armed struggle. The National Democratic Front of Bodoland was formed in 1989 as the Bodo Security Force, aims to set up an autonomous region Bodoland. The Karbi Longri N.C. Hills Liberation Front is a militant group operating in Karbi Anglong and Dima Hasao districts of Assam that was formed on May 16, 2004. The United People's Democratic Solidarity was formed in March 1999 with the merger of two terrorist outfits in Assam's Karbi Anglong district, the Karbi National Volunteers and Karbi People's Front.

The People's Liberation Army of Manipur is a leftist organisation which was formed in 1978 with the aim of liberating Manipur from India. People's Revolutionary Party of Kangleipak is an armed insurgent group in Manipur demanding a separate and independent homeland. The National Socialist Council of Nagaland was formed in 1980 to establish a Greater Nagaland, encompassing parts of Manipur, Nagaland, the north Cachar Hills (Assam). The NSCN split in 1988 to form two groups namely NSCN (IM) and NSCN (K). As of now, both the groups are in ceasefire with the Indian government.

The insurgent groups in Tripura were emerged in the end of the 1970s, as ethnic tensions between the Bengali immigrants and the tribal native population who were outnumbered by the former hailing from other parts of India and nearby Bangladesh which resulted in their being reduced to minority status even threatening them economically, socially, culturally. The National Liberation Front of Tripura was formed in March 1989. The All Tripura Tiger Force was formed by the local aboriginal tribal's in 1990. Problems in Meghalaya arise from the divide between tribals and non-tribal settlers, identity issues and growing corruption besides the fear of being reduced to minority by native tribals.

The Hynniewtrep National Liberation Council, formed in 1992, aims to free the state from the alleged Garo and non-tribal Indian domination. The Garo National Liberation Army aims to establish a separate *"Garoland"* for the Garo people. It was formed in 2009. Mizoram's tensions are largely due to the simmering Assamese domination and the neglect of the Mizo people. In 1986, the Mizo accord ended the main secessionist movement led by the Mizo National Front, bringing peace to the region. The Hmar People's Convention-Democracy is an armed insurgency group formed in 1995 to create an independent Hmar State in North East India. The Bru National Liberation Front was formed in 1997 to protect the rights and dignity of the Reangs.[34]

## Armed Forces (Special Powers) Act, 1958

The Armed Forces (Special Powers) Act is an Act of the Parliament of India which was passed on September 11, 1958. The Act has received criticism from several sections for alleged concerns about human rights violations in the regions of its enforcement, where arbitrary killings, torture, cruel, inhuman and degrading treatment and enforced disappearances have alleged to have happened. The Armed Forces (Assam and Manipur) Special Powers Ordinance 1958 was promulgated by the President Dr Rajendra Prasad on the 22nd May, 1958. It was replaced by Armed Forces (Assam and Manipur) Special Powers Act, 1958 on September 11, 1958.

The central government enacted the Armed Forces (Punjab and Chandigarh) Special Powers Act on October 6, 1983, repealing The Armed Forces (Punjab and Chandigarh) Special Powers Ordinance, 1983, to enable the central armed forces to operate in the state of Punjab and the union territory of Chandigarh. The Act was enforced in the whole of Punjab and Chandigarh on October 15, 1983.[35] In July 1990 Indian Armed Forces were given special powers under the Armed Forces (Special Powers) Act, 1958 that gives protection to Indian Armed Forces personnel from being prosecuted. The law provides them a shield, when committing human rights violations and has been criticised by Human Rights Watch as being wrongly used by the forces. This law is widely condemned by human rights groups.

On 31 March 2012, the UN asked India to revoke AFSPA saying it had the no place in Indian democracy. Many human rights organisations such as Amnesty International and the Human Rights Watch (HRW) have condemned human rights abuses in Kashmir by police such as *"extra-judicial executions", "disappearances",* and torture; the *"Armed Forces Special Powers Act",* which "provides impunity for human rights abuses and fuels cycles of violence. The Armed Forces Special Powers Act grants the military wide powers of arrest, the right to shoot to kill, and to occupy or destroy property in counterinsurgency operations. Indian officials claim that troops need such powers because the army is only deployed when national security is at serious risk from armed combatants. The judicial commission set up by the Supreme Court is trying to make the controversial Armed Forces Special Powers Act more humane and the security forces more accountable.[36]

## Conclusion

The strategy of terrorists is to commit acts of violence that draws the attention of the local populace, the government, and the world to their cause. Some of the factors that lead to terrorism are: (a) Frustration and desperation to achieve a goal; (b) Confused emotion; (c) Shortsightedness and Impulsive action; (d) Belief in a non-verifiable concept of heaven and merit; a childish concept of God favouring some and angry at others, thereby undermining the omniscience and omnipotence of the Divine; (e) Terrorism induces fear psychosis in all, increases poverty, suffering and loss of life with no apparent gains.

Al-Qaeda is a global militant Islamist and Wahhabist organisation founded by Osama bin Laden, Al-Qaeda has attacked civilian and military targets in various countries. Terrorism in Pakistan has become a major and highly destructive phenomenon in recent years. South Asia is viewed as a key arena in the fight against militant religious extremism, most especially in Pakistan and as related to Afghan stability. Jammu and Kashmir is a state in Northern India, granted autonomy under article 370 of Indian constitution. Jammu and Kashmir consists of three regions: Jammu, the valley and Ladakh. Srinagar is the summer capital, and Jammu is the winter capital. The Jammu Kashmir Liberation Front, founded by Amanullah Khan and Maqbool Bhat, is a Kashmiri nationalist organisation founded in Birmingham, England on May 29, 1977. In March 2000 Maulana Masood Azhar formed Jaish-e-Mohammed, a terrorist organisation. Lashkar-e-Taiba was founded in 1990 by Hafez Saeed, Abdullah Azzam and Zafar Iqbal in Afghanistan.

Northeastern India consists of Assam, Meghalaya, Tripura, Arunachal Pradesh, Mizoram, Manipur, and Nagaland. Tensions exist between these states and the central government as well as amongst the tribal people, who are natives of these states, and migrant peoples from other parts of India. The Armed Forces (Special Powers) Act is an Act of the Parliament of India which was passed on September 11, 1958. The Act has received criticism from several sections for alleged concerns about human rights violations in the regions of its enforcement, where arbitrary killings, torture, cruel, inhuman and degrading treatment and enforced disappearances have alleged to have happened.

## References

1. *What is terrorism?* See http://www.sagepub.in/upm-data/51172_ch_1.pdf
2. *Terrorism (2014),* Retrieved from http://en.wikipedia.org/wiki/Terrorism
3. *Terrorism: Causes, Impacts and Remedies,* Retrieved from http://libpind.blogspot.in/2010/01/terrorism-causes-remedies.html
4. *Various Definitions of Terrorism,* Retrieved from http://www.azdema.gov/museum/famousbattles/pdf/Terrorism%20Definitions%20072809.pdf
5. Amy Zalman, *Types of terrorism,* Retrieved from http://terrorism.about.com/od/whatisterroris1/tp/DefiningTerrorism.htm
6. See http://terrorism.about.com/od/causes/a/causes_terror.htm

7. See http://terrorism.about.com/od/causes/tp/Causes_of_Terrorism.htm
8. See http://www.artofliving.org/wisdom/knowledge-sheets/terrorism-cause-and-remedy
9. *What are the Causes of and Solutions to Terrorism?* See http://shil1978.hubpages.com/hub/Terrorism-Causes-and-Solutions-My-View
10. Nauro F. Campos and Martin Gassebner (2009), *International Terrorism, Political Instability and the Escalation Effect,* Retrieved from http://ftp.iza.org/dp4061.pdf
11. Aarish Ullah Khan (2005), *The Terrorist Threat and the Policy Response in Pakistan,* Retrieved from http://books.sipri.org/files/PP/SIPRIPP11.pdf
12. Rekha Chowdhary, *Terrorism and Movement: A Case Study of Kashmir*, Retrieved from http://www.lokniti.org/pdfs_dataunit/publications2011/12_terrorism_and_movement_%20a_case_study_of_kashmir-chowdhary. pdf
13. *Al-Qaeda (2014),* See http://en.wikipedia.org/wiki/Al-Qaeda
14. *September 11 attacks,* Retrieved from http://en.wikipedia.org/wiki/September_11_attacks
15. Peter R. Neumann, *Terrorism in the 21st century: The rule of law as a guideline for German policy,* Retrieved from http://www.fes.de/kompass2020/pdf_en/Terrorism.pdf
16. See http://www.state.gov/documents/organisation/31912.pdf
17. *International Terrorism: Threat, Policy, and Response (2007),* Retrieved from http://fas.org/sgp/crs/terror/RL33600.pdf
18. *Global Terrorism Index*, Retrieved from http://en.wikipedia.org/wiki/Global_Terrorism_Index.
19. *Terrorism in Pakistan,* Retrieved from http://en.wikipedia.org/wiki/Terrorism_in_Pakistan.
20. Aarish Ullah Khan (2005), *The Terrorist Threat and the Policy Response in Pakistan,* Retrieved from http://books.sipri.org/files/PP/SIPRIPP11.pd
21. K. Alan Kronstadt (2007), *Pakistan and Terrorism: A Summary,* Retrieved from http://www.law.umaryland.edu/marshall/crsreports/crsdocuments/RS22632_03272007.pdf
22. Syed Ejaz Hussain, *Terrorism in Pakistan: Changing incident patters,* Retrieved from http://www.pakistansocietyofcriminology.com/articles/TerrorisminPakistan.pdf
23. Jermie Lanche (2009), *Suicide Terrorism in Pakistan: an assessment,* see http://www.ipcs.org/pdf_file/issue/SR84-Jeremie-Suicideterrorism.pdf
24. Jammu and Kashmir (2014), Retrieved from http://en.wikipedia.org/wiki/Jammu_and_Kashmir.
25. M Amarjeet Singh, *Conflict in Jammu and Kashmir*, Retrieved from http://www.nias.res.in/docs/B%206%20Kashmir.pdf

26. *Task force report on National security and Terrorism,* Retrieved from http://www.ficci.com/SPdocument/20032/terrorism-report.pdf
27. *Kashmir, Human Rights and Terrorism,* Retrieved from http://shodhganga.inflibnet.ac.in/bitstream/10603/1315/8/08_chapter%202.pdf
28. Shaheen Akhtar, *War on Terrorism & Kashmir issue,* Retrieved from http://pu.edu.pk/images/journal/pols/Currentissue-pdf/SHAHEEN%20AKHTAR.pdf
29. B.Raman, *Terrorism in Jammu & Kashmir*, Retrieved from http://www.claudearpi.net/maintenance/uploaded_pics/TerrrorisminJandK.pdf
30. *Human rights abuses in Jammu and Kashmir,* Retrieved from http://en.wikipedia.org/wiki/Human_rights_abuses_in_Jammu_and_Kashmir.
31. *Jammu Kashmir Liberation Front*, Retrieved from http://en.wikipedia.org/wiki/Jammu_Kashmir_Liberation_Front.
32. *Jaish-e-Mohammed*, Retrieved from http://en.wikipedia.org/wiki/Jaish-e-Mohammed.
33. *Lashkar-e-Taiba (2014),* Retrieved from http://en.wikipedia.org/wiki/Lashkar-e-Taiba.
34. *Insurgency in Northeast India,* Retrieved from http://en.wikipedia.org/wiki/Insurgency_in_Northeast_India.
35. *The Armed Forces (Special Powers) Act,* Retrieved from http://en.wikipedia.org/wiki/Armed_Forces_(Special_Powers)_Act,_1958
36. *The Armed Forces (Special Powers) Act,* Retrieved from http://en.wikipedia.org/wiki/Armed_Forces_(Special_Powers)_Act,_1958

# Chapter - 14

# Disaster Management System in South Asia

*"Natural disasters are terrifying - that loss of control, this feeling that something is just going to randomly end your life for absolutely no reason is terrifying. But, what scares me is the human reaction to it and how people behave when the rules of civility and society are obliterated."*

***—Eli Roth***

## Introduction

Natural disaster is a major adverse event resulting from natural processes of the Earth; examples include floods, volcanic eruptions, earthquakes, tsunamis, and other geologic processes. A natural disaster can cause loss of life or property damage, and typically leaves some economic damage in its wake, the severity of which depends on the affected population's resilience, or ability to recover. An earthquake is the result of a sudden release of energy in the Earth's crust that creates seismic waves. At the Earth's surface, earthquakes manifest themselves by vibration, shaking and sometimes displacement of the ground. Volcanoes can cause widespread destruction and consequent disaster in several ways.

The effects include the volcanic eruption itself that may cause harm following the explosion of the volcano or the fall of rock. Flood is an overflow of an expanse of water that submerges land. Flooding may result from the volume of water within a body of water, such as a river or lake, which overflows or breaks levees, with the result that some of the water escapes its usual boundaries. Limnic eruption occurs when a gas, usually $CO_2$, suddenly erupts from deep lake water, posing the threat of suffocating wildlife, livestock and humans. Blizzards are severe winter storms characterised by heavy snow and strong winds. When high winds stir up snow that has already fallen, it is known as a ground blizzard.

Cyclone, tropical cyclone, hurricane, and typhoon are different names for the same phenomenon a cyclonic storm system that forms over the oceans. Drought is unusual dryness of soil, resulting in crop failure and shortage of water for other uses, caused by significantly lower rainfall than average over a prolonged period. Hailstorms are falls of rain drops that arrive as ice, rather than melting before they hit the ground. A heat wave is a period of unusually and excessively hot weather. Wildfires are large fires which often start in wildland areas. Common causes include lightning and drought but wildfires may also be started by human negligence or arson.[1]

Disasters are as old as human history but the dramatic increase and the damage caused by them in the recent past have become a cause of national and international concern.[2] During any disaster, communities are always the first responders. Community participation ensures local ownership, addresses local needs, and promotes volunteerism and mutual help to prevent and minimise damage.[3] Disasters have always co-existed with civilisations. With technological advancement, development initiatives resulted in the creation of a lot of infrastructure and permanent assets. Gradually material development detached man from nature on one hand, and increased vulnerability of the human population, on the other.[4]

## What is Disaster Management?

The United Nations defines a disaster as a serious disruption of the functioning of a community or a society. Disasters involve widespread human, material, economic or environmental impacts, which exceed the ability of the affected community or society to cope using its own resources. The Red Cross and Red Crescent societies define disaster management as the organisation and management of resources and responsibilities for dealing with all humanitarian aspects of emergencies, in particular preparedness, response and recovery in order to lessen the impact of disasters.[5]

Disaster management is a sequential and continuous process planning. The important elements which are to be considered at all stages during the disaster management are disaster management system and standards/ Indian Standard codes, disaster diagnosis, disaster resource planning, disaster impact assessment, investigation of disaster and hazardous risk assessment, onsite and offsite emergency planning, disaster management plans, corporate disaster preparedness programmes, emergency response plans, identification of proactive measures, systematic measurement, resource evaluation and quantification, cost analysis, environmental impact assessment, feedback towards achieving the disaster control abatement and mitigation strategies, research and development, management innovations, loss assessment and prevention measures, recovery, relief, reconstruction and rehabilitation activities, computer aided methods, state-of-art software on disaster management and enforcement of disaster compensation laws.[6]

Risk management consists of identifying threats (hazards likely to occur), determining their probability of occurrence, estimating what the impact of the threat might be to the communities at risk, determining measures that can reduce the risk, and taking action to reduce the threat. Risk management is accomplished by lessening the effects of the natural hazard or by taking actions in normal development projects that will reduce the risks to an acceptable level. Disaster preparedness refers to a broader range of activities, such as establishing emergency policies, developing evacuation plans, designating emergency shelters, and developing methods for rapid assessment of pre-positioning supplies.[7]

## Significance of Disaster Management

Disasters are defined as a serious disruption of the functioning of a community or a society. They involve widespread human, material, economic or environmental impacts, which exceed the ability of the affected community or society to cope using its own resources.[8] Disaster relief activities typically address a variety of needs. In disaster management this spectrum of human endeavours is classified by sectors. The most common are health, housing, agricultural, economic, and social sectors. These sectors are known as the prime sectors, because they are of prime concern to the disaster victims. A second group of sectors include urban settlements, transportation, lifelines, and critical facilities. These are known as secondary or support sectors, because they have indirect effects on the disaster victims.[9]

Natural Disasters causing damage to human life, property, infrastructure and economy has emerged as a global challenge. Requisite safety measures have to be provided for natural hazards. Prevention is better than cure. Once disaster occurred, it is very difficult to handle and control it. Proper planning shall always handle and mitigate the various kinds of disasters effectively, for which open, transparent and efficient systems have to be followed. There is a need for systematic identification, preparation, prediction, assessment, evaluation of disaster events and incorporation of mitigate measures.[10]

## Disaster Management: Global Perspectives

The vulnerability of mankind to disasters of various types has increased considerably all over the world. It has posed new and unconventional challenges to the nations and even compelled the policymakers to redefine the concept of security. In such an evolving environment, the concept of disaster management has gained much significance.[11] Natural disasters have exacted a heavy human toll on nations throughout the Caribbean and Central America, but Cuba is largely an exception to the rule. Despite material scarcity, Cuba has a well-informed citizenry and few casualties due to hurricanes, mudslides, earthquakes and other natural disasters.

Cuba's success in saving lives amidst natural disasters rejects joint efforts of the civil defence, meteorologists, and public administrators who assign high priority to the value of human life. Cuba is one of the few countries that use Early Advisory and Information Phases as preludes to the Hurricane Watch (48 hours before a strike is expected) and Hurricane Warning (24 hours before).[12] Developed countries which have modern early warning systems and effective mitigation programmes are able to reduce the impact of natural hazards whereas countries with less preparedness and inadequate mitigation efforts suffer more from natural hazards. In the case of India, the human and economic losses from disasters are high in comparison to many other developing nations.[13]

The Emergency Response Coordination Centre, operating within the European Commission's Humanitarian Aid and Civil Protection department, was set up to support a coordinated and quicker response to disasters both inside and outside Europe using resources from 31 countries participating in the Union Civil Protection Mechanism. It replaces and upgrades the functions of the previous Monitoring and Information Centre. It collects and analyses real-time information on disasters, monitors hazards, prepares plans for the deployment of experts, teams and equipment, and works with Member States to map available assets and coordinate the EU's disaster response efforts by matching offers of assistance to the needs of the disaster-stricken country.[14]

The European Commission has a holistic approach to disaster management; this includes prevention, preparedness, response and rehabilitation. It has developed various legal and financial instruments to support and complement the national initiatives in disaster preparedness and response of the 27 EU Member States. These include training programmes and joint exercises for civil protection experts, cooperation projects and transport co-financing. Through them, Europe aims to ensure effective response to disasters when they affect its own citizens, as well as effective assistance to other countries when they need disaster relief assistance. The European Civil Protection Mechanism facilitates cooperation in disaster response among 31 European states (EU-27 plus Croatia, Iceland, Liechtenstein and Norway). The participating countries pool the resources that can be made available to disaster-stricken countries all over the world. When activated, the Mechanism coordinates the provision of European assistance wherever it is needed.[15]

Japan's disaster management system addresses all phases of disaster prevention, mitigation and preparedness, and emergency response, as well as recovery and rehabilitation. It specifies the roles and responsibilities of national and local governments, and enlists the cooperation of relevant stakeholders in both the public and private sectors. The Basic Disaster Management Plan is the master plan and the basis for DRM activities in Japan. It is prepared by the Central Disaster Management Council in accordance with the Disaster Countermeasures Basic Act.[16]

When Japan suffered a massive earthquake and tsunami on March 11, 2011, residents turned to the Red Cross to help meet their basic needs. With support from the American public, families staying at evacuation centres received water, relief items and emotional support every day for months. The Red Cross also equipped survivors with appliances for their new homes, repaired damaged medical facilities, and helped the elderly and children. The Red Cross is supporting families moving into temporary housing units provided by the government; helping to restore a sense of normality in their live.[17]

Australia has a well-established emergency management system to manage the threats to communities from natural and technological hazards. The key elements of the system are described with particular emphasis on the impact of disasters on Australia, fundamental concepts, and principles of planning. Emergency physicians have a key role in the development of emergency plans and in the overall health response to disasters. They can enhance their understanding of local, State and national arrangements by participating in exercises and appropriate disaster medicine and emergency management courses.[18]

## Disaster Management in India

India has been traditionally vulnerable to natural disasters on account of its unique geo-climatic conditions. Floods, droughts, cyclones, earthquakes and landslides have been recurrent phenomena. About 60 per cent of the landmass is prone to earthquakes of various intensities; over 40 million hectares is prone to floods; about 8 per cent of the total area is prone to cyclones and 68 per cent of the area is susceptible to drought. Over the past couple of years, the Government of India has brought about a paradigm shift in the approach to disaster management. Disaster management occupies an important place in this country's policy framework as it is the poor and the under-privileged who are worst affected on account of calamities/disasters.[19]

India has been traditionally vulnerable to natural disaster on account of its unique geo-climate conditions. Floods, droughts, cyclones, earthquakes, and landslides have been recurrent phenomena. About 60 per cent of the landmass is prone to earthquake of various intensities; over 40 million hectares is prone to floods; about 8 per cent of total area is prone to cyclones and 68 per cent of the areas are susceptible to drought. In the decade 1990-2000, an average of about 4344 people lost their lives about 30 million people were affected by disaster every year. The loss in terms of private, community and public assets has been astronomical.[20]

In the twenty-first century, the 2001 Bhuj earthquake; the 2004 tsunami; the 2005 earthquake in Kashmir; heavy rainfall in Mumbai in 2006 when nearly 1 m rain fell in a single day; the 2008 Bihar Kosi disaster; the August 2010 cloud burst in Leh; and, most recently, the September 2011 Sikkim earthquake have seen the armed forces as first responders.[21] The prevention of loss to life and property due to natural calamities is being viewed very seriously by the Government of India. In the past, the main role played by the government in the case of various disasters was confined mainly to post-disaster activities that included providing relief and organising rehabilitation. The Uttarkashi Earthquake of 1991, Killari Earthquake of 1993 and the devastating Malpa landslide along the Kailash-Mansarovar route in 1998 acted as an eye-opener for the government. The need was felt for a proactive approach rather than waiting for a disaster to occur.[22]

Following the enactment of the Disaster Management Act, 2005, (DM Act, 2005) the Government of India constituted the National Disaster Management Authority as the apex body for Disaster Management in India with the mandate, inter alia, for laying down policies and guidelines on disaster management.[23] At the national level, the Ministry of Home Affairs is the nodal Ministry for all matters concerning disaster management. The Central Relief Commissioner in the Ministry of Home Affairs is the nodal officer to coordinate relief operations for natural disasters. Cabinet Secretary, who is the highest executive officer, heads the National Crisis Management Committee.

Secretaries of all the concerned Ministries /Departments as well as organisations are the members of the Committee. An Emergency Operations Centre (Control Room) exists in the nodal Ministry of Home Affairs, which functions round the clock, to assist the Central Relief Commissioner in the discharge of his duties. A National Contingency Action Plan for dealing with contingencies arising in the wake of natural disasters has been formulated by the Government of India and it had been periodically updated. Each State Government has relief manuals/ codes which identify that role of each officer in the State for managing the natural disasters. A Calamity Relief Fund has been set up in each State as per the recommendations of the Eleventh Finance Commission.

The States have also been asked to set up Disaster Management Authorities under the Chief Minister with Ministers of relevant

Departments as members. At the district level, the District Magistrate who is the chief coordinator will be the focal point for coordinating all activities relating to prevention, mitigation and preparedness apart from his existing responsibilities pertaining to response and relief. Indian Meteorological Department is mandated to monitor and give warnings regarding Tropical Cyclone.[24] At the National level there are different bodies for disaster management activities. They are:

1. Natural Disaster Management Division with the Ministry of Home Affairs.
2. The National Institute of Disaster Management, an autonomous institute.
3. Crisis Management Group, which was set up by the Union Government to advise, guide, supervise and co-ordinate relief measures in affected states.
4. There is also an Inter-Ministerial Co-ordination Group, and
5. Depending upon the type of disaster, a nodal Ministry is assigned the task of coordinating all activities of the State and district administration and other support departments.[25]

## Disaster Management in Bangladesh

Bangladesh and its people have been one of the worst victims of natural disasters from time immemorial.[26] A low-lying country with more than 230 waterways, Bangladesh is one of the most disaster-prone nations in the world. Fifteen per cent of its land floods annually on average. In 2003, the Ministry of Food and Disaster Management launched the Comprehensive Disaster Management Programme in partnership with DFID and UNDP. The European Commission became the Programme's third major donor in September 2006.[27]

The Ministry of Food and Disaster Management has the mandate to co-ordinate all disaster management activities within the country. A Climate Change Cell has been established in the Department of Environment under the framework of the Comprehensive Disaster Management Programme. The Cell provides the central focus for the government's climate change related work, operating as a unit of the Department of Environment under the Ministry of Environment and Forests.[28]

The National Disaster Management Council, headed by the Prime Minister, is the highest level forum for the formulation and review of disaster management policies. The inter-Ministerial Disaster Management coordination committee is in-charge of implementing disaster management policies and decisions of the committee, assisted by the national Disaster Management Advisory committee. The Ministry of Food and Disaster Management is the apex institution responsible for coordinating national disaster management interventions across all agencies. It comprises of a central Disaster Management Bureau, Director General Food, Directorate of Relief and Rehabilitation and a Cyclone Preparedness Programme Implementation Board.[29] National Plan for Disaster Management 2007-2015 is an outcome of the national and international commitments of the Government of Bangladesh and the Ministry of Food and Disaster Management for addressing the disaster risks comprehensively.[30]

## Disaster Management in Pakistan

Like other South Asian countries, Pakistan continues to suffer from a plethora of natural and human induced hazards that threaten to affect the lives and livelihood of its citizens – natural disasters including floods, earthquakes, landslides, cyclones, and drought to human induced disasters such as fires, civil unrest and terrorism, refugees and internally displaced people, health epidemics, transport accidents, industrial accidents and war.[31]

At the federal level, the Emergency Relief Cell in the Cabinet Division serves as the focal point during emergencies. At the provincial level, it coordinates with provincial relief departments/relief commissioners who are responsible for effective distribution of relief items in respective provinces. The Cell is also responsible for dealing with institutional donors and receives grants/donations/funds for distribution through the Prime Minister's Disaster Relief Fund.[32] The National Disaster Management Authority has been established as the focal point and lead agency for coordinating and facilitating the implementation of strategies and programmes on disaster risk reduction, response and recovery. Similarly, Disaster Management Authorities have been established at provincial, regional, and district levels.[33]

Pakistan National Calamities (Prevention and Relief) Act 1958 provides for the maintenance and restoration of order in areas affected by calamities, and relief against such calamities. The Calamities Act 1958 was mainly focused on organising emergency response. This act was later amended when the four provinces were created in 1971. After the abolition of one unit in 1971, the provinces adopted the 1958 Calamities Act with some changes in content as per their requirements. In province of the Punjab, a dedicated department with the name of "Relief and Crisis Management Department" was established in 1975. In other provinces, Senior Member Board of Revenue was designated Relief Commissioner ex-officio. Emergency Relief Cell was created within the Cabinet Division in 1971 and is responsible for disaster relief at national level. It provides assistance in cash and kind to supplement the resources of the Provincial Governments in event of major disaster. National Crisis Management Cell was established in July 1999 under Anti-Terrorist Act in the Ministry of Interior. District Disaster Management Authorities has been established in all the districts/agencies but priority given to the hazard prone areas. The Armed Forces have always contributed very effectively in emergency response operations and provided immediate relief through massive air and ground efforts. The Relief Commissioner is responsible for coping with any disaster situation in the province adequate.[34]

## Disaster Management in Nepal

Numbers of important measures have already been taken to tackle some serious challenges caused by disasters in Nepal. In this process, the Constitution of the Kingdom of Nepal 1990 is the law of the land which guaranteed the Right to Life and individual liberty under Article 12. The right to life includes the right to security and right to live with human dignity. In the disaster situation, affected and vulnerable people of disaster are always kept at the risk of those rights that are cherished in the Constitution and the relief responsibility has been taken as grace of the state which is not but the inherent right of the people.

Even though, Natural Disaster (Relief) Act, 1982 and other sectoral law and policies have been formulated in this field, appropriate legislation, regulation and policies is absent in a number of key sectors, and needs formulating. Disaster education, awareness-rising and management training are necessary to sensitise the citizenry, decision-makers and field workers in all sectors which is lacking in present context of Nepal.[35] The Nepal Red Cross Society is clear in its mission that is to relieve human suffering and to reduce vulnerability through community participation and mobilisation of an increased number of volunteers. Mobilisation of power of humanity, expansion and strengthening of the organisational structure of the society and building links with governmental and nongovernmental organisations are the strategic components of the mission.[36]

The National Strategy for Disaster Risk Management in Nepal endeavours to facilitate the required change in order to achieve the goal of disaster resilient Nepal by providing guidance for improving the policy and legal environment, and by prioritising the strategic interventions. UNDP Nepal, with core financial support from the European Commission Humanitarian Aid Department, provided the management support and technical leadership. The National Society for Earthquake Technology–Nepal served as the technical consultant. The Prime Minister is proposed to head the NCDRM as its Chair while the Opposition Leader in the Parliament is proposed as the Deputy Chair. Members of the Commission are proposed to be the ministers, Chief of the Army Staff, Chief of the Police departments and two representatives of the civil society. One more member is to be nominated by the Chair.[37] Ministry of Home Affairs through its department of Narcotics, Drug Control, and Disaster Management, is the national agency responsible for disaster management in Nepal.[38]

## Disaster Management in Bhutan

Forest fires are a major problem for Bhutan with 72.5 per cent of the country under forest cover and a series of fires breaking out in different parts of Bhutan every year, causing great loss to the kingdom, socially, economically and environmentally. With the serious threat of fire every year, the Royal Government frequently holds training workshops on fire prevention to train fire personnel and raise awareness of the risk. With the limited resources available, prevention measures, emergency planning and safety exercises are held, with drills and tests.[39]

The Department of Disaster Management in the Ministry of Home and Cultural Affairs is the lead coordinating agency for disaster management in Bhutan. It consists of three divisions: Preparedness and Mitigation, Response and Early Warning, and Relief and Reconstruction. The National Committee for Disaster Management is the highest-ranking executive body for disaster management, and is chaired by the Secretary, Ministry of Home and Cultural Affairs. DDM functions as the secretariat of the Committee. At the local level, there are 20 District Disaster Management Committees chaired by governors. The Department of Disaster Management under the Ministry of Home and Cultural Affairs has prepared the National Disaster Management Planning guidelines to assist the districts and blocks of Bhutan to develop their disaster management plan.

Established in 2005, Disaster Management initiatives in Bhutan had started off with its responsibilities carried out by a small division established under the Ministry of Home and Cultural Affairs. The division was upgraded to a Department in the latter half of 2008 owing to the importance given to disaster risk management. In order to prepare for and respond to disasters in the country, the Department of Disaster Management has three main divisions (a) Preparedness and Mitigation, (b) Response and Early Warning, and (c) Relief and Reconstruction. A couple of glacial lake outburst flood projects have been conducted by the Department of Geology and Mines in close cooperation with the DDM, the Department of Energy, and the UNDP with funding from organisations including LDCF/GEF, JICA-JST, and SAARC.[40]

## Disaster Management in Sri Lanka

Sri Lanka is known to be impacted by multiple hazards including floods, landslides, cyclones, droughts, rock falls, land subsidence, earth tremors, storm surges, coastal floods, coastal erosion, salinity intrusion, forest fires, high winds, tornadoes etc. Management of disasters requires in-depth understanding of hazards, causes and ways and means of minimising disaster risks and active engagement of multiple agencies and stakeholders. Accordingly, the National Disaster Management Policy of Sri Lanka has been formulated to ensure the sustainability and resilience of the nation.

Sri Lanka Disaster Management Act No.13 of 2005 provides for the coordination at the highest executive level, establishment of the institutional framework for disaster management including the National Council for Disaster Management, Disaster Management Centre and elaborates powers and functions of the institution. The Act also recognises the cross-cutting nature of disaster management. Act empowers the President to declare state of disaster. Ministry for Disaster Management was established in December 2005 and in January 2006 the function of Human Rights was added. The National Building Research Organisation and Department of Meteorology were placed under the Ministry of Disaster Management and Human Rights.[41]

## Disaster Management in Maldives

The frequency of occurrence of natural disasters in the Maldives is low. The fact that disaster preparedness became a priority of the Maldivian government only after the tsunami of 2004 was quite normal. The Department of Meteorology suggests that the islands, 199 of which are inhabited must be prepared for significant disasters. The eastern sector of the Northern and Central islands are highly vulnerable to tsunami while the Northern islands have the greatest exposure to surge hazards and cyclones. Climate change is expected to have severe impacts on the small, low-lying coral islands of the Maldives because they are highly reliant on the biological and geomorphologic functioning of the coral reef environment for their stability.

The economic base, tourism and fisheries, and livelihood are directly linked to the coral reefs. In an agreement made during the meeting with President Mohamed Nasheed on 12th July 2009, the United Nations International Strategy for Disaster Risk Reduction committed to assist the Government of the Maldives in the formulation of the country's Strategic National Action Plan for Disaster Risk Reduction and Climate Change Adaptation through a broad-based multi-stakeholder consultation. The mission team was led by the UNs champion for disaster risk reduction and climate change adaptation and the senior regional coordinator of UNISDR for Asia Pacific.

The Maldives SNAP Project recognises the commitment of the Government of the Maldives to initiate policies and measures, as well as to sustain and to build upon past gains, that contribute to the building and stabilisation of a democratic system and that promote good governance. The Third Constitution of 2008 sets forth the fundamental duties of the State and rights of the people in relation to the environment, the continued well-being of citizens, and their protection from hazards. The National Disaster Management Centre seeks a strong mandate for disaster risk management to support the fulfillment of the key pledges.[42]

## Disaster Management in Afghanistan

Afghanistan is categorised as one of the least developed countries in the world. The main hazards that have for centuries adversely affected the lives, property and livelihoods of Afghan people are earthquakes, droughts, floods, landslides, extreme winter conditions and avalanches, and sand or dust-storms. War and civil conflict during the past two decades, as well as environmental degradation, have increased the vulnerability of the Afghan people to natural disasters. Several government departments have specific units that deal with disaster-related issues, but the Office of Disaster Preparedness has the mandate to coordinate disaster management on behalf of the government. A recent study of it indicated that it does not have capability to effectively carry out its mandate. Ministry of Irrigation and Environment: is involved in disaster mitigation in relation to drought and floods as they affect agricultural production, irrigation systems and water supply and management.[43]

The National Disaster Management Plan aims to streamline disaster management systems in the country. This includes clearly identifying roles and responsibilities of the National Commission (National Disaster Management Commission) and the Afghan National Disaster Management Authority along with its provincial offices, the Provincial Disaster Management Committee and associated line ministries, NGOs, and International Organisations. The institutional framework of Disaster Management for Afghanistan comprises a National Disaster Management Commission, as the Apex body, chaired by the Second Vice President with participation of relevant ministries.

The National Commission is the principal body for setting out national policy direction towards reducing risk of disasters through vulnerability reduction, and responding to emergency situations. At province level, the Province level Disaster Management Committees / Commissions acts as the counterpart to the National Commission. The district level implementing agencies are the lowest level formally registered administration. The District Administrator plays the lead coordinating role in heading the District level Disaster Management Committee. At local level the role of NGOs and especially the Community Development Councils role are important. The National Commission may allocate funds from the National Emergency Fund after receiving recommendations from Afghanistan National Disaster Management Authority.[44]

## Effects of Disaster

While direct effects are visible on people and infrastructure, indirect effects are felt in terms of loss of revenue and productivity in the workforce. Countries later face multiplied effects including reduced government monetary reserves, higher ination and increased public expenditures.[45] Floods have been a recurrent phenomenon in India and cause huge losses to lives, properties, livelihood systems, infrastructure and public utilities. India's high risk and vulnerability is highlighted by the fact that 40 million hectares out of a geographical area of 3290 lakh hectares is prone to floods. On an average every year, 75 lakh hectares of land is affected, 1600 lives are lost and the damage caused to crops, houses and public utilities is ₹ 1805 crores due to floods. Cyclones, cyclonic circulations and cloud bursts cause flash floods and lead to huge losses.[46]

Disasters disrupt communities in many ways, including disruption to normal routines, physical harm and social disruption. In short, disasters are unexpected events and it is essential that the affected community is identified so that the needs of these groups of people can begin to be identified and then addressed. The range of impacts of disasters on a community can be described across the social, built, economic and natural environments. The effects of a disaster on the built environment depend on the disaster type, scale, magnitude, duration and location of impact. Within the built environment, impacts may include: loss of essential services, power, water, food, fuel, sewerage, gas, communications, internet; loss of community infrastructure; for example, public buildings, schools, hospitals, iconic buildings; loss/damage/disruption of transport services (for example, roads, air, marine and rail transport infrastructure, facilities and assets; and loss of property (residential, rural, industrial, public).

Impacts on the economic environment may include: (a) loss of livelihoods; (b) disequilibrium, disorientation of service providers (disasters are not a usual method of doing business); (c) reduction in cash flow for some small businesses, and injection of funds into others; (d) loss of tourism activities; (e) loss of employment opportunities for some people, and creation of employment opportunities for others.

The effects of disaster on the natural environment that impact on the community may be a result of the disaster or they may be a secondary impact or flow on from the disaster response or recovery process. Examples include air quality, water quality, land degradation and contamination, bio-security, sense of place issues and impacts on the natural environment.[47]

The growing incidence of natural disasters is highly correlated to the increasing vulnerability of households and communities in developing countries, as previous socioeconomic vulnerabilities may exacerbate the impact of a natural disaster, making more difficult the process of recovery. The impact of a natural disaster may also cause inequalities. The poor, who suffer from income fluctuations, and also have limited access to financial services, in the aftermath of a disaster may be more prone to reduce consumption and have a decreasing shock in other household indicators as a consequence. In addition, there are a number of non-poor, or close to be, who are not insured against from those risks, and then may fall into poverty as consequence of decapitalising when coping with the shock, depending the impact and likelihood of falling into poverty of the initial stock assets and coping mechanisms.[48]

## Conclusion

Disasters are defined as a serious disruption of the functioning of a community or a society. The vulnerability of mankind to disasters of various types has increased considerably all over the world. Natural Disasters causing damage to human life, property, infrastructure and economy has emerged as a global challenge. Requisite safety measures have to be provided for natural hazards. Prevention is better than cure. Once disaster occurred, it is very difficult to handle and control it. India has been traditionally vulnerable to natural disasters on account of its unique geo-climatic conditions. Floods, droughts, cyclones, earthquakes and landslides have been recurrent phenomena.

At the national level, the Ministry of Home Affairs is the nodal Ministry for all matters concerning disaster management. The Central Relief Commissioner in the Ministry of Home Affairs is the nodal officer to coordinate relief operations for natural disasters. Cabinet Secretary, who is the highest executive officer, heads the National Crisis Management Committee. While direct effects are visible on people and infrastructure, indirect effects are felt in terms of loss of revenue and productivity in the workforce. The effects of a disaster on the built environment depend on the disaster type, scale, magnitude, duration and location of impact. Within the built environment, impacts may include: loss of essential services, power, water, food, fuel, sewerage, gas, communications, internet; loss of community infrastructure.

## References


1. *Natural disaster (2014),* Retrieved from http://en.wikipedia.org/wiki/Natural_disaster.
2. *Natural hazards and disaster management,* Retrieved from http://cbse.nic.in/natural%20hazards%20&%20disaster%20management.pdf
3. *Preparation of State Disaster Management Plans (2007),* Retrieved from http://www.adrc.asia/documents/dm_information/india_plan02.pdf
4. Himayatullah Khan and Abuturab Khan, *Natural hazards and disaster management in Pakistan*, Retrieved from http://mpra.ub.uni-muenchen.de/11052/1/NATURAL_HAZARDS_AND_Disaster_Management_in_Pakistan_a_.pdf
5. *What is disaster management?* See http://www.wcpt.org/disaster-management/what-is-disaster-management.
6. *Important elements of disaster management and mitigation and design and development of a software tool,* Retrieved from http://dl.acm.org/citation.cfm?id=1369458
7. *Aim and Scope of Disaster Management, Study Guide and Course Text,* Retrieved from http://epdfiles.engr.wisc.edu/dmcweb/AA02AimandScopeofDisasterManagement.pdf
8. *The need to address disaster management,* Retrieved from http://www.wcpt.org/disaster-management/the-need-to-address-disaster-management
9. *Aim & Scope of Disaster Management, Study Guide and Course Text,* Retrieved from http://epdfiles.engr.wisc.edu/dmcweb/AA02AimandScopeofDisasterManagement.pdf
10. *Important elements of disaster management and mitigation and design and development of a software tool,* Retrieved from http://dl.acm.org/citation.cfm?id=1369458
11. Shivananda, H. and P.K. Gautam, *Reassessing India's Disaster Management Preparedness and the Role of the Indian Armed Forces,* Retrieved from http://workspace.unpan.org/sites/internet/Documents/G4IN12%20Reassessing%20India's%20Disaster%20Management%20Preparedness%20and%20the%20Role%20of%20the%20Indian%20Armed%20Forces.pdf
12. *Cuba's Domestic Disaster Management,* Retrieved from http://www.medicc.org/resources/documents/medicc-review-disaster-management.pdf

13. T Nanda Kumar, *Managing Disasters in India,* Retrieved from http://yojana.gov.in/CMS/(S(i4fktm45crrmfojby0ce3w45))/pdf/Yojana/English/2012/Final%20Yojana%20MARCH-2012.pdf
14. *Emergency Response Coordination Centre (ERCC),* Retrieved from http://ec.europa.eu/echo/en/what/civil-protection/emergency-response-coordination-centre-ercc
15. *Cooperation in disaster management: the European Union and the United States take a major step forward (2011),* Retrieved from http://reliefweb.int/report/world/cooperation-disaster-management-european-union-and-united-states-take-major-step
16. *Disaster Management Plans,* Retrieved from http://wbi.worldbank.org/wbi/Data/wbi/wbicms/files/drupal-acquia/wbi/drm_kn2-2.pdf
17. See http://www.redcross.org/what-we-do/international-services/where-we-help/asia/japan
18. *Disaster management in Australia: the national emergency management system,* Retrieved from http://www.ncbi.nlm.nih.gov/pubmed/11482853
19. *Disaster management in India*, Retrieved from http://www.unisdr.org/2005/mdgs-drr/national-reports/India-report.pdf
20. Daya Kaul, Md. Ayaz, Lohitkumar, S N, *Disaster Management In India,* Retrieved from http://unpan1.un.org/intradoc/groups/public/documents/apcity/unpan050292.pdf
21. Shivananda, H. and P.K. Gautam, *Reassessing India's Disaster Management Preparedness and the Role of the Indian Armed Forces*, Retrieved from http://workspace.unpan.org/sites/internet/Documents/G4IN12%20Reassessing%20India's%20Disaster%20Management%20Preparedness%20and%20the%20Role%20of%20the%20Indian%20Armed%20Forces.pdf
22. *National Disaster Management Guidelines: Management of Landslides and Snow Avalanches*, Retrieved from http://nidm.gov.in/PDF/guidelines/landslides_snow_avalanches.pdf
23. *National Disaster Management Guidelines,* Retrieved from http://www.ndma.gov.in/images/guidelines/flood.pdf
24. *Disaster management in India*, Retrieved from http://www.unisdr.org/2005/mdgs-drr/national-reports/India-report.pdf
25. Jacob P Alex, *Disaster Management: Towards A Legal Framework,* Retrieved from http://www.iipa.org.in/common/pdf/12.pdf
26. A.K.M. Abdus Sabur, *Disaster Management System in Bangladesh: An Overview,* Retrieved from http://iqq.sagepub.com/content/68/1/29.abstract
27. *Disaster management in Bangladesh*, Retrieved from https://www.unops.org/SiteCollectionDocuments/Factsheets/English/Success%20Stories/GBL_PJFS_CDMP_EN.pdf

28. *Comprehensive Disaster Management-Bangladesh Experience,* Retrieved from http://saarc-sdmc.nic.in/pdf/bangladesh/file4.pdf
29. *Bangladesh,* Retrieved from http://gfdrr.org/ctrydrmnotes/Bangladesh.pdf
30. *National Plan for Disaster Management 2007-2015*, Retrieved from http://unpan1.un.org/intradoc/groups/public/documents/apcity/unpan050295.pdf
31. Himayatullah Khan and Abuturab Khan, *Natural hazards and disaster management in Pakistan,* Retrieved from http://mpra.ub.uni-muenchen.de/11052/1/NATURAL_HAZARDS_AND_Disaster_Management_in_Pakistan_a_.pdf
32. *A Review of Disaster Management Policies and Systems in Pakistan,* Retrieved from http://saarc-sdmc.nic.in/pdf/pakistan/file3.pdf
33. *Climate change: Disaster Management in Pakistan*, Retrieved from http://cmsdata.iucn.org/downloads/pk_cc_dm_vul.pdf
34. *National Disaster Response Plan (NDRP)* March 2010, National Disaster Management Authority, Government of Pakistan, Retrieved from http://www.ndma.gov.pk/documents/ndrp/ndrp.pdf
35. *Disaster management system in Nepal: Law and policy*, Retrieved from http://workspace.unpan.org/sites/internet/Documents/B4NP04%20Disasters%20Management%20System%20in%20Nepal%20Law%20and%20Policy.pdf
36. *Nepal Red Cross Society: Disaster Management Strategic Framework*, Retrieved from http://workspace.unpan.org/sites/internet/Documents/*S4NP10%20Disaster%20Management%20Strategic%20Framework.pdf*
37. *National Strategy for Disaster Risk Management (NSDRM),* Retrieved from http://www.rccdm.net/index.php?option=com_docman&task=doc_view&Itemid=215&gid=17
38. Kathmandu Valley, Nepal, Disaster Risk Management Profile, *Last Review,* August 2005, Retrieved from http://emi.pdc.org/cities/CP-Kathmandu-08-05.pdf
39. Yonten Dargye, *A Brief Overview of Fire Disaster Management in Bhutan,* Retrieved from http://archives.icom.museum/disaster_preparedness_book/country/dargye.pdf
40. *DRR Policy Peer Review (2009),* Retrieved from http://www.adrc.asia/publications/drr/pdf/Peer_Review_Bhutan.pdf
41. *National Policy on Disaster Management, Democratic Socialist Republic of Sri Lanka*, Retrieved from http://www.disastermin.gov.lk/web/images/pdf/draft%20dm%20policy.pdf
42. See http://ndmc.gov.mv/wordpress/wp-content/uploads/2012/10/Strategic-National-Action-Plan-for-Disaster-Risk-Reduction-and-Climate-Change-Adaptation-2010-2020-Provisional-Draft.pdf
43. *Disaster Management Framework for Afghanistan,* Retrieved from http://saarc-sdmc.nic.in/pdf/afghanistan/file1.pdf

44. *National Disaster Management Plan, 2010 Afghanistan,* Retrieved from http://www.andma.gov.af/contents/295/Documents/226/Updated_Afghanistan_NDMP.pdf

45. *Popular mobilisation and disaster management in Cuba*, Retrieved from http://www.centerforurbanstudies.com/documents/electronic_library/cuba/disaster/disasterpreparation.pdf

46. *National Disaster Management Guidelines,* Retrieved from http://www.ndma.gov.in/images/guidelines/flood.pdf

47. *Section C Effects of disasters,* Retrieved from http://www.em.gov.au/Documents/AEMHS%202%20Community%20Recovery%20Chapter%206.PDF

48. Eduardo Rodríguez-Oreggia, Alejandro de la Fuente and Rodolfo de la Torre, *The Impact of Natural Disasters on Human Development and Poverty at the Municipal Level in Mexico*, Retrieved from http://www.preventionweb.net/english/hyogo/gar/background-papers/documents/Chap3/LAC-overview/Mexico/Mexico.pdf

# Chapter - 15

# South Asian Association for Regional Cooperation

*"Unlike a drop of water which loses its identity when it joins the ocean, man does not lose his being in the society in which he lives. Man's life is independent. He is born not for the development of the society alone, but for the development of his self."*

***—B. R. Ambedkar***

## Introduction

The world today is witnessing changes in terms of global and regional fundamentals. There is no denying the fact that the importance of peace and development through effective regional and global integration has become an important factor of these times. The strength and development of the states today is not measured in terms of military and defense capacity but in terms of how a state is able to promote trade relations, investments and economic integration within the region and globally as well.[1]

Trade bloc is a type of intergovernmental agreement, often part of a regional intergovernmental organisation, where regional barriers to trade, (tariffs and non-tariff barriers) are reduced or eliminated among the participating states. Trade blocs can be stand-alone agreements between several states (such as the North American Free Trade Agreement or part of a regional organisation (such as the European Union).[2] A block trade involves a significantly large number of shares or bonds being traded at an arranged price between parties, outside of the open markets, in order to lessen the impact of such a large trade hitting the tape.[3]

## History of the SAARC

The idea of regional cooperation in South Asia was first raised in November 1980. After consultations, the foreign secretaries of the seven founding countries (Bangladesh, Bhutan, India, Maldives, Nepal, Pakistan, and Sri Lanka) met for the first time in Colombo in April 1981. This was followed a few months later by a meeting of the Committee of the Whole, which identified five broad areas for regional cooperation. The foreign ministers, at their first meeting in New Delhi in August 1983, adopted the Declaration on South Asian Association for Regional Cooperation and formally launched the Integrated Programme of Action in the five agreed areas of cooperation: agriculture; rural development; telecommunications; meteorology; and health and population activities.[4]

The objectives, principles and general provisions as mentioned in the SAARC Charter are as follows: (a) to promote the welfare of the peoples of South Asia and to improve their quality of life; (b) To accelerate economic growth, social progress and cultural development in the region and to provide all individuals the opportunity to live in dignity and to realise their full potential; (c) To promote and strengthen collective self-reliance among the countries of South Asia; (d) To contribute to mutual trust, understanding and appreciation of one another's problems; (e) To promote active collaboration and mutual assistance in the economic, social, cultural technical and scientific fields; (f) To strengthen cooperation with other developing countries; (g) To strengthen cooperation among themselves in international forums on matters of common interests; and (h) To cooperate with international and regional organisations with similar aims and purposes.

The principles of SAARC are: (a) Cooperation within the framework of the Association is based on respect for the principles of sovereign equality, territorial integrity, political independence, non-interference in the internal affairs of other States and mutual benefit; (b) Such cooperation is to complement and not to substitute bilateral or multilateral cooperation; and (c) Such cooperation should be consistent with bilateral and multilateral obligations of Member States.[5]

## South Asian Preferential Trading Arrangement

In December 1991, the Sixth Summit held in Colombo approved the establishment of an Inter-Governmental Group to formulate an agreement to establish a South Asian Association for Regional Cooperation Preferential Arrangement by 1997. Given the consensus within South Asian Association for Regional Cooperation, the Agreement on SAPTA was signed on 11 April 1993 and entered into force on 7 December 1995 well in advance of the date stipulated by the Colombo Summit. The Agreement reflected the desire of the Member States to promote and sustain mutual trade and economic cooperation within the South Asian Association for Regional Cooperation region through the exchange of concessions.[6]

## South Asia, Free Trade Agreement

The Agreement on the South Asian Free Trade Area is an agreement reached at the Twelfth South Asian Association for Regional Cooperation summit at Islamabad, capital of Pakistan on 6 January 2004. It creates a framework for the creation of a free trade zone covering 1.4 billion people in India, Pakistan, Nepal, Sri Lanka, Bangladesh, Bhutan and the Maldives. The seven foreign ministers of the region signed a framework agreement on SAFTA with zero customs duty on the trade of practically all products in the region by end 2016.[7]

## Future and Challenges

South Asia's constellation is certainly not a simple one. India, Pakistan and the other raft of SAARC member states comprising Afghanistan, Bangladesh, Bhutan, Nepal, the Maldives and Sri Lanka are worlds apart on questions of population, territory, military power, technological development, infrastructure and political influence. India is the dominant player, due to its territorial size, large population, the current rapid pace of economic growth, its position as a nuclear power and its recent appointment as a non-permanent member of the United Nations. India's position of prominence is shown to be one of the many hurdles standing in the way of South Asia's integration. India borders every other SAARC country, but the other SAARC states do not share any mutual borders except with India. Afghanistan and Pakistan are exceptions in that they either border India or only have geographical access to the other SAARC members through India. Relation between India and Pakistan also affect on the growth of SAARC.[8]

Dwarika Dhungei in his paper "South Asian Association for Regional Co-operation: Prospects for Development" said that SAARC member nations through its annual summits have made several pledges to cooperate with each other and different task forces were formed to explore new areas of cooperation and pursue what were agreed upon or adopted. But when actual implementation is considered one could hardly feel satisfied. There was need for being selective in areas of cooperation such as poverty alleviation, trade and commerce and human resources development, etc. and emphasis on implementation through vigorous supervision and monitoring of implementation.

One could notice the gap between promises and achievements. The association is no longer in its infancy. Therefore, the main challenge before the association is to prove its effectiveness in terms of bridging the gap between the promises made and achievements, contribute to reducing poverty in the member nations and take concrete steps for easy access to the people of one country to the other and easy flow of goods and services within the region so that a win-win situation is created from all the member nations.[9]

## Conclusion

The idea of regional cooperation in South Asia was first raised in November 1980. After consultations, the foreign secretaries of the seven founding countries (Bangladesh, Bhutan, India, Maldives, Nepal, Pakistan, and Sri Lanka) met for the first time in Colombo in April 1981. In December 1991, the Sixth Summit held in Colombo approved the establishment of an Inter-Governmental Group to formulate an agreement to establish a SAARC Preferential Arrangement by 1997. The Agreement on the South Asian Free Trade Area is an agreement reached at the Twelfth South Asian Association for Regional Cooperation summit at Islamabad, capital of Pakistan on 6 January 2004. The association is no longer in its infancy

## References

1. Irum Shaheen, South Asian Association for Regional Cooperation (SAARC): Its Role, Hurdles and Prospects, *Journal of Humanities and Social Science*, Volume 15, Issue 6 (Sep. - Oct. 2013), pp. 01-09.
2. *Trade Bloc (2014),* Retrieved from http://en.wikipedia.org/wiki/Trade_bloc
3. See http://www.investopedia.com/terms/b/blocktrade.asp
4. *South Asian Association for Regional Cooperation,* Retrieved from http://cns.miis.edu/inventory/pdfs/saarc.pdf
5. See http://www.icsw.org/doc/book.pdf

6. *South Asia Association for Regional Co-operation,* Retrieved from http://fpcci.org.pk/products/subcat_pdf_105.pdf
7. *South Asia Association for Regional Co-operation*, Retrieved from http://fpcci.org.pk/products/subcat_pdf_105.pdf
8. Tomislav Deliniæ, *SAARC: 25 years of regional integration in South Asia*, Retrieved from http://www.kas.de/wf/doc/kas_21870-544-2-30.pdf?110209115423
9. Dwarika Dhungei, South Asian Association for Regional Co-operation (SAARC): Prospects for Development, *The Pakistan Development Review*, 43: 4 Part II (Winter 2004) pp. 933–941.

# Bibliography


- Abu N. M. Wahid (1996), *The economy of Bangladesh: problems and prospects*, Praeger.
- Alison Behnke (2003), *Afghanistan in Pictures,* Twenty-First Century Books.
- Amrit Man Shrestha (2007), *Nepalese economics*, G. Shrestha.
- Anu Mahmud (1997), *Inside Bangladesh Economy*, BIAM.
- Arun Kumar (2002), *The black economy in India*, Penguin Books.
- Asoka Bandarage (2008), *The Separatist Conflict in Sri Lanka: Terrorism, ethnicity, political economy,* Taylor and Francis.
- Bangladesh Economic Association (2000), *Changing rural economy of Bangladesh*, the University of Michigan.
- Charles K. Wilber (1984), *The Political economy of development and underdevelopment,* Random House.
- Chris Dixon (1991), *South East Asia in the World-Economy*, Cambridge University Press.
- Chris Johnson, and Jolyon Leslie (2008), *Afghanistan: the mirage of peace,* Zed.
- David Lewis (2011), *Bangladesh: Politics, Economy and Civil Society,* Cambridge University Press.
- Deborah Winslow, and Michael D. Woost (2004), *Economy, Culture, and Civil War in Sri Lanka*, Indiana University Press.
- Deepashree (2007), *Indian Economy-Performance and Policies,* Tata McGraw-Hill Education.
- Diwaker Chand (2000), *Nepal's Tourism: Uncensored Facts*, Pilgrims Pub.
- Emily Levitt (2011), *Malnutrition in Afghanistan: Scale, Scope, Causes, and Potential Response*, World Bank Publications.
- Fazle Karim Khan (1991), *A Geography of Pakistan: Environment, People and Economy*, Oxford University Press.
- Fazle Karim Khan (2002), *Pakistan: Geography, Economy and People,* Oxford University Press.
- Garry Rodan, Kevin Hewison, and Richard Robison (2006), *the political economy of South-East Asia: markets, power and contestation*, Oxford University Press.

- Hassan Nawaz Gardezi, and Jamil Rashid (1983), *Pakistan, the Roots of Dictatorship: The Political Economy of a Praetorian State,* Zed Press.
- Ijaz Nabi, Naved Hamid, Shahid N. Zahid (1986), *The agrarian economy of Pakistan: issues and policies*, Oxford University Press.
- Ishrat Husain (1999), *Pakistan: the economy of an elitist state,* Oxford University Press.
- Jacqui True (2012), *The Political Economy of Violence Against Women*, Oxford University Press.
- James C. Scott (1975), *The Moral Economy of the Peasant: Rebellion and Subsistence in Southeast Asia,* Yale University Press.
- James Russell Andrus, and Azizali F. Mohammed (1958), *The economy of Pakistan*, Stanford University Press.
- John Briscoe, and Usman Qamar (2006), *Pakistan's Water Economy: Running Dry*, Oxford University Press.
- K. M. De Silva, K. M. (2005), *A History of Sri Lanka,* Penguin Books India.
- K. P. M. Sundharam (1965), *Indian Economy: A Descriptive Analysis*, R. Chand.
- K. R. Gupta, and J. R. Gupta (2008), *Indian Economy,* Volume 1, Atlantic Publishers and Dist.
- Kenneth R. Hall (2010), *A History of Early Southeast Asia: Maritime Trade and Societal Development, 100–1500*, Rowman and Littlefield Publishers.
- Kishore C. Dash (2008), *Regionalism in South Asia: Negotiating Cooperation*, Institutional Structures, Routledge.
- Krishna Kumar Sharma (1951), *Evolution of Indian Economy,* Jai Prakash Nath.
- Larry, P. Goodson (2001), *Afghanistan's Endless War: State Failure, Regional Politics, and the Rise of the Taliban*, University of Washington Press.
- Madan K. Dahal (1993), *Future of Nepalese economy*, Nepal Foundation for Advanced Studies in cooperation with Friedrich Ebert Stiftung.
- Madan K. Dahal (1998), *Impact of Globalisation in Nepal, Nepal Foundation for Advanced Studies,* Friedrich-Ebert-Stiftun.
- Madan K. Dahal et al. (1999), *Development challenges for Nepal,* Nepal Foundation for Advanced Studies.
- Mahesh Chandra Regmi (1976), *Landownership in Nepal,* University of California Press.
- Mahmood Ansari (2012), *A Shangri-la Economy: Exploring Buddhist Bhutan*, Universal- Moazzem Hossain, Iyanatul Islam, and Reza Kibria (1999), *South Asian Economic Development: Transformation, Opportunities and Challenges*, Psychology Press.

- Mohiuddin Alamgir (1980), *Famine in South Asia: political economy of mass starvation,* Oelgeschlager, Gunn & Hain.
- Mumtaz Anwar (2007), *The political economy of foreign aid to Pakistan.* Nomos.
- N Ganesan, Ramses Amer (2010), *International Relations in Southeast Asia: Between Bilateralism and Multilateralism,* Institute of Southeast Asian.
- Nalani Hennayake (2006), *Culture, Politics, and Development in Postcolonial Sri Lanka,* Lexington Books.
- Nicholas Perdikis (2010), *The Indian economy: contemporary issues,* Ashgate.
- Omar Noman (1988), *The Political Economy of Pakistan*, 1947-85, KPI.
- Pakistan. Tourism Division. Economic Research & Statistics Section (1983), *Impact of Tourism on Pakistan's Economy, Economic Research and Statistics Section,* Tourism Division. Government of Pakistan.
- Parvez Hasan (1998), *Pakistan's economy at the crossroads: past policies and present imperatives,* Oxford University Press.
- Piers Blaikie (2005), *Nepal in Crisis,* Pinnacle Technology.
- Piers M. Blaikie, John Cameron, John Cameron (B.A.), David Seddon (1980), *Nepal in crisis: growth and stagnation at the periphery*, Clarendon Press.
- Rajah Rasiah, Johannes Dragsbaek Schmidt (2010), *The New Political Economy of Southeast Asia,* Edward Elgar Publishing.
- Rajesh S. Kharat (2005), *Foreign policy of Bhutan*, Manak Publications.
- Ramakant, Ramesh Chandra Misra (1996), *Bhutan: Society and Polity*, Indus Publishing.
- Rehman Sobhan (1982), *The crisis of external dependence: the political economy of foreign aid to Bangladesh,* University Press.
- Robert I. Rotberg (2007), *Building a new Afghanistan,* World Peace Foundation.
- S. Akbar Zaidi (2005), *Issues in Pakistan's economy*, Oxford University Press.
- S. B. D. De Silva (2010), *The Political Economy of Underdevelopment*, Routledge.
- S. M. Huda (1996), *The economic development of Pakistan: from self reliance to debt ridden economy,* Royal Book Co.
- Saman Kelegama, and Gamani Corea (2004), *Economic Policy in Sri Lanka: Issues and Debates*, SAGE.
- Satyendra S. Nayak (2007), *Globalisation and the Indian Economy: Roadmap to a Convertible Rupee,* Taylor & Francis.
- Sayed Askar Mousavi (1997), *The Hazaras of Afghanistan: An Historical, Cultural, Economic and Political Study,* Saint Martin's Press.

- Sayyid Ahar asan Nadîm (2002), *Pakistan: The Political Economy of Lawlessness*, Oxford University Press.
- Shahid Javed Burki (2008), *Changing perceptions, altered reality: Pakistan's economy under Musharraf, 1999-2006,* Oxford University Press.
- Sir Mokshagundam Visvesvaraya (1934), *Planned economy for India,* Printed at the Bangalore Press.
- Srî LaE ka Maha Bankuva (1998), *Economic Progress of Independent Sri Lanka*, Central Bank of Sri Lanka.
- Stuart Corbridge, John Harriss, and Craig Jeffrey (2012), *India Today: Economy, Politics and Society,* Wiley.
- Sugata Bose, and Ayesha Jalal (2004), *Modern South Asia: History, Culture, Political Economy*, Taylor and Francis.
- Tashi Choden, and Dorji Penjore, (2004), *Economic and political relations between Bhutan and neighbouring countries*, Centre for Bhutan Studies.
- TR Jain, Mukesh Trehan, and Ranju Trehan (2010), *Indian Economy*, FK Publications.
- Uma Kapila (2004), *Indian Economy,* Academic Foundation.
- Viqar Ahmed, and Rashid Amjad (1984), *The management of Pakistan's economy, 1947-82,* Oxford University Press.
- W. D. Lakshman (1987), *Dilemmas of development: fifty years of economic change in Sri Lanka*, Sri Lanka Association of Economists.
- W. D. Lakshman, and Clement Allan Tisdell (2000), *Sri Lanka's Development Since Independence: Socio-economic Perspectives and Analyses,* Nova Publishers.
- Yadav Sharma Gaudel (2003), *Monetary system of Nepal*, Adroit Publishers.
- Zonden Ukyab (2007), *Geopolitics and socio-economy of Nepal,* the University of California Publishers.
- Manoj Kumar Agarwal, and Rudra Prasad Upadhyay (2006), *Tourism and Economic Development in Nepal*, Northern Book Centre.
- Manu Goswami (2010), *Producing India: From Colonial Economy to National Space*, University of Chicago Press.
- Manzooruddin Ahmed (1980), *Contemporary Pakistan: politics, economy, and society*, Carolina Academic Press.
- Mick Moore (2007), *The State and Peasant Politics in Sri Lanka*, Cambridge University Press.

# Index

## C

## L



## M

## O



## P

**T**



**U**



**V**

## W



## Y



## Z